THE WELLNESS

OF

SAINT PAUL

CHIRHO COMMUNICATIONS

WILLIAM H. JONES

B.A., B.D., M.R.E., ED.S., M.TH., D.MIN, PH.D.

THE WELLNESS

of

SAINT PAUL

WILLIAM H. JONES

THE WELLNESS

OF

SAINT PAUL

CHIRHO COMMUNICATIONS

WILLIAM H. JONES

Abstract

1. **The Wellness and Developing Attitudes of the Apostle Paul**: This book studies the spiritual, physical and mental health of the Apostle Paul (a.k.a. Saul). Initially, the Apostle, the man in motion, appears to be trapped in an eddy of emotion, stirred to action by his conscious, subconscious and unconscious mind frames. While Saul's (later Paul) religious fervour is unmatched, Saul's application of that passion was at first appallingly misappropriated. Something was amiss in Luke's initial biography of the future Apostle, depicting him as "breathing out murderous threats against the Lord's disciples." [1] Saul acted abnormally. The book attempts to show how Paul's ability to resolve conflicts with his maturing spiritual leadership positively affected the burgeoning church he was largely instrumental in growing.

2. **Question–Why this Examination**: The dissertation seeks to discover why Paul acted the way he did. What drove him to undertake the methods he fashioned? What influences defined his life? What part did his Hellenistic ambience in Tarsus shape his thinking? What aspect did his Jewish Pharisee atmosphere control him? What were his motives in guiding his thoughts and behaviours? What purpose was he trying to reach? How did Paul overcome his initial unbridled behaviour and unbalanced discernment? The immaturity of youth is only a partial elucidation of Saul's puzzling performances. Of course, no examination can uncover all his personality factors and moods. What Winston Churchill said about Russia equally applies to the Apostle Paul–he "is a riddle wrapped in a mystery inside an enigma."[2] Can we learn to understand such a person? We will try.

3. **Rationale**: This dissertation includes probing his several correspondences, following Luke's records of his perambulations (and some not mentioned by Luke in Acts), while investigating his evolving healthier attitudes. This book attempts to view Saul/Paul from the pages of Acts, his several letters and the confrontations involving him in cultural mixtures where his tactic of involving synagogues as his main platform was often denied him. The Apostle made ready adjustments when he deemed that to be necessary. To this end we must look at appropriate ambient Greek mythology and attitudes. At the same time we must note the multiple conflicting Jewish factors tugging at Paul's life.

4. **Significance**: This research should provide Bible readers with a richer reflection on the personality and mission of the Apostle Paul by looking behind the words of scripture to understanding his apostolate. In turn, such an analysis will help moderns grasp how Paul's exertions can teach current missionaries to reach their audiences by reflecting on Paul's successes and failures. Reaching non-Christians is the forever challenge of the church. Paul's ready adjustments well serve that purpose. © William H. Jones

---

[1] Acts 9:1

[2] BBC Broadcast 01 October 1939

Acknowledgements

During the dozen years (1977–1989) of my editing and managing *The Canadian Baptist* magazine, I visited several biblical sites in the Mideast. Often, the trips were in conjunction with articles for the magazine and were supported by contra arrangements with travel groups and airlines. A re-acknowledgment is due for such help, which in a way, provided opportunity for me to draw on my research behind this book, although that was an unforeseen development at the time. For these contras I am indebted to the Israeli Government Tourist Office in Canada, the Greek Tourist Office in Canada, Diamond International Tours (Canada), Olympic Airlines, Swissair, El Al Airlines, Scandinavian Airlines, and Alitalia Airlines. Most of my other Mideastern and European visits have been made without financial assistance.

Some other aspects of this book are rooted in my long ago MSS that became a book titled *The Christian Invasion of Europe*, published by Wood Lake Books under the same title. Its roots, in turn, sprouted from my script for a four-part CTV (Canadian Television Network) series, titled, *Good News Comes to Greece*. That book has been out-of-print for several years. The original professional TV tapes were erased and recycled by the network for other programs. TV tapes are now passé, replaced by newer digital recording methods. Since then, I have revisited several of the communities in Greece, its Islands, Italy, Crete, Malta, Turkey, Jordan, Syria, Italy and specifically Rome about which some of the original *The Christian Invasion of Europe* centred. I have developed many new insights into Paul's character.

Some material from two of my previous books, *The Christian Invasion of Europe* and *Detour to Damascus* are incorporated but revised in the body of this book.

This developing book took shape from my early scripts used in four CTV television documentaries aired (and re-aired) in Canada on the CTV network. I wrote a script and designed a four-part documentary titled *Paradox* filmed in Israel (1981). *Good News Comes to Greece* was the second. Since then, I have pondered anew what made Paul tick. In this book I have added a significant measure of Greek mythology as well, because its permeating folklore factors into Paul's understanding of the culture in which Paul was preaching, teaching and ministering. He well knew Sophism, Stoicism and Epicureanism. Paul was quite familiar with the excesses of the vulgar and hedonistic mystery religions. He grew up in a Hellenistic culture. Yet the Greek religious factors must have been especially daunting to Paul and his mission team.

I wrote a script for a second, similar six-part TV series on CTV about the early missions in Asia Minor and Rome and saw first-hand some of the Turkish communities mentioned in Acts. That six-part series was titled, *The Kingdom and the Empire*. I had visited Turkey earlier for a magazine assignment on the Seven Churches of Asia Minor. Both TV series aired in the 1980s. A 13-part CTV documentary titled *The Faith Finders* followed in 1993. In that longer series, I tracked the lives of Bible personalities from Abraham to Jesus and his disciples. Another 13-week series, *Soul Liberty*–a sequel to *Faith Finders*–aired on CTV in 1997. Thank you CFTO, Baton Broadcasting and CTV.

Some material from two of my previous books, *Detour to Damascus* and *The Christian Invasion of Europe* are recycled into this current book

The research for those several television programs also fed some research for this book and provided me with visible ambience of the several biblical localities I could visualize as I wrote this volume. Since technology has changed, no tapes remain and few video players of that era could air them anyway! However, none of the series dealt with the personality of the Apostle. A further planned 13-week series on the church's missionary service did not eventuate.

I thank members of my family for supporting me in such endeavours. My wife, Glee, learned that videotaping was a "hurry-up-and-wait" operation and stood by patiently while I presented a story or assisted the crews. On some "shoots" she stayed at home, permitting me to travel without her. Over three overseas visits when I was a tour guide/leader, each of my three sons (Llewellyn, Victor, Steven) and two grands (Michelle and Evan) were able to see some of these locations themselves. What a privilege to have family members with me to learn about Bible events!

This book uses Canadian spellings. Most, but not all Bible references employ the New International Version (NIV). Dates are cited as AD (Anno Domini, the year of our Lord) rather than CE (Common Era), and BC (Before Christ) rather than BCE (Before Common Era) as sometimes are used by a few archaeologists.

William H. Jones

TABLE OF CONTENTS

PART ONE:
CONCEPTION, GESTATION AND BIRTH OF A MISSIONARY

PART TWO:
A BEACHHEAD IN EUROPE

PART THREE:
A CROSS-CULTURAL MISSION

PART FIVE:
FROM MYTH TO FAITH

INTRODUCTION
A SECOND CHANCE TO MAKE A FIRST IMPRESSION

Paul fell flat on his face as Luke introduced him to readers of The Acts of the Apostles. He was nasty, belligerent, bombastic, unforgiving, unrelenting and headstrong as we meet him in Acts, chapter nine. There is little to say that is positive about his attitude or deportment–except, perhaps for his unrelenting aspect. As this book will show in its latter pages, God had baptized Paul's "no-quit" nature in favour of the Gospel's cause. But at first perspective we see Saul as the potentate of his reflexes, the emperor of his attitudes and the champion of his own indulgences. It's not a pretty sight. Saul was a nasty piece of business.

Bruce Chilton adds his own evaluation of Paul's first emergence as Saul. "Paul is the most complex, brilliant, troubled figure in the New Testament. He speaks for himself–inviting us to trace his turbulent dramatic life."[3]

No one likes this kind of troublemaker. In this study we need to find out the nature of this personality struggle. One student of Saul (Paul) recognizes his personality deficiency. He agrees with the description of Saul in the above first paragraph and adds his own perspective:

> "His (Saul's) perception of himself and his relation to the world was highly subjective. He was racked by guilt, admittedly perplexed by the conflict between his convictions, desires, and behaviour. Today we might say he was afflicted with an overpowering superego, a phenomenon which, in that unsophisticated age, he quite readily projected on the heavens and mistook for the voice of God. To further complicate the situation, his guilt and professed unworthiness were paradoxically accompanied by the stated conviction that he had been specially appointed and called to the apostolate and that he had been specially favoured with God's revelation of his divine son."[4]

Lüdemann surely was correct about Saul's personality deficiencies. If by the Freudian term superego he meant conscience, indeed Saul must have been savagely scourged by his conscience. As for the thought that the voices were in his head, Lüdemann was partly correct: In Acts 9, the text reads that others also heard the voice of God. *"The men travelling with him stood there speechless; they heard the sound but did not see anything."*[5]

When facing a mob in Jerusalem years later, Paul recounted a slightly different explanation: *"My companions saw the light, but they did not understand the voice."*[6] In the third iteration of this account, while addressing his trial judge Agrippa, the Apostle said he heard the voice but did not mention any other witnesses, *"I heard a voice saying to me in Aramaic, 'Saul, Saul, why do you persecute me?'"*[7]

---

[3] Bruce Chilton, Rabbi Paul, p. xvi
[4] Gerd Lüdemann, Paul: The Founder of Christianity, p. 244
[5] Acts 9:7
[6] Acts 22:9
[7] Acts 26:14

Does it matter how God communicated with Saul?

To analyze the personality of Saul (later Paul) we have few tools regarding his genetic factors in his personality development. We don't know Saul's Jewish genome. We may surmise he is intelligent. To study the *Torah* on one hand and on the other to master his leather working trade is quite an accomplishment. Not many people can handle both disparate occupations with aplomb. He had multiple skills: he could parse scripture, repair sails, orate, debate and do all this with panache.

One may suspect that his rearing was rough and tough because Pharisee fathers expected much from their sons. We may correctly surmise that his Pharisee father was an unrelenting disciplinarian. To impress Saul in separating him from the pagan civic life surrounding him, his Pharisee Father undoubtedly reinforced many Jewish traditions. The temple hair on his scalp remained uncut, deferring to the *Torah* teaching of *pe'ot*, *"Do not cut the hair at the sides of your head or clip off the edges of your beard."*[8]

Saul was different than other Tarsus neighbours, his father would have ingrained in him. He was linked to Abraham by the scars of circumcision, the *dam bris*, the blood of the covenant. Such a procedure was not practised among Hellenist babies. Saul would recite the *Shema* every morning and follow the scriptural litanies set out by the Pharisee rota calendar, the *haphtarah*. When he left his abode and also when he returned home, he would touch the frame around his Father's door, and repeat words of the psalm, *"The LORD will watch over your coming and going both now and evermore."*[9]

Some of his fellow Jewish youths–probably Saul also–wore a head covering, out of respect for *Kiddush Hashem*, "the Name." But his Greek friends did not. His father would tell him that the idols displayed throughout Tarsus were impotent and objects of pagan idiocy. Saul's boyhood Greek friends did not see it that way–their Hellenistic pagan parents taught them otherwise and the children had learned to respect the idols. Saul was a marginal child; he straddled two disparate and opposing cultures.

We have much more to decipher in Saul's environmental background. His most formative, imprintable years, from one to ten, involved being a Jew in a thoroughly Hellenistic ambience. He was embossed by the *Torah* but also inscribed by some Greek humanities. Saul realized he did not fully belong to this alien society. He was above it, somewhat superior. He looked down on the pagans even while absorbing their culture. Yet the cultural divide set the future stage for his encounter with Jews who held that Jesus was Messiah and Saviour. One definitely could say, "He was a mixed-up kid."

All this, a conflict between cultures, a strict upbringing, and a sense of superiority (yet, curiously, an inferior feeling) propelled Saul into future matters that demanded resolutions. What he later wrote to Philippi, became his own challenge once God had re-routed him from the Damascus highway: *"Work out your own salvation in fear and trembling."*[10] God was doing a work in him but Saul had his own reforming to master.

---

[8] Leviticus 19:27
[9] Psalm 121:8
[10] Philippians 2:12

Looking ahead: the matter of how God dealt with Saul is followed by how Saul dealt with himself. God provided salvation for Saul—and this book will examine what happened. Saul was responsible, with God's help, for smoothing out his own puzzling and contentious attitudes. This dissertation will probe how and to what degree that also was accomplished.

PART ONE:
THE CONCEPTION, GESTATION AND BIRTH OF A MISSIONARY

CHAPTER ONE
GROWING UP PHARISEE

We know the name of the early church's foremost missionary as Saul of Tarsus. Only sometime after he was ordained and commissioned for missionary service by the Antioch Church do we know him as Paul. Luke, a later companion and note-taker, wrote about the change of names while he reported on Saul's evangelizing in Paphos, Cyprus: "*Saul, who is also called Paul, filled with the Holy Spirit . . .*"[11]

We assume Luke authored Acts. Few are the scholars will argue that. Luke himself writes, "*In my former book, Theophilus, I wrote about all that Jesus began to do and teach until the day he was taken up into heaven.*"[12]

From Paphos on, Luke refers to Paul, not Saul, in his reporting. *Paulos* is the Greek version of his alternate (cognomen) name. *Paulus* is the Latin spelling. Evidently Paul perhaps thought his Hellenistic name's version made him more acceptable to Gentiles than using his Hebrew appellation.

The change, however, may not have endeared him to the Jews who heard him teach and preach.

The name change has another explanation. It mirrors a change in Paul's self image. Saul, the proud Pharisee, represented a historic pride in Israel's first king–a name any Jewish father would gladly give his son. A Jewish father is most unlikely to dub his child as Paul! In Latin, Paulus means "small, insignificant." It amplifies Paul's remade, humbler attitude that, "*I am the least of all saints.*"[13] Saul/Paul seemed to struggle with humility.

Tarsus

During Saul's lifetime, Tarsus was a major community in what is now Turkey and near Adana. Paul called it, "*no mean city.*"[14] The River Cydnus ran through it as it wended its way some 20 kilometres to the Mediterranean Sea. Tarsus served as capital of Cilicia. It had a reputation for its schools of "oratory," a gift that the young child Saul may have recognized for his future work. Tarsus was founded by Phoenicians and enjoyed a sizeable Semitic population. Its textile industry made it possible for Jews to choose that craft because it was "kosher-neutral." Yet, Jews in the Asia Minor Diaspora

---

[11] . . . and the story continues in Acts 13:6–12
[12] Acts 1:1–2
[13] Ephesians 3:8
[14] Acts 21:39

often lived on the edges of their communities in order to avoid the indulgences and influence of Gentile proclivities, not to mention statues of pagan gods. Each community had its own deity; Tarsus bowed to Tarku as its patron deity.[15]

Both Alexander the Great and the Assyrian conqueror Antiochus Epiphantes had their way with Tarsus. The foreign colonizing Seleucids inflicted Hellenism upon them. Antiochus "Epiphanes" was worse. He not only asserted everything in Greek culture but factored in the Greek deities he imagined he revered. Antiochus abused anything Jewish. That Saul grew up in Tarsus where Jews were an irrelevant minority gave a young boy ample opportunity to peer through his Hebrew window to observe the atmospheres of a Gentile style of living. His indelible pre-teen years imbedded the Hellenistic version of Judaism into Saul's growing mindset. "The Hellenistic Diaspora, not 'Palestine,' was the seedbed of Paul's life and thought," wrote Bruce Chilton.[16]

Calvin J. Roetzel writes about the Greek ambience into which Saul was born:

"Paul was a child of a thoroughly Hellenized urban setting that engaged the Diaspora Jewish community in a vital reciprocity. Either in Tarsus or in some other Hellenized urban setting Paul learned his first language, Greek. It is important to realize that language does not express ideas, it shapes ideas."[17]

Antiochus' imposition made living more difficult for the monotheistic Jews who had settled there. Jews had sought an Asia Minor Diaspora in seeking a better economic life but also for opportunity to practise their own faith in relative freedom.

A few Pharisees also joined the Diaspora. Pharisees were a religious, social and political party. They arose after the Hasmoneans won victory over the insurgent Assyrians in the 160s BC. They based themselves in synagogues and taught the *Torah*. The word Pharisee means, "separatist."[18] They banded together in a form of political entity they called *haburah*,[19] meaning "brotherhood." They sought Levitical "purity." Pharisees also paid weighty deference to Jewish "traditions," something ignored by the Sadducees.

Soon, Romans replaced the Seleucid culture, imposing their own traditions. Rome offered some benefits, however, among them, an invaluable Roman citizenship. If the Emperor deemed it amenable, other ethnics could be invested as citizens of the empire. Jews seldom earned Roman citizenship but apparently Saul's father did. Saul's father was both Roman and Jewish. Moreover, the father was a Pharisee ("*Brothers, I am a Pharisee, the son of a Pharisee*).[20] Paul also claimed his heritage as that of Benjamin. Marcel Simon wrote,

"The Pharisee, was above all a schoolman and a scholar. But the school was that of life, and study guided content. The law formed a whole. To be sure, a distinction can be made between the moral commandments and the ritual

---

[15] Bruce Chilton, op cit., p. 9, 10
[16] Bruce Chilton, op. cit., p. 14
[17] Calvin J. Roetzel, Paul: The Man and the Myth, p. 3
[18] W. O. E. Oesterley, A History of Israel, p. 317
[19] members were called *haberim*, "brothers"
[20] Romans 11:1

prescriptions. But both express the divine will to the same degree . . . Occasionally the ritual aspects took precedence over the ethical. Yet this can be seen as a temptation that waylays every religion to the degree that it expresses itself outwardly."[21]

The tribe of Benjamin's claim to being Jewish perhaps was a borderline interpretation. "Jew" meant Judah, not necessarily Benjamin. Yet Benjaminites, thinking of themselves as part of the Southern nation of Israel/Judah, maintained they were legitimate Jews. Purist natives of Judah may not have been so sure.

Generally, a Pharisee's occupation was handed down from his father. Saul's father had two important duties. The first was to link him to Abraham. The second was to choose a trade for his son. Bruce Chilton argues that Saul's Pharisee father was also a tentmaker, and a wealthy one at that. Possibly he taught young Saul his trade. "Tent-making firms such as Paul's family ran made a huge profit–providing portable stalls and accommodations, and repairing damage to the canvas and felt that protected the caravan's wagons and to the leather that harnessed its animals."[22]

The *Torah* and Training

The much later *Talmud* reflects a very long established qualification of a Jewish scholar–(1) to circumcise his son and (2) teach him a trade, lest he become a thief. "Work" is an important concept for Jews. Initially, they considered work a judgment from God. The *Talmud* is an extension of the *Mishnah*, which was the written version of the oral rabbinical code. There is little reason to suspect that the *Talmud* did not reflect Jewish regulations at the time of Saul.

> *"To Adam he* [God] *said, "Because you listened to your wife and ate fruit from the tree about which I commanded you, 'You must not eat from it,'"Cursed is the ground because of you; through painful toil you will eat food from it all the days of your life. It will produce thorns and thistles for you, and you will eat the plants of the field. By the sweat of your brow you will eat your food until you return to the ground, since from it you were taken; for dust you are and to dust you will return."*[23]

In time, "work" became a Jewish purpose in living and an imitation of God's creative process. In the Old Testament, a reader will note that, *"surely the LORD your God has blessed you in all your works."*[24] A reader is invited to note that, *"Hezekiah prospered in all his works."*[25] Again, The Chosen people are told to observe God's works. *"Bless the LORD all his works, in all places of his dominion."*[26]

An underlying current in Jewish belief is that work is a way of winning God's favour. When a legal expert approached Jesus with a serious question, he posed, *"What*

---

[21] Marcel Simon, <u>Jewish Sects at the Time of Jesus</u>, p. 31
[22] Bruce Chilton, <u>op. cit.,</u> p. 7
[23] Genesis 3:17–20
[24] Deuteronomy 2:7
[25] 2 Chronicles 32:30
[26] Psalm 103:22

shall I do to inherit eternal life?"[27] The emphasis clearly is on the verb, "do." The inference is that work and "doing good" (Hebrew, *tzedakah*) are primary passages to a Pharisee's preservation–that's what puts a smile on God's face. It does, of course. But there is more to it. Later, the ex-Pharisee Paul just as clearly told believers pointedly . . .

> *"But because of his great love for us, God, who is rich in mercy, made us alive with Christ even when we were dead in transgressions—it is by grace you have been saved. And God raised us up with Christ and seated us with him in the heavenly realms in Christ Jesus, in order that in the coming ages he might show the incomparable riches of his grace, expressed in his kindness to us in Christ Jesus. For it is by grace you have been saved, through faith—and this is not from yourselves, it is the gift of God— not by works, so that no one can boast. For we are God's handiwork, created in Christ Jesus to do good works, which God prepared in advance for us to do."*[28]

The Pharisees' outlook on life stemmed from Isaiah's theology of hope.[29] God was already "resurrecting" Jews from their exile and enslavement in Babylon, although Isaiah did not live long enough to personally experience it. Yet his prophetic words offered a mood of aspiration in the Jewish people. He wrote: *"But your dead will live, their bodies will rise. You who dwell in the dust, wake up and shout for joy. Your dew is like the dew of morning; the earth will give birth to her dead."*[30]

In John Bright's A History of Israel he notes that, "Later Pharisees were driven to embrace it (i.e., the belief in a future life) because only so could the justice of God, which they refused to question, be harmonized with the facts of experience."[31]

The Pharisee movement seized upon this concept. Unlike the Sadducees who opted for the "here and now," Pharisees saw past death to a hopeful future. Resurrection became a key element in their theology. It became fundamentally central in Paul's hermeneutic. The Pharisee conviction of resurrection melded easily with the Gospel facts.

Gerald Borchert noted at the time of Lazarus resurrection,[32] "that when Jesus announced to her (Martha) that her brother would rise again, she responded by quoting good orthodox Pharisaic theology that her brother would rise at the end of time. Jesus, in turn, reminded her that "he was the resurrection and the life and that believing in him would bring forth life even to the dead."[33]

Saul/Paul was later to realize, in Jakob Jocz' words, "the Kingdom of God is not a theological concept but an overwhelming fact in history by the resurrection of Jesus from the dead. The risen Christ is the focal point of that Kingdom which was initiated on Easter Sunday and is now in the process of spreading the world over."[34]

---

[27] Mark 10:17; Luke 10:25; 18:18

[28] Ephesians 2:4–10

[29] Isaiah 40:1, *ff*

[30] Isaiah 26:19

[31] John Bright, A History of Israel, p. 434

[32] John 11:21 *ff*.

[33] Gerald R. Borchert, The Resurrection Perspective in John, Review and Expositor, Vol. 85, No. 3, Summer 1988, p. 504

[34] J. Jocz, The Spiritual History of Israel, p. 218

Jakob Jocz underlined the essential nature of Paul's later and fuller understanding of Jesus' resurrection. "No one reading St. Paul can fail to notice the importance he ascribed to the resurrection of the Messiah. *'If Christ has not been raised, then our preaching is in vain and your faith is in vain . . . if in this life we who are in Christ have only hope, we are of all men most to be pitied'* (1 Cor. 15:14 ff). Pauline theology is resurrection–theology *par excellence*."[35]

The primary duty of a Pharisee was to learn and then teach each detail of the *Torah*. A Pharisee must do this while seeking an environment of purity. The second duty of a Pharisee was to send his son to a theological school at age 10. We may surmise that after age five, Saul's Pharisee parent would have enrolled him in some form of apprenticeship connected to leather working, a trade he would nurture in Jerusalem, once there.

Thus Saul's father would have sent him to rabbinical school in Jerusalem. Paul's school was the elitist English Eton of today. Gamaliel, reputed as a conciliatory jurist, was its principal. He was adjoined to the renowned House of Hillel. Gameliel was the grandson of the reputed Hillel, and became the first chair of Jerusalem's Sanhedrin.

Gameliel's purpose, says the authoritative *Jewish Encyclopedia*, was "the improvement of the world." We learn from Paul that he was brought up in Jerusalem: "*Under Gameliel I was thoroughly trained in the law of our fathers and was just as zealous for God as any of you* (Paul's accusers) *are today.*"[36] Despite Paul's speaking of his zeal, Pharisees connected more with the common people than did the Sadducees. The Pharisees have been dubbed, "blue collar Jews."

Some sayings attributed to Hillel sound much like those of Jesus. A report proposes that a Gentile once approached Hillel to summarize the wisdom of the *Torah* while standing on one foot. Hillel responded, "What is hateful to you, do not do to your fellow. That is the whole *Torah*; the rest is an explanation–now go and study."[37] That sounds much like the Golden Rule proposed by Jesus.[38] Pharisees, like Gamaliel and Hillel, regarded Moses as the ultimate Pharisee/Rabbi.

How long was Saul's education? We can only surmise. The Pharisees-in-training needed to achieve a mature age before rabbinical officialdom recognized them. They needed to memorize the scriptures. Students in the school needed to buy into all Pharisee theology that included belief in the resurrection. Many of them, if not all, needed to be married. No record of Paul's marriage exists!

---

[35] J. Jocz, <u>op. cit.</u>, p. 188

[36] Acts 22:3

[37] The great Jewish sage, Rabbi Hillel, lived in Palestina (Israel) in the First Century BC. *The Talmud, Shabbat* 31a, relates the following story: "A prospective convert to Judaism asked Hillel to teach him the entire *Torah* while he stood on one leg. Hillel replied: "that which is hateful unto you do not do to your neighbour. This is the whole of the *Torah*, the rest is commentary, Go forth and study."

[38] Matthew 7:12

Jesus and The Pharisees

Despite their resurrection tenet, Jesus was generally unimpressed by the Pharisees. They thrived in being "separatists"; he saw them as being apart from the Kingdom of God. They didn't sense that God ruled in human hearts. Their flaws were pride and upmanship. In general, their regulations were neither redemptive nor refreshing. Theirs was an unholy connection to the people of Israel. Their influences were corruptive and corrosive. They placed religious burdens on people that were so weighty they forgot finding God in order to keep track of the multitudinous required Pharisaic observances. Jesus lashed out at them."

"Then Jesus said to the crowds and to his disciples, 'The scribes and the Pharisees sit on Moses' seat, so do and observe whatever they tell you, but not the works they do. For they preach, but do not practise. They tie up heavy burdens, hard to bear, and lay them on people's shoulders, but they themselves are not willing to move them with their finger. They do all their deeds to be seen by others. For they make their phylacteries broad and their fringes long, and they love the place of honour at feasts and the best seats in the synagogues and greetings in the marketplaces and being called rabbi by others. But you are not to be called rabbi, for you have one teacher, and you are all brothers. And call no man your father on earth, for you have one Father, who is in heaven. Neither be called instructors, for you have one instructor, the Christ. The greatest among you shall be your servant. Whoever exalts himself will be humbled, and whoever humbles himself will be exalted.

"'But woe to you, scribes and Pharisees, hypocrites! For you shut the kingdom of heaven in people's faces. For you neither enter yourselves nor allow those who would enter to go in. Woe to you, scribes and Pharisees, hypocrites! For you travel across sea and land to make a single proselyte, and when he becomes a proselyte, you make him twice as much a child of hell as yourselves.'"[39]

Jesus offered to replace the taxing, chafing, uneven[40] religious yoke imposed by the Pharisees with his own undemanding yoke. *"Take my yoke upon you and learn from me,"* he said, *"for I am gentle and humble in heart, and you will find rest for your souls."*[41] Jesus was surprised at the ignorance of one particular Pharisee, Nicodemus. Nicodemus made a secret appointment with Jesus to find out more about his teaching.

"Now there was a Pharisee, a man named Nicodemus who was a member of the Jewish ruling council. He came to Jesus at night and said, "Rabbi, we know that you are a teacher who has come from God. For no one could perform the signs you are doing if God were not with him." Jesus replied, "Very truly I tell you, no one can see the kingdom of God unless they are born again." "How can someone be born when they are old?" Nicodemus asked. "Surely they cannot enter a second time into their mother's womb to be born!" Jesus answered, "Very truly I tell you, no one can enter the kingdom of God unless they are born of water and the Spirit. Flesh gives birth to flesh, but the Spirit gives birth to spirit. You should not be surprised at my saying, 'You must be born again.' The wind blows

---

[39] Matthew 23:1–36
[40] Deuteronomy 22:10; 2 Corinthians 6:14
[41] Matthew 11:29

wherever it pleases. You hear its sound, but you cannot tell where it comes from or where it is going. So it is with everyone born of the Spirit."
"How can this be?" Nicodemus asked.
"You are Israel's teacher," said Jesus, *"and do you not understand these things?*[42]
Jesus found this ignorance odd because the Pharisees made a point of insisting on ritual immersions at their *mikve'ot*. The principle of the *mikveh* was that it represented both the tomb and the womb. Jews called the act of immersion, *tevilah*. Rabbi Aryeh Kaplan wrote: "When a person immerses he is temporarily in a state of non-living, and when he emerges, he is resurrected with a new status."[43] "The *mikveh* represents the womb," wrote the Rabbi. "When an individual enters the *mikveh*, he is re-entering the womb, and when he emerges, he is as if born anew."[44]

But Nicodemus didn't even "get" that explanation of the immersion he practised almost daily! It was a ritual, nothing more–and it was lost on him.

Thus, when the junior Pharisee Saul joined the rank of this small sect within Judaism, this is the milieu in which he would be constructing his faith, his ideas and his behaviour.

---

[42] John 3:1–10
[43] Aryeh Kaplan, Waters of Eden: The Mystery of the Mikvah (sic), p. 14
[44] Aryeh Kaplan, ibid.,

CHAPTER TWO

WELLNESS AND GAINING ACCEPTANCE

Few would question the mental or spiritual acuity of the cadet Pharisee, Saul of Tarsus. His spiritual development was begun, undoubtedly by his spiritually-minded parents. How was his state of wholeness, his wellness? Wellness is a term used differently by various groups, religious, medical professionals (who usually define it as the opposite of illness). In many instances, health officials believe their emphasis on wellness is a useful prophylactic against illness.

Stephen Covey, author of a multi-million book best seller, The 7 Habits of Highly Effective People, proposes seven principles of what Covey calls an "abundance mindset." They are: (1) Be proactive, not reactive; (2) Focus on the end result; (3) Always put first things first so as not to let less important things capture your incentives; (4) Think win/win so that there are no losers; (5) Listen to what others say before you speak; (6) Involve teamwork, value the differences in others; (7) Take care of yourself first (self care) in order to care for others. This is one version of wellness. It is commendable in itself.[45]

Covey's wellness is not under discussion in this dissertation. "Wellness" as used in this book can be minimally stated as a positive approach to living–an approach emphasizing the whole person. It is the wholeness integration of the body, mind, and spirit; and the appreciation that everything one does, thinks, feels, and believes creates a unity within one's relationship to God.

Jews use the word *shalom* to convey many implications of wellness. *Shalom* may be interpreted as peace, but it also means "may it be well with you," "Good morning," "goodbye" (God be with you), "to your health" and a host of other positive attributes to become a blessing to those receiving *shalom*. *Shalom* is a word of health, wellness and it is a word that every Jewish parent, especially every Pharisee father, would impart to his children. "*Shalom*, my son." On Sabbath, the Jewish greeting is, *Shabbat Shalom*.

As we meet Saul in the Scriptures he may have recited righteous words yet he did not possess *shalom*–wellness. Like the king of Denmark in Shakespeare's Hamlet, Saul might have admitted, "My words fly up, my thoughts remain below: Words without thoughts never to heaven go." But at this stage in his life, he never would admit that. Saul was neither at peace with himself nor anyone else, for that matter.[46]

In addition to teaching his son *shalom*, Saul's Pharisee father obviously obeyed the letter and the spirit of the *Shema*, and taught his son the basics of Jewish tenets.

"Hear, O Israel: The LORD our God, the LORD is one. Love the LORD your God with all your heart and with all your soul and with all your strength. These commandments that I give you today are to be on your hearts. Impress them on your children. Talk about them when you sit at home and when you walk along

---

[45] (General outline, The 7 Habits of Highly Effective People.)
[46] William Shakespeare. Hamlet, Prince of Denmark. Act 3, Scene 3, lines 100–103

the road, when you lie down and when you get up. Tie them as symbols on your hands and bind them on your foreheads. Write them on the doorframes of your houses and on your gates."[47]

All parents know that one may teach the children spiritual truths but it doesn't mean the offspring "buy," follow or implement them. Saul's father cannot be judged for not teaching his son the basics of his faith. In this instance, young Saul seemed to accept the truths as his own. He also bought into the traditional Jewish understanding that Jews differed from Gentiles and possibly were a notch loftier, certainly more loved and respected by God.

God chose Jews as his chosen, covenantal people,[48] didn't he? This attitude surfaced as he not only accepted the separation of superior Jews from inferior *goyim*, but also as Saul grew into the Pharisee's notion of being separate from Jewish laity. Saul then deemed he was "double-separate!" Pharisees also held little esteem for the home-grown, non-observants–the unwashed Jewish *am ha'aretz* people of the land.

Saul's mental acuity was stellar. As moderns evaluate intelligence, Saul likely would have a genius IQ. Were he to be tested today, he likely would have bested the most able Mensa members. He learned to debate the meaning of Scripture as well as anyone, likely better. He honed his oratorical gifts with skill. As a pre-teen, he must have listened to the highly regarded and the gifted Tarsus' Hellenist speakers joust with each other in rhetorical contests. The observations sank in.

How was his emotional health, his EQ (Emotional Quotient)? What about his personality development, his emotional wellness? First, we understand that all growing up is grueling. We have many obstacles to challenge us, including the inheritance of imperfect parents. They colour our perceptions and unknowingly donate their many prejudices to us. Then, in turn, we parents inflict our deficiencies onto our own offspring. It is ever thus. Moreover, everyone alive is addled by one's adolescence when hormones and self-discovery reign supreme.

Saul also inherited obvious basic familial environmental challenges, to grow out of the peccadillos our parents unwittingly, unintentionally and unconsciously unloaded on us. Now we must add other factors inherent in his juvenile development. Was an early imposed absence from Saul's parents a limiting factor in male and female emotional support? Did he sense his parents' rejection by their shipping him to a Jerusalem religious academy at an early age? At least his father occasionally, yearly probably, would journey to Jerusalem to attend one or more of the great Jewish religious feasts of *Pesach*, *Shavuot* and *Sukkoth* (Passover, Pentecost and Harvest).

Swiss psychiatrist Paul Tournier was well aware of the dynamics of parent/child relationships. "Call a child stupid," he wrote, "and you make him stupid showing what he has it in him to do."[49] He continued, "A pretty girl may always have been told by her

---

[47] Deuteronomy 6:4–9

[48] Three covenants of the *Brit bein HaBetarin*, Genesis 12:1–3; 15:18–21; 17:9–14

[49] Paul Tournier, <u>The Meaning of Persons</u>, p. 50

mother that she is plain, either in order to preserve her from becoming conceited, or else from a subconscious motive that operates more often than one might imagine, namely fear that she might outshine her mother." Tournier adds, "The girl comes to have so little confidence in her looks that if a man stares at her she mistakes his admiration for scorn."[50]

We simply don't know the parental relationship of Saul's parents with their child. We don't know what dynamics were in play that led him to become a "Christian hunter." Was Saul attempting to make his Pharisee-father proud of him by his adopting an "ultra" form of Pharisee separation? What part did his mother have in forming his attitudes? Did the adolescent Saul sense a need to outdo his father? Had bad blood developed between them—or all of the above?

In Jerusalem, Saul was something of an outsider, being a Hellenist from Tarsus. Perhaps Saul was a tad short on the elite scale. He used what finicky Pharisees considered a Hellenistic Bible, the *Septuagint*. Many hyper-religious Jews considered the Septuagint not quite pure, not written in Hebrew, but a Greek version of the Bible. Never mind that the *Septuagint* was the Bible everyone used because 70 superior scriptural consultants translated it into the Greek language, finalizing this version in 150 BC in Alexandria. Perfectionist Pharisees would have mused, "Can any good thing come out of Egypt?"

Calvin J. Roetzel notes that Paul's Bible was a degree lower on the authentic scale than the versions used by Jerusalem's Pharisees. "The formative influence of this Hellenistic environment on Paul is most evident in his use of the Septuagint. While known in Jerusalem it hardly enjoyed the unrivalled preeminence there that it enjoyed in Alexandria and Tarsus."[51]

Then Paul had to live with the fact his tribal ancestry was from the clan of Benjamin, not the tribe of Judah. On all those counts, his fellows at Pharisee school would deem him a titch inferior. That's enough to give a young man a complex, isn't it? But add to that: Saul was a Jew in the Diaspora and Diasporan Jews owned a sense of slight inadequacy, when compared to the Jews born in Judea or even in Galilee. Diasporan Jews tried harder to gain the recognition of those born and bred in Jerusalem. Diasporan Jews tried to outdo the homeland variety.

It showed. Saul had to prove himself. Proving oneself is what even some late adolescents do to get attention and acceptance. When the deacon Stephen began to speak about Jesus' work and atonement, a group of Hellenistic Jews provoked Jerusalem's Jewish elders (the Sanhedrin) into stopping this radical blaspheming firebrand from spreading his desecration of the true faith (as they saw it). The Hellenists' caucus got the Sanhedrin's consent. Their Diaspora version solution was to stone Stephen. Isn't that what you do to people who disturb you by their example of faith? Isn't that what *Torah*[52] teaches? Drop the bomb on them if you disagree with people!

Saul thought so. He implicated himself in the heinous act of stoning by gawking at Stephen's untimely extermination, and most cheerfully being noticed by the other

---

[50] ibid
[51] Calvin J. Roetzel, op cit., p. 16
[52] Leviticus 20:12

Hellenistic Jews from his native Cilicia. He didn't quite get fully involved (a "chicken" perhaps?), not picking up the death rocks to execute deacon Stephen. He did consent to the act, however. Saul held the clothes of the perpetrators who hurled their abominable ammo and bashed Stephen to death.[53]

Saul heard the testimony of deacon Stephen as he was dying. Steven stated that he saw the resurrected and exalted Jesus. *"But Stephen, full of the Holy Spirit, looked up to heaven and saw the glory of God, and Jesus standing at the right hand of God. "Look," he said, "I see heaven open and the Son of Man standing at the right hand of God."*[54] The words and the "event" surely sank into Saul's consciousness and lingered in his unconscious mind.

Many leaders suffer from such inferiority feelings. Winston Churchill and Napoleon Bonaparte are among them. Everyone bears the eternal scars of growing up and mastering our challenges.

So, such leaders, especially alpha ones, compensate for their negatives by being much more assertive than others. Saul/Paul certainly exhibited assertiveness. He was an alpha leader. He applied for attention and acceptance. And he was seriously flawed. Paul Tournier wrote that he was reading paper and came across a Spanish proverb: "Habits begin like threads in a spider's web, but end up as ropes."[55] So it was with Saul.

---

[53] Acts 6:11, *ff*; 7:57
[54] Acts 7:55, 56
[55] Paul Tournier, op. cit., p 51

CHAPTER THREE
GOD'S DIVERSIONS

Meanwhile Paul had become a firebrand of sorts. He had stepped from the sidelines of being an accessory by holding the cloaks of Stephen's killers, to become a hit man himself. We could speculate that this was yet another undertaking to prove himself in front of other Pharisee zealots in an attempt to gain their admiration and accent their adoption of him among them. Saul saw his Christian prey as "radicalizers." Psychologist David Belgum proposes that those with Saul's behaviour reflect their need to be approved by gangs like Saul's Hellenistic Jewish friends in Jerusalem:

"For many of us good behaviour is prompted by the desire to have loved ones and significant others think well of us. As children we want the approval of meaningful authority figures, the acceptance of our playmates; and in exchange for this 'do right.' that is the must conscience of childhood. Hopefully as we mature into adulthood, we will internalize a sense of morality and the capacity to make ethical decisions. This may be called the ought conscience of the responsible adult member of society."[56]

People feeling inferior often do that. It's an unhappy natural downward progression and a human commentary on immature development. Does that compare to the schemes of Nazism, or of ISIS, the Islamic State of Iraq and Syria (or ISIL, the Islamic State of Iraq and the Levant)? The Bible reads,

"*Meanwhile, Saul was still breathing out murderous threats against the Lord's disciples. He went to the high priest and asked him for letters to the synagogues in Damascus, so that if he found any there who belonged to the Way, whether men or women, he might take them as prisoners to Jerusalem.*"[57]

The "Way" is a great term for new Christians, those who had come to believe in Jesus as the Messiah, Saviour and Lord. Its Jewish antecedent is the Hebrew word *halakah*. *Halakah* is how we live. It is our lifestyle for behaviour and piety. In Deuteronomy [8:2], Moses wrote, "*Remember how the LORD led you all the 'way'*" (double entendre). Psalm 37:34 states, "*Wait for the LORD and keep his way.*" Isaiah wrote, "*Whether you turn to the right or to the left, your ears will hear a voice behind you, saying, 'This is the way; walk in it.'*"[58]

Jesus told his disciples that he is "the way."[59] That helps to explain why the earliest Christians became known as "The Way."[60] To critics like the junior Pharisee Saul, this term used by Jesus' disciples was a perversion of *halakah*. It was an insult to his immature Jewish understanding.[61] Saul needed to personally discover that "The Way" is a very long, concentrated and demanding walk along a very constricted roadway.

---

56 David Belgum, Alone, Alone, All Alone, p. 48
57 Acts 9:1, 2
58 Isaiah 30:21
59 John 14:6
60 see Acts 9:2; 19:9, 23; 22:4; 24:14
61 see Paul Tournier's comment on immaturity observed by Freudian

Jesus put it this way: *"Go in by the narrow gate. For the wide gate has a broad road which leads to disaster and there are many people going that way. The narrow gate and the hard road lead out into life and only a few are finding it."*[62] As Paul, no longer Saul, the Apostle reset the goal's end. Jesus was the destination. Paul told the Philippians, *"I press on* (not yet having arrived) *toward the goal to win the prize* (Jesus Christ himself) *for which God has called me heavenward in Christ Jesus."*[63]

One may anticipate but never quite know how long is the road, or what blessings or banes one may encounter along the roadway. David Belgum offers this thought: "Man is never a finished product: he is always in the process of becoming. If he chooses to exercise his full potential, he can have a great deal to say about what he becomes from day to day."[64] Luke wrote of the four-part youth Jesus, *"Jesus grew in wisdom and in Spirit and in favour with God and man."*[65] Jesus set the pattern for a "wellness" life.

Saul's Epiphany

Saul set out to stop this development. By now, "The Way" had emerged in various parts of the Roman world. He learned that a believers' outbreak had occurred in Damascus and set out to influence like-minded Jews connected to a Syrian synagogue to smother this fearful fire. A funny but serious thing happened as Saul rushed to root out, corral and punish his prey.

God intervened. Outwardly, Saul adjudged any member of The Way to be a schismatic, and scurrilous one at that! Inwardly–subconsciously and/or unconsciously–Saul admired the members of the group. They had as much stick-with-it-ness as he had, if not more. Explanations for what happened next are difficult to interpret, God hit him with a kind of "divine electro-shock" that allowed his spiritual synapses to work satisfactorily.

Freudian psychoanalysts have a name for what happened. They call it, "reaction formation."[66] It is a person's developed defence mechanism to hide one's true subconscious or unconscious feelings. People use many defence mechanisms to ignore the truth. They practise rationalization, transference, repression, denial, projection and reaction formation to avoid reality.[67] The anxiety defence mechanism that created "reaction formation" was masking Saul's true feelings by his behaving in an opposite way!

Anna Freud argued, for example, without referencing Saul, that people like Saul employed reaction formation as a defence mechanism to hide their true feelings by

---

psychologists, "it is the Freudians . . .who have shown us how many infantile attitudes and reactions persist into what we fondly call adulthood," Paul Tournier, op. cit., p 58

[62] Matthew 7:13, 14. J. B. Phillips Paraphrase
[63] Philippians 3:14
[64] David Belgum, op. cit., p.55
[65] Luke 2:52
[66] Anna Freud, The Ego and Mechanisms of Defence, p. 9
[67] Helen Schacter, Understanding Ourselves., pp. 75–81

behaving in the exact opposite manner. Dr. Freud wrote, "reaction-formation secures the ego against the return of repressed impulses from within."[68] It was Anna Freud's hypothesis that defence mechanisms were developed to act as a shield to one's ego. She describes reaction formation as "obsessive neurosis."[69] Anna Freud expands her theory of reaction formation:

> "Reaction-formation . . . is one of the most important measures adapted by the ego as a permanent protection against the id. Such formations appear almost unheralded in the ego in the course of a child's development. We cannot always say that the ego's attention had previously been focussed on the particular contrary instinctual impulse which the reaction-formation replaces. As a rule, the ego knows nothing of the rejection of the impulse or of the whole conflict which has resulted in the implanting of the new characteristic. Analytic observers might easily take it for a spontaneous development of the ego, were it not that definite indications of obsessional exaggeration suggest that it is of the nature of a reaction and that it reveals a long-standing conflict. Here again, observation of the particular mode of defence does not reveal anything of the process by which it has been evolved."[70]

The phrase "reaction formation" especially applies with individuals having an obsessive or possessive personality, an identifiable neurosis. In other words, deep down, unconsciously, Saul really wanted to follow Jesus. Saul was part of an Olympian inner war with himself. This situation was much like the dilemma of Job, *For the thing which I greatly feared is come upon me, and that which I was afraid of is come unto me.*[71] The difference between Job and Saul, however, is that Saul's fear was deeply buried in his unconscious mind. Job recognized his fear overtly.

What was entrenched in Saul's subconscious or unconscious was a truth denied (another defence mechanism). The "event" on the Road to Damascus was the climax of the anxiety conflict and Saul surrendered to his true inner convictions. Had Saul heeded what he read and knew in the Jewish scriptures, he might have understood his dilemma earlier. *The Lord gave us mind and conscience; we cannot hide from ourselves.*[72] Saul was hiding from himself.

"Every man's behaviour is a human contradiction because there is more than one of him."[73] John Homer Miller may be suggesting that such a person may have multiple personalities. In this book we prefer suggesting that Saul had only one personality but it was a confused and conflicted one. Saul did not have an *ought* conscience, at least not a conscious *ought* conscience. Saul's understanding was befogged by his neurotic, adamant, biased, and inbred closed mind regarding issues taught in the *Torah*. He had allowed his Pharisee-interpreted theology to trump basic Scriptural truth.

---

68 Anna Freud, op. cit., p. 190
69 Anna Freud, op. cit., p. 46
70 Anna Freud, op. cit., p. 9
71 Job 3:25 KJV
72 Proverbs 20:27
73 John Homer Miller, Why We Act The Way, p. 156

The first book of the Pentateuch made it abundantly clear that God's intentions included sharing and encompassing his love within Gentiles. God made it perfectly plain to Abraham that his job description included bringing Gentiles into the fold of his blessings. "*You* (Abram) *will be a blessing. I will bless those who bless you, and whoever curses you I will curse; and all people on earth will be blessed through you.*"[74]

Isaiah likewise foretold that God would show himself to everyone. "*The glory of the LORD will be revealed and all mankind together shall see it.*"[75] It was not that Saul did not know these texts; but by his obstinacy, he simply failed to parse them properly. Jesus was part of that blessing to the world. Saul's bias could not allow him to comprehend that Jesus was the anticipated Messiah and now the Saviour of the world.

Saul's misinterpretations gave him no leg to stand on. He was plain wrong! We needn't rely on defence mechanism explanations to show Saul's psychological errors even though they are compelling and seem to be scientifically and medically correct. The scripture says it quite well and hardly needs little further explanation. God entered into Saul's private innermost waged war and helped him discover *shalom*. God stormed Saul's ego fortress and extracted Saul's sturdy defences. Here's the story:[76]

> "*As he neared Damascus on his journey, suddenly a light from heaven flashed around him. He fell to the ground and heard a voice say to him, "Saul, Saul, why do you persecute me?"*
> "*Who are you, Lord?" Saul asked.*
> "*I am Jesus, whom you are persecuting," he replied. "Now get up and go into the city, and you will be told what you must do."*
> *The men travelling with Saul stood there speechless; they heard the sound but did not see anyone. Saul got up from the ground, but when he opened his eyes he could see nothing. So they led him by the hand into Damascus. For three days he was blind, and did not eat or drink anything.*"

The fact that two other slightly varying versions of this account appear in scripture does not negate the reality of what happened. In this account, Saul alone saw a light, heard a voice (as did others), and he alone fell to the ground.[77] Later, at the entrance steps of Jerusalem's Fortress Antonia (Praetorium), Paul told the unruly mob what happened on the Damascus Road. Again, Saul saw a light, then heard a voice and he alone fell to the ground. In a later version, the text reports that all saw the light and fell to the ground and then he heard a voice.[78] The modest differences are unimportant. The three days of Saul's blindness mirrored Jesus' three days in the tomb.

Saul needed a spiritual spanking, a thorough debasing. God put him down, did not leave him disconsolate, but raised him up again. It was a form of necessary chastening, a personal demise and an individualized resurrection. Saul described himself as "wretched" when it happened, but he thanked God for rescuing him.[79]

---

[74] Genesis 12:2b, 3
[75] Isaiah 40:5
[76] Acts 9:3–9
[77] Acts 22:6, 7
[78] Acts 26:13

Saul/Paul continued to wrestle with this new humility but somehow, somewhat managed with God's help to control it. Saul was wretched because he had assented to Stephen's assassination but also because he had opposed God. He was thankful that God rescued him from his sin and his faulty spirituality, restoring him by grace to God's service. Like the Prodigal Son,[80] Saul was lost and then was rescued.

Paul restated his inner wars in another way when he penned his letter to Roman Christians:

> *"By dying to what once bound us, we have been released from the law so that we serve in the new way of the Spirit, and not in the old way of the written code . . . I do not understand what I do. For what I want to do I do not do, but what I hate I do. And if I do what I do not want to do, I agree that the law is good. As it is, it is no longer I myself who do it, but it is sin living in me. I know that nothing good lives in me, that is, in my sinful nature. For I have the desire to do what is good, but I cannot carry it out. For what I do is not the good I want to do; no, the evil I do not want to do – this I keep on doing. Now if I do what I do not want to do, it is no longer I who do it, but it is sin living in me that does it. So I find this law at work: When I want to do good, evil is right there with me. For in my inner being I delight in God's law; but I see another law at work in the members of my body, waging war against the law of my mind and making me a prisoner of the law of sin at work within my members. What a wretched man I am! Who will rescue me from this body of death? Thanks be to God–through Jesus Christ our Lord! So then, I myself in my mind am a slave to God's law, but in the sinful nature a slave to the law of sin."[81]*

Conversion is an inexplicable, deep and mysterious experience. One needs to hit bottom before rising to a new way of life. It's another form of God's metamorphosis' miracle of resurrection. One dies as a caterpillar and rises as a butterfly. Jesus articulated the principle: *"I must fall and die like a kernel of wheat falls into the furrows of the earth. Unless I die I will be alone–a single seed. But my death will produce many new kernels–a plentiful harvest of new lives."*[82]

Confession is always necessary for someone's death to self. Psalm 51 is a classic example of the necessary step to forgiveness and rehabilitation. Not only do the religious people need to confess sins, mental health requires it. The basis of the various "steps" programs, i.e., Alcoholic Anonymous, is to be upfront about one's impotence to solve a hurtful way of life. Read Paul Tournier on this matter:

> "It is not necessary for me to insist on the medical value of confession. A bad conscience can, over a period of years, so strangle a person's life that his physical and psychical powers of resistance are thereby impaired. It can be the root cause of certain psychosomatic afflictions. It is like a stopper that can be pulled out by confession, so that life begins at once to flow again. That is why Dr. Sonderegger called the doctor the 'natural confessor of humanity'; and why Michelet wrote that 'a complete confession is always necessary in medicine.' At the beginning of

---

[79] Romans 7:24
[80] Luke 15:11–32
[81] Romans 7: selected verses
[82] John 12:24 TLB

this Century Dr. Dubois, of Berne, who did not call himself a Christian, wrote: 'Confess your patient.'"[83]

The Good News is God's way of helping us find out who we are. Confession assists in this search. We learn that we are loved and that we are children of God. When converted, new Christians discover they have royal blood coursing through their veins. In the words of Peter,

> *"But you are a chosen people, a royal priesthood, a holy nation, God's special possession, that you may declare the praises of him who called you out of darkness into his wonderful light. Once you were not a people, but now you are the people of God; once you had not received mercy, but now you have received mercy.[84]*

Professor Jakob Jocz saw it that way too.

"The biblical call to self-discovery is different in nature from the Greek motto: *gnōthi seauton* (know yourself). Whatever that inscription may have meant to the worshippers attending Apollo's temple at Delphi, to Plato it certainly does not mean the discovery of self as a sinner . . . The self discovery of man as a sinner was the most revolutionary ferment which changed the whole structure of ancient society."[85]

When Paul, the former Pharisee discovered this mercy and grace en route to Damascus, God turned him into an able apostle and a potent proselytizer.

On Damascus' highway, Saul made major self-discoveries. His first admission was his inability to know why he acted as he did. "*I do not understand my own actions,*"[86] he wrote to Rome. The next discovery was God-planted because faith is generated by God.[87] He realized his depravity and his failure. When the Lord asked him, "*Saul, Saul, why do you persecute me,*"[88] he understood the ugly truth that he was working against the God whose cause he thought he was serving. Saul was warring with *YAHWEH*. Saul discovered Jesus. Like Carter opening King Tut's tomb, Saul began to uncover God's will. And like Howard Carter[89] peering into the newly unsealed Tut tomb, Saul could say, "Yes, I see wonderful things!" He was finding God's purpose for his life and he realized for the first time, his true identity. What an epiphany!

Confession is but one phase of reconciliation with God, certainly an essential first step in justification. What must follow are: repentance, forgiveness, assurance of pardon, restoration and commissioning. Such steps would not surprise a confessing Saul. He knew Isaiah's great promise about God's steps to restoration. "*I, I am he who blots out your transgressions for my own sake and I will not remember your sins.*"[90] The

---

[83] Paul Tournier, op. cit., p. 157
[84] 1 Peter 2:9, 10; Exodus 19:6
[85] J. Jocz, op. cit., pp. 198, 199
[86] Romans 7:15
[87] Ephesians 2:8
[88] Acts 9:4
[89] Nicholas Reeves, John H. Taylor, Howard Carter Before Tutankhamun, p. 188
[90] Isaiah 43:25

prophet repeated himself in assuring confessors of God's just redemption: *"I have swept away your transgression like a cloud, and your sins like a mist: return to me, for I have redeemed you."*[91] The term transgression suggests going beyond God's boundaries. Redemption implies that a confessor was a slave to his sin, and that God purchased his freedom.

Jeremiah said as much and more. *"I will cleanse them from all the guilt of their sin against me, and I will forgive all the guilt of their sin against me, and will forgive all the guilt of their sin and rebellion against me."*[92] That assurance provided Saul with remission of both sin and its guilt. Saul served a restorative God, one who offered second chances.[93] Saul needed both remissions.

The word "salvation" connects with similar words, i.e., "salve," meaning "health" or "saliferous," meaning "conducive to health." Among other meanings, salvation means a restoration of health, wellness. This is pointed out by one of John's letters. *"If we confess our sins, he who is faithful and just will forgive us our sins and cleanse us from all unrighteousness."*[94] Cleansing leads to wholeness.

Saul/Paul appropriated these truths declared by Isaiah, Jeremiah (and would have seconded John's motion) for himself and assured new Christians elsewhere of their justification by God himself. Saul confessed, repented, received pardon, restoration and a commission from God. Paul wrote to Rome to underline them:

> *"But God demonstrates his own love for us in this: While we were still sinners, Christ died for us. Since we have now been justified by his blood, how much more shall we be saved from God's wrath through him! For if, while we were God's enemies, we were reconciled to him through the death of his Son, how much more, having been reconciled, shall we be saved through his life! Not only is this so, but we also boast in God through our Lord Jesus Christ, through whom we have now received reconciliation."*[95]

Saul realized all aspects of reconciliation with God. His comprehension led to his prayer for Christians in Rome: *"May your hearts* [i.e., feelings] *and your minds* [i.e., thinking] *rest in the promise and assurance of freedom from condemnation through Jesus Christ"* (i.e., the entire person).[96] Paul here was expressing his own deliverance from slavery to sin and ironically, his freedom found in a new acceptable slavery, his service to his Saviour. Saul had confessed, repented, was restored, reconciled and commissioned, ergo, "saved." He experienced all the steps to full healing.

As a part of this salving, Saul was rapidly realizing that the newly-minted friends of The Way provided him with a human warmth he had not known in his previous Pharisee existence. Theirs was a different *halakah*, a "way" of life he had not experienced previously. These were joyful people. They shared their lives with one another. All their

---

[91] Isaiah 44:22
[92] Jeremiah 33:8
[93] see also Matthew 18: 21, 22
[94] 1 John 1:9
[95] Romans 5:8–11
[96] Romans 8:2

possessions belonged to the Lord so they had no sense of personal ownership and they shared these possessions freely, willingly and gladly.[97]

Saul, later called Paul, recognized that the aura apparent in The Way was best described with a Greek word, *koinonia* (fellowship). This must be first interpreted as a community of partnership, communion, love, mercy and grace, where a spirit of joy permeated human relationships.[98]

This fellowship, this partnership was marked by a joyous mood even in persecution. Saul was learning a new way of walking, a new *halaka*, and an exuberant way of worship. The crowd of Christians known as The Way sang from the heart and soon were composing their own psalms praising God in the manner of King David.

One of their poems-hymns is found in Paul's letter to Philippi. Perhaps Paul wrote it, or possibly it was already so well known that it suited Paul to prompt the Philippians of their proper point of priority. Saul discovered that the believers began their worship meetings with joy set in musical form. It continues to this day. Believers must sing!

> *In your relationships with one another, have the same mindset as Christ Jesus:*
> *Who, being in very nature God,*
> *did not consider equality with God something to be used to his own advantage;*
> *rather, he made himself nothing*
> *by taking the very nature of a servant,*
> *being made in human likeness.*
> *And being found in appearance as a man,*
> *he humbled himself*
> *by becoming obedient to death—*
> *even death on a cross!*
> *Therefore God exalted him to the highest place*
> *and gave him the name that is above every name,*
> *that at the name of Jesus every knee should bow,*
> *in heaven and on earth and under the earth,*
> *and every tongue acknowledge that Jesus Christ is Lord,*
> *to the glory of God the Father.*[99]

James Orr proposes that it is

"not necessary to discuss at length the reality and objectivity of the appearance of the glorified Jesus to Saul the persecutor when his mad rage was in full career. The sudden and revolutionary change then wrought, with its lasting moral and spiritual effects is one which no '*kicking against the goads*' (Acts 26:14) is Saul's consciousness which had been silently gathering to a head, can satisfactorily explain . . . Most certain it is that St. Paul himself was convinced both at the time of the vision and ever after, of the reality of Christ's appearance to him and of the call he then received to be the Apostle to the Gentiles."[100]

---

[97] Acts 4:34

[98] Acts 2:42; 2 Corinthians 6:14; Galatians 2:9; Philippians 3:10

[99] Philippians 2:5–11

[100] James Orr, The Resurrection of Jesus, p. 209

What also astonishes Bible readers is that Paul's epiphany on the Damascus Road included seeing the Lord himself. He used that claim as a validity of his apostleship. Theologian Robert Reymond notes the importance of this vital affirmation:

"It is arguable that no postascension act by the risen Christ has ever rivaled, in the significance of its effect on the on-going worldwide life of the church, his appearance to his arch-foe, Saul of Tarsus, on the road to Damascus, sometime between AD 32 and 35, the record of which is found in Acts 9:3–18; 22:6–16; and 26:12–18 (see also 1 Cor. 9:1; 15:8). Indeed, so significant is Saul's conversion to Christianity that it is not saying too much to declare that if he was *not* converted as the Acts accounts report, not only is Luke/Acts (as well as Luke's personal integrity as a careful historian) rendered immediately and directly a false witness to history, but the Pauline corpus is also rendered invalid as a rule of faith and practice, because Paul claimed in all of his letters to be a legitimate apostle, meeting all the requirements of one who would be an apostle, particularly the one Peter mentions in Acts 1: 22: *"a witness of his resurrection."* Paul claimed that Jesus *'last of all . . . appeared to me also'* (1 Cor. 15:8). He claimed that he had received his commission as an apostle *'not from man nor by [any] man, but by Jesus Christ'* (Gal. 1:1)."[101]

A Gracious Welcome

What followed Saul's epiphany is remarkable. First, God humbled him and followed it by offering Saul a helping hand to stand again. Resurrection (*anastasis*) means "stand again." As James wrote, God *"gives us more grace . . . God opposes the proud but gives grace to the humble."*[102] The psalmist also knew this from personal experience. *"The humble will see and be glad–you who seek God, may your hearts live!"*[103]

God had already prepared someone to administer his resurrection grace to Saul. Some companions led Saul, still blinded, into Damascus and followed divine instructions for Saul to find a man named Ananias dwelling on Straight Street. (Straight Street still exists in Damascus!). Until he met Ananias, Saul neither ate nor drank. The irony and evidence of the account is that Ananias was one of the main targets of Saul's posse. Ananias was also a bull's-eye! So the very man Saul was seeking to arrest and perhaps to stone him like Stephen, ministered to Saul. Love does that.

Yet, Ananias was not naïve. He questioned God about reaching out to Saul, but the Lord allayed any anxiety Ananias exhibited. Grace was alive and active in Damascus.

"This man is my chosen instrument," God revealed to Ananias. He *"will carry my name before the Gentiles and their kings and before the people of Israel. I will show him how much he will suffer for my name."*[104] Thus God allowed Ananias to hear what plans the Lord had prepared for Saul.

Saul now had come under the tutelage of Ananias. He had died as a proud Pharisee and now would spend three days humbled by his blindness and leaden regrets

---

[101] Robert L. Reymond, <u>A New Systematic Theology of the Christian Faith</u>, p. 1113
[102] James 4:6
[103] Psalm 69:32, 33
[104] Acts 9:15, 16

until Ananias observed him newly born as a believer and missionary. Like Jesus, Saul had experienced death and soon a resurrection.

The Damascus saint went to the house where Saul's travelling companions had taken him. Ananias symbolically placed his hands on Saul's eyes, reinforcing the new vision God had given Saul. He was about to see again, but what he saw was totally different from what he had perceived previously. He had moved from a form of grave spiritual illness-nigh unto death–into the threshold of spiritual wellness.

Clifford W. Beers (30 March 1876–09 July 1943), a frequent resident of a New Haven mental institute wrote a book on his experience, A Mind that Found Itself.[105] He suffered from depression and paranoia. Beers died in a mental institution but during his periods of clarity and sanity, he described what he was going through and how he found stretches of wellness. The book (1908) became the basis of modern mental health treatment. In a way, Saul, like Beers, had found his soul. He now knew he was a child of God's love and a servant forever of his grace.

Ananias prepared Saul to receive the Holy Spirit. He called Saul, "Brother." He then instructed Saul to be immersed as a believer in Jesus the Christ.

Saul no longer needed to undertake his constant ritual washings in the Jewish ritual of supposed spiritual cleansing, but in the one lifetime ordinance that symbolized death to the old Saul and his resurrection of a new existence. The Jewish immersion vats (*mikve'ot*) that served to provide ritual cleansing represented wombs and tombs; the rising from the baths represent being born anew. But this Jewish custom was a multi-repeatable baptismal form lacking any sense of repentance.

Saul had followed Jesus' example of baptism, the reflection of death and resurrection Jesus showed when John the Baptist immersed him in the River Jordan. "*Immediately, something like scales fell from Saul's eyes, and he could see again. He got up and was baptized, and after taking some food, he regained his strength.*"[106] Jesus submitted himself to a human agent, a symbol of Jesus' emptying himself to live like human beings. He later would submit himself to human magistrates, human courts and human execution squads. Saul would do the same.

Even prior to his anticipated Arabian desert Spirit-tutoring ahead of him, Saul began to exercise a change of attitude–his spiritual healing was underway. The miracle of incorporeal metamorphosis had begun. Saul had to learn to trust the believers he formerly had vowed to annihilate. Saul was now among a brotherhood (*haburah*) exponentially richer than that of the Pharisees.

He first needed to trust Ananias, who assured Saul that he now was among friends, not opponents and that it was the Lord Jesus he had seen on the highway. He obediently followed this faithful Damascus contact who now promised him a returned sight. Saul obeyed Ananias' command to be immersed as a believer. Was not Jesus–the Son of God, the Saviour of the world, the Messiah–immersed by human hands when he committed himself at the Jordan for his ministry? So was Saul!

[105] Clifford Willingham Beers, A Mind That Found Itself
[106] Acts 9:18, 19

Saul was overwhelmed by his conversion experience. That was another kind of baptism. He was inundated by guilt, shame and regret. David Watson explained that baptism had an application in this feeling as well:

> "The verb *baptizo* was used in pre-Christian Greek to mean 'plunge, sink, drown, drench, overwhelm.' A person could be overwhelmed (lit. baptized) by debts, sorrow, calamity; or overcome (lit. baptized) by wine or sleep. Euripedes in the Orestes uses *bapto* when water is splashing into a ship, but *baptizo* when the ship is waterlogged or sinking."[107]

And when Saul learned of plots against him, he vested his life into the care of the Damascus trusteeship of The Way. These were those he believed would help him escape at night over the Damascus wall. He grew in the "power" of God's Spirit as he realized how faith in new friends and brimming reliance in Jesus quickly authorized him to preach and teach about "The Way" of which he now was assuredly a vital part.

Saul soon began to realize his potential as an advocate of his reborn life, of all Spirit-reborn lives. God had humbled him for a good reason. Now God was warranting him to speak for Christ's kingdom on earth. He was proud to do so, not in an arrogant way but in an overjoyed yet modest manner. The secret of this new boldness was in the confidence of the Holy Spirit, and not in the human ego-centred drive that marked his previous outrages. Saul was healing and approaching "wellness."

---

[107] David Watson, I Believe in the Church, p. 126

CHAPTER FOUR
SAUL'S SEMINARIES

One realizes how swiftly the belief of Jesus' death and resurrection in Jerusalem had now rooted itself in distant places. Disciples abounded everywhere. Could Saul put out the brushfire/virus that by now had swept ferociously and infectiously into Syria?

No wonder Saul was terrified at the increase of what he thought was bogus Judaism now seriously advanced into Syria. Saul had been brainwashed while in Jerusalem. He had bought into the mindset of fanatical critics from the Hellenist-Jewish sect searching out those who had rallied around the crucified and risen Jesus. Jesus' followers now heralded their Lord as the long expected Messiah (Christ).

The Damascus Seminary

This Pharisee-ingrained mindset was like a bad seed. Saul had viewed his self-assignment as if he were treating a wide-spread bacterium now acutely infecting far too many Jews. Saul saw the seed as corrupting his God-given *Torah* faith, the Law. "The Way," thought Saul, had twisted *Torah* teachings not to mention warping the fragile faith of predisposed Jews. The truth was just the opposite. Jesus explained the *Torah*.

Saul, in his prejudiced mind, saw "The Way" as a diabolical twist of the Jewish central principal (*halaka[h]*) of following God's prescribed pathway as outlined in the *Torah*.[108] "*Halaka* is walking in the 'way of the LORD,'"[109] wrote Toronto Rabbi Stuart Rosenberg. "What the priests made into cold and impersonal commands of scripture, Rabbinic *halaka* (interpreted it) with warmth of a new zeal: to build God's kingdom on earth by learning to do his will within the human situation." "*Halaka* is symbolic of a return to an Eden in which humankind can walk shamelessly in the garden with the LORD God."[110]

During his ministry, Jesus cautioned his disciples about the single-mindedness of many Pharisees. Jesus did not brand all of them as bad or biased, but he described some of their influence as unhealthy leaven. "*Be on your guard against the yeast of the Pharisees and Sadducees.*"[111] Saul had bought into the Pharisees' unacceptably perverted leaven.

Ananias comes across as a humble, fearless disciple who is attentive to God's leading. He knows who is in charge of life. He reflects David's response to the Philistines: "*You come against me with sword and spear and javelin, but I come against you in the name of the LORD Almighty . . . This day the LORD will deliver you into my hands . . . And the whole world will know that there is a God in Israel.*"[112]

---

[108] Herbert Danby, The Code of Maimonides, p. xiii
[109] Stuart Rosenberg, To Understand Jews, p. 40
[110] Genesis 3:8
[111] Matthew 16:11
[112] 1 Samuel 17: 45, 46

Saul's virulent predispositions demanded debriefing and reordering. Perhaps Ananias reminded Saul of an adage in Proverbs. *"A hot-tempered man . . . gets into all kinds of trouble."*[113] At first, God assigned that training task to Ananias. The wise and patient Ananias began to deprogram his charge, Saul. Disciples in Damascus joined with Ananias in detoxifying Saul's previous skewed, brain-washed attitudes.

After several days, Ananias, like a wise and mature Master at Teacher's College, took his charge Saul to several synagogues around the outskirts of Damascus and under observation set him free to teach and preach.

Saul was now rid of his former persuasions. He delighted in talking about Jesus as the Son of God. It was a C-turn in Saul's troubled life. These practice-teaching/preaching sessions were auditions to check his revised faith before Ananias gave positive affirmation in recommending him elsewhere.

Saul's Arabian Desert Theological College

Ananias knew could not teach him everything. Saul took his post-graduate three years of studies somewhere in Arabia. Arabia is not necessarily Saudi Arabia. Karen Armstrong conjectures that Paul (Saul) arrived in Nabatean cities such as Petra, and that he may have preached in synagogues because many Jews lived in these regions.[114] However, in that wilderness area Saul had no human instructor.

The Holy Spirit privately tutored him about the new faith he had enjoined. The Holy Spirit enabled Saul to see his true identity as a child of God. The Spirit helped to heal Saul of his defence mechanisms, his reaction formation. The Spirit reformed Saul and shaped him for the service of God to which God undeniably called him. The Spirit helped Saul to see his purpose in life. Saul did what the early Coptic ascetics such as St. Anthony did, namely use the desert for contemplation, pondering the word of God, personal reflection, assimilation and prayer. Oh the healing he needed to recover from his self-reproach, guilt and regret! The Holy Spirit did his work now that Saul had come down from his "high horse." God's service and human conceit are incompatible.

Saul had much to unlearn, learn and relearn. Likely, it was in this seminary, with God's Spirit as tutor and teacher, that he began to realize that the Law he had so avidly respected as an obedient Jew, was trumped by God's revelation of a new covenant God made with all mankind through Jesus, Saviour, Messiah. Father Jerome Murphy-O'Connor points this out.

> "The next step followed naturally, because Paul had anticipated it mentally, and was prepared for it. If Jesus was the Messiah, then the time of the Law was over. What the Law laid down as the prerequisites for salvation no longer had any validity. Gentiles, therefore in terms of their hope of salvation were no longer in any way different to Jews. It was not the obedience to the Law that mattered, but acceptance of Jesus. The Messiah was not just for Jews. He was Lord of the whole world."[115]

---

[113] Proverbs 29:22 TLB
[114] Karen Armstrong, St. Paul: The Apostle We Love to Hate, p. 19

Saul began to find his purpose. God was revealing to him that his work was to share his faith in Jesus with those who did not know the oracles of God. Purpose is needed in every life. Had Saul not found his purpose he would have continued undisciplined, wandering aimlessly as a lost nomad, like the mythical "wandering Jew." Purpose gives us direction and destination. Bless the solitude of a desert in which to communicate with God and he with you!

Rick Warren was onto something when he wrote The Purpose-Driven Life, asking the question, "What are we here for?" Purpose is our North Star. Warren persuades his reader that (1) We were planned for God's pleasure; (2) we were formed for God's family; (3) we were created to become like Christ; (4) we were shaped for serving God; (5) We were made for mission.[116]

Purpose gives everyone direction. Purpose tells everyone where they are. It tells us who we are. The Damascus Road experience of Saul/Paul was an epiphany–a eureka moment–to be sure. But not only did Saul discover Jesus as Lord and Saviour. He found his purpose in life. He found his mission. He found himself. He was like the prodigal in Jesus' parable, who Jesus described as having a eureka moment,[117] *"When he came to himself."* Saul/Paul "came to himself," saying, *"To me, living is Christ."*[118] While travelling the Damascus Road, that became Saul's discovery of his life purpose. That is when Saul uncovered his pathway to wellness.

Paul defined his purpose more succinctly than most church confessions. He stated it in six words. *"Our aim is to please him."* That was his sole purpose in being an Apostle. All else falls under that favourable fixation. *"Whether we are at home or away our aim is to please him."* The verb Paul uses (*euaresteo*) means, "be well pleased with," "to take pleasure in." It is the goal of a slave whose own life is richly enhanced if his work gives joy to his master. Both slave and master take delight when a task is done the best possible way and without self-interest. When the goal is completed satisfactorily, it puts a smile on the face of both slave and master. Petersen (The Message) translates the passage with a lilt in his paraphrase: *"Cheerfully pleasing God is the main thing, and that's what we aim to do regardless of our conditions."*

Paul's "aim" may be an echo from Jesus' parable about a faithful slave. *"Who then is the faithful and wise slave, whom his master has put in charge of his household, to give the other slaves their allowance of food at the proper time? Blessed is that slave whom his master will find at work when he arrives. Truly I tell you, he will put that one in charge of all his possessions."*[119]

God's Spirit did more than reform Saul. "Reform" is too belittling a word to describe the changes in Saul's psyche. Bible readers can get a glimpse of God's desert work in Saul by reading the early sentences in Romans 12.

---

[115] Jerome Murphy O'Connor, Paul: His Story, p. 24
[116] Rick Warren, The Purpose Driven Life
[117] Luke 15:17
[118] Philippians 1:21a
[119] Matthew 24:45–47

"Therefore, I urge you, brothers and sisters, in view of God's mercy, to offer your bodies as a living sacrifice, holy and pleasing to God—this is your true and proper worship. Do not conform to the pattern of this world, but be transformed by the renewing of your mind. Then you will be able to test and approve what God's will is—his good, pleasing and perfect will."[120]

The key word in this text is not "conform" but "transform." The Greek word is *metamorphousthe*. It means becoming an entirely different person or creature. The word is used to describe a caterpillar becoming a butterfly. God was not removing Saul's natural prickliness or other personality traits but rather his learned attitudes while simultaneously turning Saul's outlook to face in the opposite direction. To Rome, in this chapter 12, Paul was explaining what God's Spirit did to him during his three year private tutoring sessions at the Arabian Desert Theological College. Paul also sought this change for any Christian neophytes in Rome. God had remade Saul into a new being.

Matthew Henry explains:

"Metamorphousthe – Be you metamorphosed. The transfiguration of Christ is expressed by this word (Matthew 17:2), when he put on a heavenly glory, which made his face to shine like the sun; and the same word is used 2 Corinthians 3:18, where we are said to be changed into the same image from glory to glory. This transformation is here pressed as a duty; not that we can work such a change ourselves: we could as soon make a new world as make a new heart by any power of our own; it is God's work, Ezekiel 11:19; Ezekiel 36:26, 27. But be you transformed, that is, 'use the means which God hath appointed and ordained for it.' It is God that turns us, and then we are turned; but we must frame our doings to turn . . ."[121]

Thomas Harris, a psychiatrist advocating Transactional Analysis for some patients, dotes on the word "transformational." He writes that this type of psychotherapy is a new answer to people

"who want to change rather than to adjust, to people who want transformation rather than conformation. It is realistic in that it confronts the patient with the fact the he is responsible for what happens in the future no matter what has happened in the past. Moreover, it is enabling persons to change, to establish self-control and self-direction, and to discover the reality of freedom of choice."[122]

Dr. Harris describes how all of us act differently every day depending on the circumstances we are in. We may act like an adult, an adolescent or a child at any time of the day, on any day. Saul started that bad day acting like an immature child. But good days followed and he began acting like a mature human being–most of the time.

No doubt Saul also scanned through all the Scriptures he had memorized as a bona fide Pharisee, reprocessing, reinterpreting and reapplying them in the framework of Jesus' life, death and resurrection. The rest is a mystery that no one except God himself

---

[120] Matthew 24:45–47 NRSV
[121] Matthew Henry, Commentary on the Whole Bible
[122] Thomas A. Harris, I'm OK–You're OK, preface

can or should need to explain. Once one hits bottom, anything else is up. Saul had hit bottom and would recover.

CHAPTER FIVE
MANAGEMENT RELOCATION

Before Saul journeyed to his Arabian desert seminary, he returned to Jerusalem. However, he realized he was the bulls-eye target of some likeminded Pharisee firebrands who now turned on him. They deemed him to be a turncoat. Now he had become the quarry of their vindictiveness.

Saul's many new believer friends acted as his antennae, and knew about a lately hatched plot to kill him. The same friends' "ears" heard that Damascus' gates were closely watched, so they put him in a large basket and at night lowered him over the city's walls. He retraced his route back to Jerusalem to face those of his former "associates in diabolical intrigue."

The Lord's disciples in Jerusalem were more than cautious about accepting Saul into their gatherings. They still saw him as a virus, as toxic as poison ivy, or worse. Maintaining a connection with him would likely bring harm to the believers among them. If it were not for Barnabas, he might still be barred from gathering with the disciples but Barnabas, "son of consolation,"[123] told the Jerusalem believers of Saul's conversion, and how Saul personally had seen the Lord and conversed with him.

Barnabas' intervention made a difference. Saul had become one of them, and now walked freely among the disciples, preached and taught just as they had. And he did so enthusiastically. Luke summarizes what happened:

> "But Barnabas took him and brought him to the apostles, and declared unto them how he had seen the Lord on the way and that He had spoken to him, and how he had preached boldly at Damascus in the name of Jesus. And he was with them, coming in and going out at Jerusalem."[124]

A severe test of Saul's improving spiritual health was in his facing both Christ's believers and former Hellenistic-Jewish cohorts in Jerusalem. What would happen when he returned to the milieu in which previously he was once "breathing out threats against the Lord's disciples?"[125] This is an inexact illustration, but it was something akin to a pilot who having crashed his plane, escaped death, is about to skipper another airplane, except that the new aircraft belonged to a competitive airline.

Saul no longer had any Hellenist Jewish friends in Jerusalem. His former Hellenistic-Jewish soul mates were now his antagonists. Members of "The Way" were just as wary of him, in an understated way, to allow their former persecutor to access their "mailing lists" or address books. Saul did not rail against the situation. He understood.

Fortunately, the compassionate disciple Barnabas sponsored him among the Jerusalem believers and Saul acclimated himself to the challenging issues of being a new disciple amid a cautious family of new friends. With God's help and the support of the

---

[123] Acts 4:36
[124] Acts 8:27, 28
[125] Acts 9:1

formerly wary believers, Saul preached "fearlessly" and moved about "freely," yet with staunch and steadfast strictures from his former allies, the Hellenistic Jews.[126]

Jerusalem Moves North and West

Saul needed to know what was going on elsewhere in The Way's orbit. Soon Jerusalem began fading as the centre of "The Way." The book of The Acts of the Apostles cites some the most important events taking place in the fledgling church, including the reality that many other places such as Samaria wanted to receive and act upon the Good News Jesus had brought to the world. Saul returned to Tarsus for a spell.

In Jerusalem, severe punishment came to the believers for their faith. Herod, wrote Luke, killed John's fisherman brother James by sword to "please the Jews" (i.e., the Sanhedrin).[127] Yet, Peter and John preached and taught openly.

Peter was arrested for his part, but God sent an angel who opened the prison doors in answer to the believers' prayer requests. His arrest did not daunt Peter's boldness. He told the Sanhedrin, *"We must obey God rather then men."*[128]

Nor did the persecution stop the disciples' actions. *"The apostles left the Sanhedrin rejoicing because they had been worthy of disgrace for the Name."*[129] In other words, they had been honoured for the dishonour on Jesus' account. The disciples were not discouraged but emboldened.

The gospel message made its way into Samaria and was gladly received there. This was miraculous. In a former time, Samaria was a place where Jesus couldn't find overnight accommodation when he went through that area. *"Foxes have holes and the birds of the air have nests but the Son of Man has nowhere to lay his head."*[130] Previously, Samaritans and Jews had a toxic relationship. Now, a miracle of love was changing attitudes.

Not only had the Gospel broken out from its Jerusalem roots, but it gained acceptance in alien terrain that once had been considered anathema by Jews. The face of the faith was now transforming into much more than a specific, private Jewish possession. What had happened?

Many events led to this breakthrough. Most of the advances were opened by the Holy Spirit. The start was at *Shavuot* or Pentecost when Jesus' followers received the Holy Spirit and the Church was born.

The Church's birth had been a dramatic event, with an emboldened Peter preaching to the *Shavuot* swarms assembling at the Ophel below the Temple Mount. In preparation to enter the Ophel Temple area, the males immersed themselves ritually as a required process for Temple prayers and sacrifices. At Pentecost, on the steps of this

---

[126] Acts 6:9–11; Acts 9:29
[127] Acts 12:2 *ff*
[128] Acts 5:29
[129] Acts 4:11
[130] Luke 9:58

stone stairway leading to the Temple, Peter had urged his captive audience to hear about Jesus, crucified and now resurrected.

Next, Peter urged those gathered to confess their sins and to accept Jesus as Saviour and Lord, showing the resolve of each person to submit to believers' baptism (not just self ritual washing but using the myriad immersion vats on the Ophel) as a sign of their belief. Some 3,000 of "the gathered" obeyed that invitation to receive faith and be immersed–and became members of the birthday church.

That church, however, was no longer just in Jerusalem. Wherever the newly converted returned home, they left Jerusalem bringing the Gospel with them. They spread it throughout the Roman world. Many of these pilgrims at *Shavuot* were Hellenistic Jews. Some were Gentiles, or proselytes. This event set the stage for the early church to embrace Gentile people in addition to Jews.

The writer of Acts, Luke, introduces us to Philip, an evangelist, deacon and prophet. God ordained him to meet an Ethiopian high official, a eunuch, who had been to Jerusalem and couldn't make sense of the events taking place there.[131]

A Eunuch No Longer a Dried Tree

The Bible gives no time frame for the Ethiopian's Jerusalem visit. If he was not there for *Shavuot*, possibly he met a bevy of believers bearing witness about Jesus and his fulfillment of Isaiah's prophecy.[132]

The Way's believers saw Jesus as a fulfillment of Isaiah's prophecy. That prophecy also meant that those either bearing or not wearing genital mutilation were now both fully acceptable in the new faith's worshipping community. The Gospel was inclusive.[133] Isaiah prophesied that in God's renewed kingdom, those forbidden to enter God's house would have accessibility.

The Ethiopian could embrace Isaiah's foretelling: "*Let no foreigner who is bound to the Lord say, 'The Lord will surely exclude me from his people.' And let no eunuch complain, "I am only a dry tree."*"[134] That would countermand the *Torah* prohibition of a eunuch's being disallowed entrance to the House of God. "*No one who has been emasculated by crushing or cutting may enter the assembly of the LORD.*"[135]

That was a strange ban because all Jewish males had been "cut" in the process of circumcision at eight days after birth.

What, wondered the Ethiopian, did Isaiah mean when Jerusalem's new believers now talked about Jesus? "*Who has believed our message and to whom has the arm of the Lord been revealed?*"[136]

[131] Acts 8:26–40
[132] Isaiah 53
[133] Isaiah 49c
[134] Isaiah 56:3
[135] Deuteronomy 23:1
[136] Isaiah 53

Philip explained to the Ethiopian government official that the prophecy pointed to Jesus. Likely, the foreigner was a black Jew, with kinship to The Queen of Sheba's long ago dalliance with King Solomon.

Some Israelis won't fellowship with the immigrant black Jews, calling them by a pejorative name, "Falashas." "Falasha" is the Jewish equivalent of an American calling a negro a "Nigger." It is an appellation not to be used, even in Israel today. In the Bible, however, Luke relates that Simeon was called "Niger."[137] That was not considered pejorative.

Philip explained the Gospel convincingly. The Ethiopian came to faith in Jesus as the atoner of his sins and Saviour of the world. Philip immersed him, symbolizing the foreigner's death to his old self and rebirth to the new life to be lived in the authority and power of a resurrected Jesus. This immersion was a mirror symbol of Jesus' death and resurrection.

Luke presents Philip several times in the Acts of the Apostle. First we meet him as an appointed deacon in the new-born church. Guided by the Holy Spirit, the church chose servants (*diakonoi*) to meet the social needs of the church, to free up the Apostles for evangelism.[138]

Diakonos means servant, but the definition did not deter a deacon from exhortation, as we saw in Stephen, also elected as a deacon, who became the first church martyr. The first seven deacons were responsible for the welfare of widows overlooked by Jewish society when there were no males to sponsor their causes.

Philip relocated in Samaria following his fellow-deacon's stoning. In Samaria, Philip led a magician, Simon Magus, to Christ, baptizing him as a believer.[139] However, Simon's understanding of the Christian faith was immature. When the magician wanted to "buy" the Holy Spirit for his magic acts, Peter and John chastised him for his motive and warned him to repent, lest he be condemned by God.[140]

Subsequently, deacon and evangelist Philip met the Ethiopian eunuch returning from Jerusalem. As reported earlier in this document, Philip explained the meaning of Jesus' death and resurrection. He then immersed the Ethiopian as a believer.

Next we learn that Philip had relocated again, this time in the Roman coastal city of Caesarea Maritima. His description is that he had four daughters who prophesied (preached?). Philip hosted Paul as he returned from his last mission in Asia and was on his way to Jerusalem.[141]

A tradition posts Philip as an overseer (bishop, *episcopos*) at Tralles in Anatolia, southern Asia Minor (present Turkey).

---

[137] Acts 13:1
[138] Acts 6:5, 6
[139] Acts 8:13
[140] Acts 8:22
[141] Acts 21:8, 9

A Joppa Journey and Return

Next came another attitude alterer that Saul needed to enter into his mind-set. A time gap developed after *Shavuot*. His fellow apostle Peter was visiting believers (staying with an observant *kosher* tanner named Simon) in the coastal community of Joppa. Peter got weary and hungry and had a mid-afternoon nap that effected a vision. God is good at providing visions.

Visions, for the most part, are mysteries not to be analyzed but accepted at face value. A cautionary word at this point is that not all visions are God-given. Some visions are merely projections of human imagination. Human fancies can deceive the dreamer.

While Peter was raptured during his siesta, a God-inspired Roman military travelling group from the coastal capital of Caesarea Maritima wended its way South to see the Apostle. The delegation consisted of soldiers sent by a Roman centurion named Cornelius. He asked Peter to venture North and explain a vision the Italian Regiment centurion received from God.

Cornelius was not a devotee of the Roman pagan deities. He was, without becoming a proselyte to Judaism, a monotheist who believed in the Jewish God. He was also generous in many ways. Now God instructed him to bring Peter to his garrison's HQ.

Cornelius' guards arrived in Joppa just as Peter roused from his vision. The apostle's fresh vision meshed with that of Cornelius. As Luke tells it, Peter

> *"became hungry and wanted something to eat, and while the meal was being prepared, he fell into a trance. He saw heaven opened and something like a large sheet being let down to earth by its four corners. It contained all kinds of four-footed animals, as well as reptiles and birds. Then a voice told him, 'Get up, Peter. Kill and eat.'*
> *'Surely not, Lord!' Peter replied. 'I have never eaten anything impure or unclean.'*
> *The voice spoke to him a second time, 'Do not call anything impure that God has made clean.'*
> *This happened three times, and immediately the sheet was taken back to heaven."*[142]

The vision rattled Peter. What did it mean? The Holy Spirit directed Peter to meet the delegation and go with them from Joppa North to Caesarea Maritima. Some believers joined Peter on the mission God gave to him.

The message was clearly that God was sending Peter to minister to a Gentile. He would have food fellowship with them and talk about Jesus, Saviour of the world and not just for the "chosen" Jews. Were not the Jews chosen to serve God, not selected to hoard his love for only themselves?

This vision gave Peter God's permission to eat victuals other than *kosher*. It also told Peter that the Gospel was for Gentiles (*goyim*) (the faith-children of Abraham) and not just for the genetic children of Abraham.

---

[142] Acts 10:10 *ff*

Had not God told Abram, "*I will bless you and . . . all peoples on earth will be blessed through you.*"?[143] Had not Isaiah said, "*I will make you . . . a light for the Gentiles.*"[144] "*that you will may bring my salvation to the ends of the earth?*"[145]

Cornelius met Peter with an awesome reverence, by bowing to him. Peter dissuaded him from any untoward veneration. "*Stand up,*" said Peter, "*I am only a man myself.*"[146] What followed was Peter's statement to Cornelius and his household about Jesus and his atonement. The Holy Spirit entered the lives of these Gentiles.

Immersion followed their faith decisions. Peter asked, "*Can anyone keep these people from being baptized with water? They have received the Holy Spirit just as we have. So Peter ordered that they be baptized in the name of Jesus Christ.*"[147] They may have used the convenient Mediterranean Sea.

Cornelius, his family and friends hosted Peter and his friends for a "few days." Saul/Paul later brought that story out of his memory bank and discussed it with Peter.[148]

A Samaritan Breakthrough

Jews and Samaritans had thrived on mutually insulting terms. Nehemiah, rebuilder of Jerusalem, thought Samaritans to be unworthy of joining in the city's reconstruction.

To the Jews, Samaritans had no virtues. They remembered their vilification by the prophet Micah.[149]

Jews tended to disregard the many prophetic judgments on Judah made by their seers but they nursed every adverse judgment on Samaria. Jesus faced the discrimination head on too. Jews bore a cherished inconvenient amnesia; the hatred had lingered for centuries. "*The Jews do not associate with the Samaritans.*"[150]

It was strange then, miraculous really, that the Gospel crossed Samaria's invisible border and met the once deemed-unworthy people of that jurisdiction. Jewish believers of The Way escaped the persecutions of Herod and Rome. Samaria was now safer than Jerusalem, and it became their mission field.

The paraphrase offered by *The Message* (MSG) translated in Acts 8:4 as, "*Forced to leave home base, the Christians all became missionaries.*"[151] They began their Diaspora in Samaritan territory. Never mind the past Samaritan enmity with Jews, Jewish "Christians" found a reception of sorts in the region of Samaria. Possibly, some Samaritan citizens thought, "the enemy of my enemy is my friend."

---

[143] Genesis 12:2, 3
[144] Isaiah 42:6
[145] Isaiah 49:6
[146] Acts 10:26
[147] Acts 10:46 *ff*
[148] Galatians 2:11–14
[149] Micah 1:6–16
[150] John 4:9
[151] Acts 8:4

Philip was chosen by the Jerusalem Church to be a deacon and was the one who evangelized the Ethiopian from Queen Candace's court. He now established himself in Caesarea and Samaria. Later, he hosted Paul returning from a final mission tour. Possibly, it was this Philip who softened the ground for the Gospel seed to be planted and germinate in Samaritan soil. Philip preached about Christ there. Luke says he *"preached the good news of the kingdom of God and the name of Jesus Christ and the people who came to faith were baptized, both men and women."*[152]

The mother Jerusalem Church heard of this and sent a two-apostle delegation of Peter and John to confirm that the conversions were authentic. The two disciples were impressed. They prayed with the converts to the effect that the converts had received the Holy Spirit. Luke records that, *"They simply had been baptized into the name of the Lord Jesus. Then Peter and John placed their hands on them, and they received the Holy Spirit . . . Peter and John returned to Jerusalem, preaching the gospel in many Samaritan villages."*[153]

One person who heeded his message was a sorcerer in Samaria–Simon Magus (Simon the Great). Having seen the Jerusalem leaders place hands on the converts, he too wanted to "distribute" (read, "franchise") the Holy Spirit. Simon offered the disciples some money as a bribe. The two bluntly told Simon that God is not for sale.

"When Simon saw that the Spirit was given at the laying on of the apostles' hands, he offered them money and said, 'Give me also this ability so that everyone on whom I lay my hands may receive the Holy Spirit.'

"Peter answered: 'May your money perish with you, because you thought you could buy the gift of God with money! You have no part or share in this ministry, because your heart is not right before God. Repent of this wickedness and pray to the Lord in the hope that he may forgive you for having such a thought in your heart. For I see that you are full of bitterness and captive to sin.'

"Then Simon answered, 'Pray to the Lord for me so that nothing you have said may happen to me.'"[154]

As Paul's cautioning word to Corinth, written later, put it, *"We do not peddle the word of God for profit."*[155] Simon's sin is branded as "Simony."

Peter had not quite absorbed the full intentions of that dream and visit from the centurion. He lacked the courage at times to speak boldly about the oneness of Jew and Gentile. Paul noticed it. In a full discussion of the Jew/Gentile mission, Paul bluntly told a fence-sitting Peter about his vacillation and lack of courage to face criticism on this. Paul records his annoyance in his letter to the Galatians:

"When Cephas came to Antioch, I opposed him to his face, because he stood condemned. For before certain men came from James, he used to eat with the Gentiles. But when they arrived, he began to draw back and separate himself from the Gentiles because he was afraid of those who belonged to the circumcision

---

[152] Acts 8:12
[153] Acts 8:15 *ff* . . . Acts 8:25
[154] Acts 8:18 *ff*
[155] 2 Corinthians 2:17

group. The other Jews joined him in his hypocrisy, so that by their hypocrisy even Barnabas was led astray. When I saw that they were not acting in line with the truth of the gospel, I said to Cephas in front of them all, "You are a Jew, yet you live like a Gentile and not like a Jew. How is it, then, that you force Gentiles to follow Jewish customs?"[156]

Paul was not backward in coming forward!

If the "blood of the martyrs is the seed of the church," as Tertullian[157] exclaimed, then the martyrdom of Stephen planted a very large forest of trees. The faith was now firmly set in Caesarea and Samaria. The Jerusalem Church leaders saw an opportunity to extend their reach and undertakings to Diaspora Jews who had moved to Phoenicia, Syrian Antioch and Cyprus. Cyprus was a copper resource nation (giving the island its name), settled by Phoenician traders and now in-filtered for their own safety by migrating Jews from the Asian mainland around Jerusalem.

Jerusalem Examines Antioch

The Jerusalem leaders delegated the trusted the Jewish Cypriot Barnabas to visit the developing Church at Antioch. Barnabas was attracted to that church, and "*saw the evidence of the grace of God amid the believers.*"[158] Luke describes this disciple as "*good man, full of the Holy Spirit and faith.*"[159] After his reception in Antioch, a "great number" of people came to the Lord. Very quickly Barnabas chose to find Saul, now dwelling back in his hometown of Tarsus. He found and visited with Saul, bringing him to Antioch to meet, witness and instruct their church leaders.

The sainted Barnabas wove his influence in and out of Paul's life. Barnabas was among the first to accept Saul following his conversion en route to Damascus. Since Barnabas had great credibility with the Jerusalem Church, he introduced Saul to his new family of The Way.

Barnabas was a Cypriot Jew whose heart beat strongly for his Island's Jewish countrymen. He was a positive person and an encourager. He had a PMA, a "Positive Mental Attitude," not an NMA, a "Negative Mental Attitude." He saw the potential in people. He was prepared to take the time necessary to see immature believers grow into reliable, fully developed disciples. He lived up to his name that meant, "Son of Encouragement, Son of Consolation."

Credit Barnabas with the wisdom and serenity to work with an exasperating Paul even when they disputed about the inclusion of Mark in their mutual mission. Barnabas saw far beyond their disagreements to their hopeful accomplishments.

Here at Antioch, members of "The Way" became known as "Christians."[160] They wore the new badge graciously. "The name that is above all names"[161] became the

---

[156] Galatians 2:11–14
[157] Apology, Chapter 10
[158] Acts 11:23
[159] Acts 11:24
[160] Acts 11:26

moniker that Jesus' followers would use as the handle for all believers. Jews and pagans alike would recognize that honorific. The Jerusalem Church knew that recent leaders in Antioch needed schooling in the faith, not to mention the *élan* that both Barnabas and Saul could offer them.

Their next step was to receive a visit from a godly man, Agabus, who foresaw a severe famine soon to develop in Jerusalem's surroundings. The Antioch Christians sized up the situation, gladly gathered some money and entrusted Saul and Barnabas to deliver the aid to the Jerusalem elders and believers.

When Barnabas and Saul returned to Antioch, they brought Barnabas' nephew John Mark with them. We will meet Mark early in Paul's mission journeys. Paul was hesitant to believe Mark had the stamina of someone able to face the hard knocks of criticism and persecution. Mark became a cause of friction between Paul and Barnabas. Barnabas had a sense of Mark's potential (perhaps also clouded by a family connection). Paul saw Mark as an unworthy, immature companion in his missionary service, sensing he was a quitter.

Decades later, when Paul was in chains as a prisoner, we read of his commendation of Mark. Perhaps Barnabas' mentoring helped the young man mature into a reliable and solid believer. Maybe, Paul's improving "wellness" kicked in and he had a new appraisal of one he formerly dismissed so readily and so abruptly. Thus, Paul wrote to Timothy, "*Get Mark and bring him with you, because he is helpful to me in my ministry.*"[162] Again we hear Paul's later commendation of Mark in Paul's letter to Colossae, "*My fellow prisoner Aristarchus sends you his greetings, as does Mark, the cousin of Barnaba*s."[163] Maybe Paul changed his opinion of Mark or Mark grew in spiritual strength and resolve, or both. In any event, Paul and Mark had grown to respect one another.

We owe John Mark the Spirit-gift of the Gospel bearing his name.

---

[161] Philippians 2:10
[162] 2 Timothy 4:11
[163] Colossians 4:10

CHAPTER SIX
CHECKPOINTS

With Jerusalem now hampered by famine and persecution, Antioch quickly became the nerve centre of Christian activity. The native Antiochenes, like many residents in their cultural Hellenistic orbit, thrived on hedonism. Lewdness and debauchery were a way of life in this Asian version of New Orleans, "The Big Easy." Christians had a challenge here. The growing Christian component in this Cilician capital meant that Antioch soon supplanted the Jerusalem mother church, certainly not in honour, but in practical mission activity.

Antioch was as cosmopolitan a city as any in the known world. Its then half-million people had grown into a wide heterogeneous ethnic amalgam of Europeans, Africans and Asians. Antioch now embraced an omnibus of careers–longshoremen, teachers, politicians, traders, hawkers, sail makers, seamen, textile workers, perfumers, goldsmiths, metal workers, clothiers, soldiers, philosophers, physicians, priests, tax collectors, freemen and slaves. Name the occupation! Diaspora Jews added to the mix.

By the time Barnabas and Saul arrived in Antioch, they realized that the Gospel had found a friendly, firm footing in this global city. Skin colours in Antioch included Viking white, Italian olive, Egyptian brown and Nubian black. Antioch was the multicultural Toronto of the ancient world.

Antioch was nearly 400 years old when Saul and Barnabas arrived from Jerusalem. It was founded by a general of Alexander the Great, Seleucus I Nicator, and sits along the Orontes River. Today it is in ruins, but the modern Turkish city of Antakya abuts the ruins. Its wealth came from being on the Silk Road and the accompanying spice trade.

When the gathered, newly-dubbed "Christians"[164] of Antioch met to adore and pray to God, the Holy Spirit broke into their assembly. "*Set aside Barnabas and Saul for me for the work to which I have called them.*"[165] Apart from this unusual direct intervention from God, note that (1) Barnabas is the first mentioned and (2) neither one mumbles any rejection. Saul obviously is the apparent apprentice in this situation. That will change. Barnabas was a Hellenistic, Cypriot Jew, with Levite credentials. As a Levite he had priestly duties in the Temple. Luke reports that, "*a large number of priests became obedient to the faith.*"[166] Perhaps because of Barnabas' seniority and priestly preferential status is why Paul was given learner status in this pilot undertaking.

Contrast the acceptance by these two willing servants of God with the kvetching excuses offered by Israel's revered leader, Moses. His initial response to God's invitation to serve him was a litany offering of excuses–"*Who am I? . . . "Who are you Lord?" . . . I stutter.*"[167]

---

[164] Acts 11:26
[165] Acts 13:2
[166] Acts 6:7

Saul was in Tarsus when Barnabas fetched him to Antioch, as Bible tells us, "*The Grecian Jews tried to kill him . . . When the brothers learned of this, they took him to Caesarea and sent him off to Tarsus.*"[168] This turn of events was something like that of Peter, who after the resurrection of Jesus, went back to his fishing enterprise to sort out the implications God had in store for him.

Saul readily saw that he was not entirely welcome in Jerusalem and willingly accepted this co-ordinated hijack to Tarsus where he could regroup. Probably Saul needed time to himself and wait for God's further instructions. "*Understand what the Lord's will is,*"[169] wrote Paul to Ephesus, knowing personally how important that truth was to Paul himself. Just as essential was Paul's need to learn patience while awaiting God's further instructions.

Patience is always God's advice to those he loves. "*Be still before the Lord and wait patiently for him; do not fret when men succeed in their ways, when they carry out their evil schemes.*"[170] From learned experience, and from his developing strong spiritual health (his wellness), Paul reminded his troubling believer allies in Galatia, that when the Holy Spirit indwells you, he also gives you evidence of his indwelling, and one such evidence is patience. "*The fruit of the Spirit is love, joy, peace, patience, kindness, goodness, faithfulness, gentleness and self-control.*"[171]

We do know that "The Way" missed him and that Barnabas sought his presence. Barnabas knew his location and summoned him to nearby Antioch. Antioch had become a refugee assembly locale for persecuted Christians suffering in Jerusalem and other parts of the Roman province of Palestina.

By this time, Peter's ministry[172] had spread to Gentiles. Neonate Gentile ministry drew attention as far away as Jerusalem, the "mother church." The parent church sent one of its most reliable and very effective evangelist members, Barnabas, to gather evidence and prepare a report. Upon his arrival in Antioch, Barnabas then asked Saul (now in Tarsus) to join him and other believers not far away in Antioch.

After being introduced by Barnabas to the Antiochene Christian leaders, Saul speedily saw that he was among friends. He accepted this introduction as a signal to get to work. He began to teach "*great numbers of people.*"[173] Saul's practised patience in Tarsus had properly prepared him for ministry in Antioch–and for the remainder of his apostolic mission.

---

[167] Exodus 3, selected verses
[168] Acts 9:29, 30
[169] Ephesians 5:17b
[170] Psalm 37:7
[171] Galatians 5:22–23
[172] Acts 11:19–23
[173] Acts 11:26

Mission 1; Voyaging to Cyprus

The Antioch Church family fasted and prayed about the guidance the Holy Spirit had given them. They surmised that God had prepared a special place for these two missionaries to travel to Cyprus and specifically to the Jews living there.[174] The time period for this Gospel foray probably was sometime between 46–48 AD.

Barnabas' nephew, John Mark, accompanied them. Why John? He had not been commissioned by the Antioch Church. He should have been a useful resource on this mission, since he probably knew Jesus' work and ministry first-hand and likely witnessed the death and resurrection of Jesus. Some Bible scholars speculate that John Mark is the unnamed youth mentioned in Mark, *"A young man, wearing nothing but a linen garment, was following Jesus. When they seized him, he fled naked, leaving his garment behind."*[175] Seemingly, that young man had a weak spine. Did Paul know about this allegation?

Cyprus, Barnabas' homeland, was under Roman jurisdiction when Barnabas, Saul and John Mark arrived on its Eastern shores. Prior to the Romans, Assyrians, Ptolemaic Egyptians, Greeks and Phoenicians governed the Island. It can claim Neolithic settlements as far back as 7500 BC. Cyprus benefitted from being on a favoured maritime trade route and a major source of mined copper. The island's name means "copper."

The pair whom Antioch elders commissioned to share their faith abroad, plus John, probably would have walked from Antioch the 13 kilometres to the port, Seleucia Pieria. That would be proper hospitality and an action of morale boosting by the Antioch Church.

Likely, a few church elders and other Christians accompanied them to the wharf. Once there, they inquired about ships lading goods and headed with their cargoes to Salamis on the Island of Cyprus. "Do you have room for three passengers?" they would have asked the captain. And so they found their transport. Salamis was a 200 or so kilometre voyage; thus the trio would have slept while curled up on deck amid the merchandise.

They arrived at the chief city of Salamis (six kilometres from present day Famagusta) and met Jews in the city's synagogue. Barnabas and Saul did the preaching. Luke describes John Mark as their *"helper."*[176] Luke offers no report of their reception at Salamis, only that, *"They travelled the whole island until they came to Paphos."* Paphos was the seat of government of Cyprus. According to mythology, Paphos also was the birthplace of Aphrodite (aka Venus) where she was worshipped by the Greeks.[177]

The unordinary has a way of telling its own news. Paphos' governing leader, a Roman proconsul named Sergius Paulus, got wind of Barnabas' and Saul's activities and sent for them to explain their philosophy, or as Luke framed it, he *"wanted to hear the word of God."*[178] Sergius Paulus had an appointment secretary, an evil, eccentric man

---

[174] Acts 13:5
[175] Mark 14:51, 52
[176] Acts 13:5
[177] Mark P. O. Morton and Robert J. Lenardon, Classical Mythology, p. 496
[178] Acts 13:7

named bar-Jesus aka Elymas (obviously Jewish) who did his best to prevent the missionaries from meeting the proconsul. Elymas, also called "the Sorcerer," attempted to intercept the two from telling Sergius Paulus about Jesus' death and resurrection.

Roman officials were a superstitious bunch. They employed "spiritual" advisors of various sorts, to help with predictions and auguries such as examining animal or bird entrails. Elymas, a padre/assistant of sorts, obviously thought that his job was in jeopardy when Paul and Barnabas found favour with Sergius Paulus. His job was in definite jeopardy!

It was not the tactful Barnabas who confronted Elymas, but the infuriated Saul who felt Elymas was working against God. So Saul called him out on his blocking God's plan of salvation for Paphos' proconsul. He called him, *deceitful and perverting the Gospel.*[179] Saul told him God would blind him. Immediately Elymas was blinded. And Sergius Paulus *believed and was amazed about the teaching of the Lord.*[180]

Disciples needed to know God's method of intersecting with potential converts, moderation or assertiveness. Saul's aggressiveness worked here, whereas Barnabas's method suited him ideally when he introduced Saul to the Jerusalem Church leaders.

Some details are unwritten but implied. First, at this point, Luke records that Saul is also known as Paul (same name as the Gentile proconsul). Was this when Saul understood he might have more influence on his Hellenistic audience if he used his Roman name? Secondly, we see a shift in the leadership of the missionaries.

No longer does Luke write, *"Barnabas and Saul,"* but *"Paul and his companions."*[181] Paul had become the lead missionary. Are Saul and Barnabas having a tiff? Would that be surprising?

Another sign of Saul's developing wellness was apparent here in Cyprus. Saul was more of a "follower" of Barnabas' supervision when the pair began a mission to that island. Part way through the mission, Saul ceased to be a follower and became a leader. Saul took charge of the mission, confronting the spiritual advisor (bar Jesus) of Sergius Paulus, the island's proconsul.

Barnabas might not have done that. Joseph Barnabas was a mediator, a negotiator, described in the Bible as "a man of consolation (encouragement)."[182] Saul, by seizing the leadership role, showed clearly that he now fully understood that his maturing "wellness" meant taking on the purpose that God had prepared for him.

Direction for continuing the Cyprus mission had now moved from Lieutenant Barnabas to Captain Saul. Not everyone is a captain. God also has a place for lieutenants. Furthermore, Saul's exerting his leadership qualities was not a coup d'état or mutiny but stemmed from Saul/Paul's clear understanding that a direct confrontation with the sorcerer bar Jesus was an imperative, the Lord's order, an opportunity not to be missed.

[179] Acts 13:10
[180] Acts 13:12
[181] Acts 13:13
[182] Acts 4:36, 37

The Onset of Oppression

From the Western end of Cyprus the trio found transport to mainland Perga in Pamphylia, in Asia Minor. The two of them journeyed onward to Antioch in Pisidia. John Mark had left the two at Perga and sailed back to Jerusalem.

Paul didn't mind. He sensed that John Mark was unfit for the task and unworthy of the responsibility. Mark's inclusion on this mission already had created a tension between Barnabas, who was John Mark's uncle, and the single-minded Paul. John Mark's participation was Barnabas' idea, not the commission of the Antioch elders. Perhaps Paul saw trouble looming that he surmised John Mark could not handle the complexities and risks of mission work.[183]

Clearly, Paul took an attitude of "fish or cut bait." Paul was in a hurry. Barnabas was more laid back. The latter realized that some things take time, and that John Mark's missionary service was one of them.

Fishing

When Jesus first called some of his fishermen disciples, he changed the course of their lives. *"Come, follow me,"* he said, *"and I will make you fishers of men."*[184] Saul/Paul had heeded that invitation and in his developing spiritual healing he now was fishing God-style.

What's important in fishing is (1) to know where the fish are; and (2) to know what bait or lure attracts them. Expert fisherfolk know the habitat of the fish they seek. Few fishermen will divulge their secret. They also know the best lures for the species they want to haul in.

On Lake Galilee, some fishermen still work at night. With something of a torch at one end of the dory, they draw the tilapia fish toward the light and into their nets.

The Galilee fishers pretty much knew where to catch their prey and when to do so. But not always! Thermal springs empty into the Sea of Galilee and the locations of the streams sometimes vary after the waters have left their exit into the lake. The schools of fish also move to their preferences of warmer or cooler water.

The Bible tells readers of a night's fishing that was fruitless for Jesus' disciples. To use fishermen's jargon, "They were skunked." Jesus asked them about their success. They answered "Nada," or something like that–a "wasted, long night's work." Jesus urged them to put their nets on the other side of the boat, and voila, the nets were full.[185]

To Paul and Silas, the best fishing was at the synagogues. Jews would know the Scriptures exceedingly well but not so the Gentiles. Moreover, most Jews living under Pharisee-dominated centres, would accept the doctrine of resurrection. Greek philosophers balked at that as Paul quickly heard in Athens–*"When they heard about the resurrection of the dead, some of them sneered."*[186]

---

[183] Acts 15:36–41
[184] Matthew 4:9
[185] John 21:6

Synagogues, like the modern meaning of churches, were buildings, but first they are people who meet in the buildings. Synagogue means "get together, congregated" or close to that. It's where people studied (*shul*) prayed and fellowshipped. This is much the same meaning as "church" which first of all means a called-out people (*ekklesia*), and secondarily is a building where people gathered for purposes quite similar to Jews.

The Cypriot missionaries were sure that those gathering in synagogues would also want to hear about their Messiah, the promised Saviour-King expected by most Israelites (except Sadducees). Paul and Barnabas' chances of success would increase dramatically over "cold turkey" preaching, or so the pair thought. That became their strategy. Go first to the synagogues! Meet the Jewish people and palaver with them. If Gentiles listen in, they are welcome.

After disembarking at Attalia from Cyprus, the pair, minus Mark, trekked to Perga where they quick-planned an itinerary. What may have been a clear sail for John Mark back to Jerusalem was anything but clear sailing for Paul and Barnabas now sharing the Gospel in the mainland of Asia Minor. Their first stop would be at Pisidian Antioch but no one knows why. Were the two guided by God's Spirit to this destination?

Pisidian Antioch

Asia Minor embraced 16 cities named Antioch, all of them once-named to honour the maniacal autarch Antiochus Epiphantes so hated by the Jews for his desecration of the Jerusalem Temple and who imposed Greek culture upon them.

Paul and Barnabas made themselves known once they mounted the Taurus Mountains and ensconced themselves in Antioch of Pisidia. Soon they stirred enough interest among Hellenistic Jews living there that these Jews wanted further explanations about Jesus from the itinerant pair.

Pisidian Antioch's synagogue was the venue for the now-invited Paul and Barnabas to state the Gospel to its worshippers. They listened to synagogue leaders reading the prescribed *Torah* (Law) and prophetic lectionary readings for the day.[187] The collective readings were called the *haphtarah*.

The president of the synagogue then invited their visitors to add to the interpretation of scriptures just read. That invitation was a synagogue tradition.[188] *"Brothers, if you have a message of encouragement for the people, please speak,"*[189] suggested the synagogue moderator. Paul jumped right in. Indeed Paul did have Good News to share with them and he spoke.

The now-metamorphisized Paul preached dynamically, chilling some of the Hellenistic Jews (but not all) and thrilling many of the Gentiles who also attended. Wrote

---

[186] Acts 17:32
[187] Luke 4:17 is an example of a passage designated for that Sabbath's day service
[188] Luke 4:16–21
[189] Acts 13:15

Luke, "*When the Gentiles heard this, they were glad and honoured the word of the Lord; and all who were appointed for eternal life believed . . .*"[190]

The Jews invited Paul and Barnabas to return on the next Sabbath and explain themselves further. Obviously the two used the days between Sabbaths to share their faith among community members. Luke tells his readers that after the first message from Paul, "*Many of the devout Jews and devout converts to Judaism followed Paul and Barnabas, who talked with them to continue in the grace of God.*"[191]

Paul and his cohort Barnabas had picked the right fishing spot. Paul made little mention of Jesus as Messiah, but rather of Jesus as Saviour. Perhaps that is because Pharisees were not "gung ho" on Messiah as much as on resurrection. The two missionaries spent the week between Sabbaths in sharing their faith among the people. By this time, however, enough opposition to the missionaries' message interfered with their public speaking. "Don't fish in our pond," the Hellenistic Jews implied.

The Hellenistic Jews in this city violently expelled Paul and Barnabas from their region when Paul told them that henceforth he would no longer share the Gospel with Jews but only with Gentiles. The duo repeated this threat at other places where Jewish critics stonewalled their message.

They then shook the dust off their cloaks as a symbol of God's judgment on unbelievers, and left. Shaking the dust off one's clothes was telling the villagers that they were to "keep the dust in their own village." It was a condemnation on the village or town. However, the two undaunted missionaries remained upbeat and unflinching, as Luke records, "*The disciples were filled with joy and the Holy Spirit.*"[192]

Good and Bad Receptions

Paul and Barnabas had moved into the area of Southern Galatia. It would take the strong suits of each of them in this new phase of their exciting ministry. Paul offered his extraordinary endowments of rhetoric, exegesis and forthrightness. Barnabas' gifts of moderation, empathy and encouragement supplemented Paul's shortcomings. Despite being "transformed" on the Damascus roadway, Paul did not shake off his nature to be curt and frank. Together, as a team, they began to exercise a remarkable mission into Asia Minor communities populated with an atypical mélange of Gentiles (*goyim*) and Hellenistic Jews.

Iconium

If Paul and Barnabas seemed to be barred from sharing the Gospel in Antioch, they thought they might try Iconium. Iconium is 160 kilometres from Pisidian Antioch–a very long and arduous trek. Iconium, in the Southern part of the Roman province of

---

[190] Luke 4:16–21
[191] Acts 13:15
[192] Acts 13:52

Galatia, was a much larger community than the one they had just left. Today it is called Konia and its population is over a million souls.

The two missioners followed their planned strategy by zeroing in on the local synagogue. Again, they were invited to speak. Paul once more extolled the Gospel as he saw it, and once again he received a mixed reception from Hellenistic Jews and Jewish proselytes.

Some hearers accepted Paul's message with enormous enthusiasm and others received it with epic enmity. The specter of death by stoning reared its ugly head, causing Paul and Barnabas to leave town. A dead missionary can't preach. Or can he? Even in death, the martyr Stephen had a voice–and Saul had heard it.

Lystra

Paul and Barnabas opted to visit other cities in the general region 30 kilometres away. The scripture says that the two "fled" Iconium for Lystra. Lystra, like Philippi, was a Roman colony and likewise on a military highway. The Jewish population was minimal. Instead, its religious activities centred mostly about the Greek and Roman deities.

So when Paul offered healing to a man lame from birth, the citizens of Lystra deemed the missionaries were actually Olympian deities. *"The gods have come down to us in the likeness of men,"*[193] they exclaimed. Well, God did come to them in the form of a man–Jesus. We wonder if Paul played with that concept.

For a very short time, Paul and Barnabas became Hermes (the god's mythic messenger and interpreter) and Zeus (the mythic Greek CEO at Mount Olympus). The guise was short-lived because the apostles told the people not to do that. This gave the missionaries opportunity to declare the Gospel.

Some vexatious Jews from Antioch and Iconium had followed Paul and Barnabas to Lystra. They now stirred the crowds against them. Soon, it was Paul who was stoned as Jews followed their code that blasphemers should be executed by stoning. This was more than stoning. The perpetrators dragged Paul's inert body outside the city limits, the garbage dump where the dogs fed, perhaps. It was an indignity plus.

One wonders if the incident stirred any pangs of remorse in Paul about Stephen's untimely execution in Jerusalem. Paul did not die from this stoning. [194] After the would-be assassins left, Barnabas and some converts watched Paul rise to his feet. Helped by the many new believers, he and Barnabas found a suitable refuge for overnight.

It is a sad commentary on the Hellenistic Jews who travelled a great distance to Lystra with soiled motives. It is also an honourable commentary on the new believers in the city who, while unable to intervene, remained with the wounded body of Paul to ensure he could be revived. No doubt the resolve of Paul, willing to pay any price to

[193] Acts 14:11
[194] Acts 14:19

share his faith, was a powerful influence on the hearers and a strong signal of his spiritual health.

His is not the only story of suffering for one's beliefs. Through the ages it has be replicated time and again: What follows is from records in Boston's First Baptist Church.

(Boston, First Baptist Church) "In Boston, Massachusetts, on September 5, 1651, Obadiah Holmes was sentenced to 30 lashes by the Puritan Pilgrims. Had Obadiah paid the £30, he would be spared the lashing on the Boston Common. His crime was insisting on believers' baptism by immersion. He stuck to his belief. Although he was severely beaten (it took months for him to recover) he said during the whipping, 'You have struck me as with roses.' Afterwards he could eat only while leaning on his elbows and knees. The Puritan colony's leaders ordered him 'to desist, and neither to ordain officers, nor to baptize, nor to break bread together, nor yet to meet upon the first day of the week . . .'"[195]

Derbe

The morning found Paul sufficiently well to continue his mission. His destination was Derbe, 50 kilometres Southeast of Lystra–quite a hike for an injured Apostle. It must have a multi-day walk.

Why Derbe? Why not? Like David Livingston, Paul and Barnabas were as much explorers as they were missionaries. They had entered into territory unreached by the Gospel and they were now searching for audiences who might welcome the Good News. Even faced with rejection, disappointment and persecution, this was a venture they believed they must attempt.

Derbe supplied the two with a ready audience. This book writer surmises that Paul and Barnabas had company and helpers on the road–new disciples from Lystra. The new converts must have travelled with the two both to learn more about Jesus and to support them in Derbe. We read that in Derbe, *"When they preached the gospel to that city* (they) *made many disciples."*[196]

Lystra

In some way, perhaps by friendly messengers from Lystra, Paul and Silas learned they could return there without further persecution. The angry mob that had attacked them, had returned by now to their home bases in Iconium and/or Pisidian Antioch.

Paul and Barnabas had unfinished business in Lystra. They had left untrained disciples in Lystra. These converts needed more teaching, more discipling, more substance to their faith. So the two of them, with perhaps the accompaniment of new converts from Lystra and now Derbe resumed their mission.

Paul preached again. Then he and Barnabas "appointed" elders (presbyters) to secure the new converts in their newly found faith. The very word translated as

[195] Plaque in First Baptist Church, Boston
[196] Acts 14:21

"appointed" implies an election, a vote of hands–*cheirotoesantes* (Greek). Appointment was not an executive action by Paul but a vote by valid members of the fledgling church.

The term "elder" goes back a long time in Jewish tradition, meaning judges or overseers. The elders mentioned in the Old Testament met outside the city gates of a city and exercised their judgments. Now Paul was applying this term (Hebrew: *zekenim*) to church life.

Perga

Barnabas and Paul retraced their paths until they returned to Pisidian Antioch. They then continued to Perga, where the two offered the Gospel to its inhabitants. Barnabas' nephew had left earlier from there.

The pair continued from Perga to Pisidian Antioch where they gathered the recently created church and spent "*no little time*"[197] teaching, encouraging and consoling them in the Gospel.

They also reported on their inland mission to Iconium. Lystra and Derbe, thus ensuring that the Pisidian Antiochenes were fully valid partners with them in the wider mission of Jesus Christ.

Attalia

The Bible tells that Paul and Barnabas "*went down*" from Perga to the port of Attalia to board a ship to Syrian Antioch. "Down" is the operative word, for it was a steep descent from the mountainous communities they so recently had visited. At Attalia, they did what John Mark would have done to reach Jerusalem; they would have scoured the wharf to find a freighter ship suitable to accept them along with the captain's laded merchandise heading east to Syrian Antioch.

Accountability and Evaluation

The two commissioned missionaries finally arrived in Antioch. After receiving a warm greeting from the church, they did what any church delegates should do, report back to those who commissioned them. Theirs was an important de-briefing. Paul wanted to be accountable. He wanted the Antiochenes to know what had occurred during the mission he and Barnabas has just completed. Paul wanted the Christians in Antioch to be mission-sharers.

Mission sharing is a necessary principle in the work of Christian mission. When William Carey addressed a potential sponsoring group meeting in Andrew Fuller's (a Particular Baptist) home in October of 1792, the would-be cobbler-missionary to India told his host, "I will go down the well, if you will hold the rope."[198] That worked. Carey went to India; Fuller raised support funds.

---

[197] Acts 14:28
[198] William Gordon Blaikie, <u>Dictionary of National Biography</u>, Fuller, Andrew

One wonders if Paul explained why he now used his Roman name, but perhaps he disclosed that when he told about the successes among Gentiles. The two of them were on a "high," something like Jesus when he talked to a Samaritan woman and his disciples asked him if he was hungry.

Jesus responded, *"I have eaten meat that you don't know about."*[199] Again, hear Jesus talking to the Satanic tempter: *"It is written, man does not live on bread alone."*[200] Actual food to Paul and Silas likewise, was nothing at all compared to seeing people come to Christ, believing him to be the Lord and Saviour of the world.

Key to the reporting of Paul and Barnabas was whether the Holy Spirit affirmed their mission. The evidence of God's gift to believing people was in that divine grace.

We learn much more of Paul's personality in this mission. He began it by accepting Barnabas' lead but took over the command part way through the mission. He was intolerant of John Mark's lack of focus and zealousness. Paul expected more. He changed his name, in part to reach the Gentiles he encountered, and also to show a little more humility with a name that means "less."[201] Paul gradually had seized his rightful role as leader and was working on his humility. The humility task remained a life-long test.

1885–1900, Volume 20
[199] John 4:32
[200] Luke 4:4
[201] see the discussion of Paul's name in earlier in Chapter 6

CHAPTER SEVEN
SETTING PRINCIPLES

Faith as a Gift

The return of Paul and Barnabas to Antioch raised a fundamental question about the faith the missionaries were spreading. Does faith emanate from God or is it merely a human reaction? This question stirred–really rattled–the Antioch Church.

The main factor in this enigma was the report that God bestowed the Holy Spirit on Gentiles (*goyim*). That proclaimed fact shook the Christian Antiochenes! Gentiles fully acceptable in God's sight? If God chose to anoint Gentiles, how could the church not recognize them as legitimate partakers in God's salvation? This was enough to disquiet the Hellenistic Jews' deep-rooted, entrenched theological positions.

Later Paul wrote to Corinth arguing that faith was God's gift to them. *"God gives faith by the same Spirit."*[202] When Paul wrote to believers in Ephesus, he said something similar, *"For by grace you have been saved through faith; and that not of yourselves, it is the gift of God; not as a result of works, that no one should boast."*[203]

Clearly, not only is grace the Spirit's to give, but so is faith! Believers have no grounds to brag about their faith–it is God's gift to unbelievers and believers alike so that they will know God's planned purposes. Faith is a gift from God, coming as it does as prevenient grace.

The Holy Spirit is the initiator of faith. When Jesus cured a woman with "an issue of blood" i.e., likely a menstrual disorder, he told her, *"Daughter, your faith has healed you!"*[204] Jesus in fact was saying, "The faith God has given you in trusting me, has cured you."

Must Gentiles Be Jews?

Nonetheless, some believers with Pharisee credentials insisted that the Gentile believers must also submit to the *Torah* laws, effectively becoming proselyte Jews. This ultra conservative group wanted all Christians to become Jews, obeying various Jewish obligations including circumcision. Paul and Peter queried the questioners, citing the reality that God already recognized their accepted status with him.

We read in the Galatian letter that Peter only came to this conclusion after Paul lectured him face to face in front of the Antioch Church. The Bible does not say what brought Peter to Antioch. Was it to help establish basics for the early church? We do know that the ever-forthright and maturing Paul, "had it out" with Peter, as noted in the Galatian letter:

"When Cephas (Peter) came to Antioch, I opposed him to his face, because he stood condemned. For before certain men came from James, he used to eat with

---

[202] 1 Corinthians 12:9
[203] Ephesians 2:8–9
[204] Mark 5:34

the Gentiles. But when they arrived, he began to draw back and separate himself from the Gentiles because he was afraid of those who belonged to the circumcision group. The other Jews joined him in his hypocrisy, so that by their hypocrisy even Barnabas was led astray.

"When I saw that they were not acting in line with the truth of the gospel, I said to Cephas in front of them all, 'You are a Jew, yet you live like a Gentile and not like a Jew. How is it, then, that you force Gentiles to follow Jewish customs?'"[205]

Karen Armstrong, writing in the 20th century about Paul's lack of prejudice in the First Century, wrote:

"All his life Paul struggled to transcend the barriers of ethnicity, class, and gender, that sadly, are still socially divisive in the 21st Century . . . Like Jesus, he would always insist that in the Kingdom of God, everybody must be allowed to eat at the same table. In our secularized world, we no longer place such rules for ritual purity; but racism and class divisions are still a noxious force even in what used to be called the free world. Again, Paul would have rejected such prejudice, just as Jesus did. Jesus continuously and provocatively ate dinner with 'sinners', touched those who were ritually impure and contagiously sick, crossed social boundaries and consorted with people despised by the establishment."[206]

This was but one issue both the Antioch and the mother Jerusalem Church needed to synthesize. Paul felt that his mission was primarily to the Gentiles and that Peter's was to the Jews. "They saw that I had been entrusted to take it (Gospel) to the Jews; for the same God who was at work in Peter's mission to the Jews was at work in mine to the Gentiles."[207]

Yet Paul told the Romans, *"In the first place the Jews were entrusted with the oracles of God."*[208]That may explain why he first went to the synagogues when he preached. However, Paul considered himself an apostle to the Gentiles.[209] The healthy discussion that followed this reality became a doctrine for all Christians for all time. And what must be done? The Antioch group wanted to share their report and concerns with the mother church. Paul and Barnabas voyaged to Jerusalem for further advice.

Jerusalem's Assent

James, the main leader of the Jerusalem Church who had listened keenly to the Antioch missionary's report, offered his own conclusion:

"It is my judgment, therefore, that we should not make it difficult for the Gentiles who are turning to God. Instead we should write to them, telling them to abstain from food polluted by idols, from sexual immorality, from the meat of strangled animals and from blood. For the law of Moses has been preached in every city from the earliest times and is read in the synagogues on every Sabbath."

---

[205] Galatians 2:11–14
[206] Karen Armstrong, The Apostle We Love to Hate, p. 14
[207] 1 Thessalonians 4:11; Romans 13:1–3
[208] Romans 3:2
[209] Romans 1:5

"Then the apostles and elders, with the whole church, decided to choose some of their own men and send them to Antioch with Paul and Barnabas. They chose Judas (called Barsabbas) and Silas, men who were leaders among the believers. With them they sent the following letter:

The Jerusalem Council's Letter to Gentile Believers

The apostles and elders, your brothers,
To the Gentile believers in Antioch, Syria and Cilicia:
Greetings.
We have heard that some went out from us without our authorization and disturbed you, troubling your minds by what they said. So we all agreed to choose some men and send them to you with our dear friends Barnabas and Paul— men who have risked their lives for the name of our Lord Jesus Christ. Therefore we are sending Judas and Silas to confirm by word of mouth what we are writing. It seemed good to the Holy Spirit and to us not to burden you with anything beyond the following requirements: You are to abstain from food sacrificed to idols, from blood, from the meat of strangled animals and from sexual immorality. You will do well to avoid these things.
Farewell."[210]

The letter from James and the Jerusalem Council allayed some adverse rejoinders about Gentile believers. It did not stop all criticism, however. Paul had to lay down another clear principle for the nay-sayers who continued to argue with the challenge.

"So in Christ Jesus you are all children of God through faith, for all of you who were baptized into Christ have clothed yourselves with Christ. There is neither Jew nor Gentile, neither slave nor free, nor is there male and female, for you are all one in Christ Jesus. If you belong to Christ, then you are Abraham's seed, and heirs according to the promise."[211]

This same letter of Galatians is often described as the Magna Carta of the early Church, a declaration of emancipation from legalism. Galatia continued to be a "thorn" in Paul's flesh which may explain why he made several return visits to the churches of that area.

That settled the issue for the majority of the church. Yet there remained a rump unwilling to follow the inclusive decision proposed by Paul and supported by both Antioch and Jerusalem branches of the church.

Equality of Church Members

Chapter Six made mention of how Barnabas and Saul were "set aside" or "commissioned" by the Antioch Church. The commissioning was done by a vote in a democratic fashion among the church membership.

In his book, *Theological Sentences*, Professor Samuel J. Mikolaski notes the democratic polity practised among the Antiochene Christians. Referring to the "setting aside" of Saul and Barnabas, he noted,

"The laying on of hands probably means nominated or chosen by show of hands, or signified by hand, as in Acts 14:23 and 2 Corinthians 8:19. The church added

---

[210] Acts 15:19–29 NIV
[211] Galatians 3:26–29

its consent with the fraternal mood and consensual decision-making indicated in 1 Clement.

This initial policy of the first Christians reflects an egality among them. None saw the other believer as having more authority than any other. That did not mean they did not recognize that some Christians enjoyed different gifting or traits than others."[212]

Later, writing to the Corinthian and Roman churches, Paul clearly stated that equality of Christians was established by God but that God chose certain individuals for specific service and gifted them individually for the work they were to undertake for him and his church.

> *"The body is a unit, though it is made up of many parts; and though its parts are many, they form one body . . . There are different kinds of gifts but the same Spirit. There are different kinds of service but the same Lord. There are different kinds of working but the same God works all of them in all men . . . God has combined the members of the body , , , you are the body of Christ, and each one of you is a part of it."*[213]

In Romans, Paul cautions against an elitist spiritual caste system, *"I say to every one of you; do not think of yourselves more highly that you ought."*[214] Sadly, the later development in the churches removed the egalitarian equations and offered increased authority to multi-tiered church leaders.

When Paul wrote to believers in Ephesus he emphasized both the diversity and unity of the church. He claimed that the various functions of members resulted from gentle gifts of grace presented by God himself. *"So Christ himself gave the apostles, the prophets, the evangelists, the pastors and teachers, to equip his people for works of service, so that the body of Christ may be built up."*[215]

No Christian could claim superiority to another because all fitted in with God's plan for the church Christ said he was building. Equality of value to God was no different from one to another. So when the church elected to send missionaries, it was "one man (or woman) and one vote."

Sharing Possessions

Further evidence of the egality of the early believers in Jerusalem is in the generosity of the entire company. The basis for this equality is the creed, "Jesus is Lord." If that is true, ergo, everything belongs to the Lord. And if it is the Lord's, it is his to disseminate as needed.

> *"There were no needy persons among them. For from time to time those who owned land or houses sold them, brought the money from the sales and put it at the apostles' feet, and it was distributed to anyone who had need. Joseph, a Levite from Cyprus, whom the apostles called Barnabas (which means "son of*

---

[212] Samuel J. Mikolaski, Theological Sentences, p. 652
[213] 1 Corinthians 12, various verses
[214] Romans 12:3
[215] Ephesians 4:11–12

encouragement"), sold a field he owned and brought the money and put it at the apostles' feet."[216]

Another understanding among the early church was the imminent second coming of Jesus Christ. Was this a factor in the believers' readiness to rid themselves of their belongings? It may have been for some. The benefit of the doubt must go to the willingness of believers to put their trust in spiritual matters, to follow the instructions of Jesus himself,

> *"So do not worry, saying, 'What shall we eat?' or 'What shall we drink?' or 'What shall we wear?' For the pagans run after all these things, and your heavenly Father knows that you need them. But seek first his kingdom and his righteousness* (both spiritual purity and justice)*, and all these things will be given to you as well. Therefore do not worry about tomorrow, for tomorrow will worry about itself. Each day has enough trouble of its own."*[217]

---

[216] Acts 4:34–37
[217] Matthew 6:31–34

CHAPTER EIGHT
RETESTING MISSION

Paul and Barnabas together with the other Christian Antiochenes delighted in the reporting from the pair who had successfully shared their faith in Cyprus and Asia Minor. The mission had not gone smoothly. The missionaries met many barriers on multitude occasions.

Despite all the daunting blockades experienced by Paul and his mission partner Barnabas, many Jews and Gentiles had responded to the faith-sharing of both apostles. They reported that churches had formed in Salamis, Paphos, Pisidian Antioch, Iconium, Lystra, Derbe and Perga. That was a measurable result.

The simple Gospel achieved dynamic results among those who responded to it. First, the newly-born believers experienced the presence and infusion of the Holy Spirit. The converts now understood their full acceptance by God, forgiveness of all their sins and guilt, and a sense of joy that accompanies such liberation.

Implications for Believers

The Antioch Christian brain and spirit trust began to realize that the simple gospel was not so simple. Part of it was uncomplicated; some of it produced unanticipated consequences. Did Gentiles need to become Jews when they became believers? Did Jews need to maintain their legal obligations required by *Torah* law? What about work–if Christ is returning soon, need the believers continue in their day jobs? When is Jesus returning? What about eating meat that was sacrificed to pagan idols? The list goes on and on and on.

The church was becoming more than an agent of disseminating the truth of God's grace; believers now wrestled with the implications of saving faith and resurrection. When the believers said, *"Jesus is Lord,"* that statement implied denial of the divine Caesar, a renewed concept of generosity, a sense of justice for humanity far greater than anything Jews accepted as justice defined by the *Torah*. Look at how Jesus redefined "neighbour!"[218]

As to the basic tenets of resurrection and that, *"Jesus is Lord,"* Paul stressed that credo in his letters penned to give "his" (pastorally his, that is) churches a firm foundation. *"No one can say, 'Jesus is Lord' except by the Holy Spirit."*[219]

"If you confess with your mouth, 'Jesus is Lord,' and believe in your heart that God raised him from the dead, you will be saved."[220] *"Regarding his (God's) Son, who as to his human nature was a descendant of David, and who through the Spirit of holiness declared with power to be the Son of God by his resurrection from the dead: Jesus Christ our Lord."*[221] *"For what I received I passed on to you as of first*

---

[218] Luke 10:13–24
[219] 1 Corinthians 12:3
[220] Romans 10:9
[221] Romans 1:3, 4

importance: that Christ died for our sins according to the Scriptures, that he was buried, that he was raised on the third day according to the Scriptures, and that he appeared to Cephas, and then to the Twelve. After that, he appeared to more than five hundred of the brothers and sisters at the same time, most of whom are still living, though some have fallen asleep. Then he appeared to James, then to all the apostles . . ."[222]

The need for guidelines should not surprise anyone. Jesus more than hinted at the implications[223] this Gospel to the church which he said he would build.[224] Simply said, the church was now under construction. Paul defined its foundation.

Now the swelling church would need to resolve its parameters by the believers themselves working through issues and guided by the Holy Spirit. The church remains a work in progress. It has changing targets as new factors emerge in the changing world. Peter called the building structure of the church, "living stones." *"And you are living stones that God is building into his spiritual temple. What's more, you are his holy priests. Through the mediation of Jesus Christ, you offer spiritual sacrifices that please God."*[225] A "live" church meets the challenges of each new day.

Cementing Churches; Constant Coaching

Paul itched to return to see the believers he had catecumened. He also mused about what horizons extended beyond Pisidia and Pamphylia where these new churches now existed. He realized that new congregations needed support in many ways, encouragement, teaching, skills in sharing, and organization. Moreover, if the first mission went so successfully, if not smoothly, could there be places beyond the existing new churches that could be evangelized?

Paul broached Barnabas. Barnabas was willing and eager to pick up where they had left off their combined Cypriot and Galatian mission. But the latter had baggage attached to his consent. Barnabas wanted to take John Mark (now in Jerusalem) with them. Paul's response was an adamant No! *Not* Mark!

Paul had little regard for the young man who had deserted them at Perga on their initial mission. Paul viewed John Mark as a toxic missionary. Paul was not challenging John's commitment to Jesus but to his focus, courage and dependability.

Was Paul's evaluation of John accurate? Perhaps John Mark thought Paul to be exceedingly overbearing in his leadership and wanted out of that situation. Overbearing? It's a strong probability. But Paul required a competent and uncompromising cohort in his ministry.

Let's consider Barnabas' point-of-view. Undoubtedly he had a conflict of interest since John Mark was a close relative. Yet he believed his nephew possessed both potential and purpose. Barnabas was patient, an encourager and a believer in second

---

[222] 1 Corinthians 15:3–7
[223] Matthew 25:34–36
[224] Matthew 16:18
[225] 1 Peter 2:5 New Living Translation

opportunities. Had he not stood up for Saul when he re-entered Jerusalem after Saul's detour on the Damascus highway?[226] He thought then that Paul deserved a second chance. Paul's refusal and Barnabas' insistence of John Mark joining a second mission was a watershed in the relationships between Paul from Tarsus and Barnabas from Cyprus.

"Some time later Paul said to Barnabas, "Let us go back and visit the believers in all the towns where we preached the word of the Lord and see how they are doing." Barnabas wanted to take John, also called Mark, with them, but Paul did not think it wise to take him, because he had deserted them in Pamphylia and had not continued with them in the work. They had such a sharp disagreement that they parted company. Barnabas took Mark and sailed for Cyprus, but Paul chose Silas and left, commended by the believers to the grace of the Lord. He went through Syria and Cilicia, strengthening the churches."[227]

In a peculiar way, Paul endorsed Barnabas and his mission. What mattered most to Paul was the Gospel declaration. *"The important thing is that in every way whether from false motives or true, Christ is preached. And because of this, I rejoice."*[228]

We can't quarrel with Barnabas' decision to foster John Mark. Some teachers are more patient with their students than are other lecturers. Barnabas saw an opportunity to coach the young man in the Lord's purposes. They walked together across the Island of Cyprus sharing their faith and growing together in Christian maturity.

If it were not for Barnabas, would the Gospel of Mark have been written? Mark set the template for Luke and Matthew to follow with their own versions of the life and work of Jesus. The Bible does not detail what the two did in Cyprus during their mission. Egyptian Coptics believe that Mark brought the Christian faith to Egypt. The main cathedral in Cairo is named St. Mark's. The Coptic patriarch, always chosen from ascetic hermit desert monks, has a dwelling across the road from it.

Paul's New Team Player

The supposed schism between Paul and Barnabas did not dissuade Paul from trying again. Silas became Paul's new companion. The name Silas is Greek. It may derive from an Aramaic word *Seila*, meaning Saul! But the name's meaning is guesswork. In other New Testament references Silas seems to also be called Silvanus. For purposes of this book, we believe we may correctly assume that Silas and Silvanus are one and the same– but we could be wrong. It's not worth a wager.

We first meet Silas as part of a delegation including a Judas who travelled to Antioch with Paul and Barnabas. Their purpose was to bring greetings and solidarity from the Jerusalem Church to the church in Antioch. Jerusalem's decision centred on an acceptance of Gentiles into the Christian community. The two main centres of the burgeoning Christian group were singing from the same page in their hymnals.

Probably, as was noted, Silas' name derives from Silvanus, the Roman god of trees and forests. Orthodox Christians propose that Silvanus was among the 70 disciples that

[226] Acts 9:27
[227] Acts 15:36–41
[228] Philippians 1:18

Jesus sent out as described by Luke, as a herald of Jesus' imminent visit in Galilee and Judea. *"The Lord appointed 72 others and sent them two by two ahead of him where he was about to go."*[229]

Could this be the same Silas (abbreviation for Silvanus) who joined Paul on a mission to Asia Minor and Europe, and was jailed in Philippi? Why not? If so, he had personal acquaintance with Jesus himself, and not just from any secondary connection to the Lord.

Paul had great confidence in this early Christian man. He was a steady disciple, ready to suffer for his faith, and evidently respected in the churches Paul, Silas and Timothy had visited. With his strong credibility, Paul invited him, along with Timothy, to pen the two letters to the Thessalonian Church. Silas and Timothy had more influence in that city because Paul went on the lam when Hellenist Jewish critics harassed him, chasing him from Thessalonika.

Silas (Silvanus) is a recurring and esteemed name in the book of Acts, and the various Epistles.

This voyage offered Paul an opportunity to discuss missionary work with Silas. No doubt the previous impression Silas made on Paul was sufficient enough for Paul to approach Silas as a potential partner in proclaiming the Gospel. For Silas' part, he must have wanted to see the new mission stations first-hand and meet the new converts.

Paul and his new companion Silas left Antioch for points West. The route was around the bay enclosing Antioch, past present-day Payas and Adana, through Cilicia (Paul's home area of Tarsus) and onto the inland route to the cities of Southern Galatia.

Maybe Paul and Silas took the inland route to avoid letting the Hellenist Jews in Iconium and Pisidian Antioch hear of his travel plans and thus avoid their interference. Maybe also the two could evangelize along the way. It's very limiting to do mission while sea-bound on a ship, although not impossible.[230] Any contact is an open opportunity.

Acts 16 tells us only that they came to Derbe. Paul's previous visit to Derbe was a success story. *"They preached the Good News in that city and won a large number of disciples."*[231] Now Paul returned, and with Silas, a different evangelistic companion. No doubt their intention was twofold, (1) to anchor the faith of those who came to Christ earlier, and (2) to see if further hearers would receive and accept the Gospel message. Establishing a church required continued steadfast instruction, spirited encouragement and ongoing upbuilding.

Lystra held mixed memories for Paul. No doubt Paul had briefed Silas on them. This is the community that at first thought Paul and Barnabas were Greek deities, and they bowed down before them. Then, when Hellenistic Jewish hecklers and agitators arrived on the scene to blockade the Gospel message, Lystrans joined the uproar against the two. They created a brouhaha. In Lystra they stoned Paul and left him for dead.

---

[229] Luke 10:2
[230] Acts 27:15
[231] Acts 14:21

No stoning occurred on this next visit. The two visitors came to Lystra to upbuild the church, founded by Jesus,[232] and add to the number of saints. The initial visit to Lystra was short on details about the believers who were won by the missionaries to Christ. But this second visit notes that a visit to Timothy was one intention of their travels. The new Christians in both Lystra and Iconium *spoke well of him.*[233]

Timothy's father was Greek; his mother was a Jewess. If a mother is a Jew, her son, no matter the father's ethnic background, is also automatically a Jew. This visit had long-term results. The two from Antioch invited Timothy to join them on their current mission. Timothy had no qualms about joining them. He was eager and willing.

Paul insisted that Timothy be circumcised, not so much to fulfil the Jewish law or contradict his teachings to Galatian Hellenistic Jews, but to make Timothy acceptable without question when dealing with a Jewish audience–and a requirement for visiting Jerusalem's Temple. Timothy began his enrollment in the Lystra "seminary" training as he sat and studied for many days at the feet of both Silas and Paul. They ensured he was both biblically conversant and deeply rooted in the life of Christ.

Timothy grew on Paul. He and Silas saw the superlative potential in this young man. Paul loved the family connection too and later wrote of its spiritual rootage.

> *"That precious memory triggers another: your honest faith—and what a rich faith it is, handed down from your grandmother Lois to your mother Eunice, and now to you! And the special gift of ministry you received when I laid hands on you and prayed—keep that ablaze! God doesn't want us to be shy with his gifts, but bold and loving and sensible."*[234]

When Paul and Silas thought Timothy was ready for the mission, they set out together. Acts says they *"travelled town to town."* Their message about the atonement was provided by Jesus' death and resurrection for all the world, not only for Jews, but Gentiles as well. *"As they travelled from town to town they delivered the decisions reached by the apostles and elders in Jerusalem for the people to obey."*[235]

These decisions, as indicated in Chapter Six, were as follows: *"It seemed good to the Holy Spirit and to us not to burden you with anything beyond the following requirements: You are to abstain from food sacrificed to idols, from blood, from the meat of strangled animals and from sexual immorality. You will do well to avoid these things.*

The church reporter Luke, in summarizing the Asian part of this mission, noted, *"So the churches were strengthened in the faith and grew daily in numbers."*[236]

---

[232] Matthew 16:18
[233] Acts 16:2
[234] 2 Timothy 1:5 MSG
[235] Acts 16:4
[236] Acts 16:5

CHAPTER NINE
CHOOSING COMPATIBILITIES

Paul/Saul appeared to be as prickly a person as one could ever meet. He seemed to have a short fuse. He did not hesitate to berate the Apostle Peter who was highly revered by early Christians. He argued with Barnabas. But he was never a quitter, although it looks as if Barnabas had given up co-operating with him. What else is new? The church is comprised of imperfect people but still God has called them into his service and has *"set eternity in their hearts."*[237]

This should encourage any church, to know what God sees in his trophies collected by the atonement of Jesus and what he can do with impatient, peevish, persnickety performances. One thinks of the child's prayer: "Please God, make all the bad people good; and make the good people nice." How can you use someone with attention deficit hyperactivity disorder (ADHD)–impulsive and hyperactive behaviour? God knows how!

In Rogers and Hammerstein's *Sound of Music*, a song went like this, "What do you do with a problem like Maria? How do you hold a moonbeam in your hand?" That was God's question about Saul/Paul. "What can I do with a person like Paul? God answered his own question: "I'll turn him into a missionary / teacher / preacher. I'll send him afield and thereby prevent him from constantly disrupting local established churches like Jerusalem and Antioch. I'll use him to grow and develop believers."

God did just that! The Lord had a unique place for Paul. The Lord said, "I'll take you, Paul, just as you are," which is the way the Lord takes everyone.

This gives rise to another key question. "How do you work with a person like Paul?" The answer is "with great perseverance and difficulty." Paul was a short-term person, constantly on the move, with "ants in his pants." His longest tenure in a church was three years in Ephesus and less than two years in Corinth. Some of that short tenure was God's doing; some of it was Paul's peculiar obsessive, compulsive personality.

There is no mistaking it. God and Paul were lovers. The Lord saw past Paul's flaws and loved him despite his nastiness. He might have sung the Jerome Kern/Oscar Hammerstein ballad to Paul:

"But you're lovely, never, never change. Keep that breathless charm
Won't you please arrange it? 'Cause I love you, just the way you look
Just the way you look tonight."

Paul might have responded in the same way as lovers do, using Charlotte Elliott's song,

"Just as I am, Thou wilt receive, Wilt welcome, pardon, cleanse, relieve;
Because Thy promise I believe, O Lamb of God, I come, I come."

So we know how God worked with Paul. We also know how Paul worked with God. Barnabas had difficulty with "the least of all saints." *Although I am less than the*

---

[237] Ecclesiastes 3:11

*least of all the Lord's people, this grace was given me: to preach to the Gentiles the boundless riches of Christ.*²³⁸ Yet, once Mark had left them on Mission One, Barnabas did not hold back from working tirelessly with Paul. He followed his missionary teammate through thick and thin and stayed with him until they reported to the Antiochene church, after Mission Number One.

John Mark didn't work well with Paul–not in this mission, anyway. We can only guess that their personalities clashed or that Paul had little time for some tyros. Maybe he resented Barnabas foisting John Mark on him. Salvation was serious business, thought Paul. One doesn't toy with such an evangelistic responsibility.

Paul figured that John Mark had not been serious enough about the Gospel, treating it as a cherished treasure they held in "fragile clay pottery."²³⁹ John Mark, however, came to his faith in less of an explosive manner than Paul and was less mature in every way and maybe, just maybe, Paul thought his tenderfoot was inadequate for the main mission of life.

One senses that Paul was all business all the time. He would have little time for a morning coffee with friends or an evening of relaxation watching TV. He knew about athletics–racing, boxing and the Olympic sports. Yet one can hardly picture him on a team or sitting in the stands rooting for other people at play. He always wanted to be somewhere else, or so it seems. He needed to be in the "action." He might easily take over any conversation. He may have been "transformed,"²⁴⁰ but he would always have a leader's personality–and why not?

It's not easy to work alongside such a person. Yet, it is important to co-operate with all people. The Gospel is about people, not legalities, not agendas. The psalmist wrote: *"But as for me, my contentment is not in wealth but in seeing you and knowing all is well between us. And when I awake in heaven, I will be fully satisfied, for I will see you face-to-face."*²⁴¹

---

²³⁸ Ephesians 3:8
²³⁹ 2 Corinthians 4:7
²⁴⁰ Romans 12:2
²⁴¹ Psalm 17:15 TLB

PART TWO: A BEACHHEAD IN EUROPE

CHAPTER TEN
VISAS DENIED

Paul and Silas must have spent quality time in Lystra. When the missionaries deemed that they could leave several qualified new disciples happily ensconced in Lystra and competent for faithfully undertaking the Lord's work, they pushed on. Except that Paul wanted Timothy to join the fishing expedition. So now there are three. They will soon be joined by a fourth member, the sometime physician and full-time church reporter, Luke.

Paul and Silas began writing their own script for this part of their seemingly God-chosen mission–Mission Two. That was not an illegitimate choice. God gives his servants much leeway to do their "thing." Jesus told parables to that effect.[242] God is not a puppeteer who holds humans at the end of strings he controls! He can and does however, if necessary, change the scripts we write for ourselves.

The Bible is full of testimonials as to how people make their decisions but God desires to amend them. "*In their hearts humans plan their course,*" wrote the author of Proverbs, "*but the Lord establishes their steps.*"[243] In the story of Joseph, God critically rewrote that drama's libretto.

> "*Joseph said to (his brothers), "Don't be afraid . . . You intended to harm me, but God intended it for good to accomplish what is now being done, the saving of many lives. So then, don't be afraid. I will provide for you and your children." And he reassured them and spoke kindly to them.*"[244]

Paul and Silas, the original two missionaries of Mission Two, were now seeing mind-blowing dividends from their work. The opposition Paul once had experienced during a prior evangelistic foray into Galatia, had considerably abated. Paul and Silas now had a new, youthful and energetic missionary companion in Timothy. He seemed like a suitable comrade; compatible, committed, ebullient, enthusiastic and absolutely ineradicable in the Gospel.

The three moved in and out of sundry settlements in central Galatia and Phrygia. The populace received their message gleefully. This had become an exciting experience about which to write home to the Antioch Church.

As noted, Luke wrote, "*As they travelled from town to town, they presented the simple guidelines the Jerusalem apostles and leaders had come up with. That turned out to be most helpful. Day after day the congregations became stronger in faith and larger in size.*"[245]

The implications are many. First, each day's Gospel declaration led to daily

---

[242] Matthew 25:27 *ff*
[243] Proverbs 16:9
[244] Genesis 50:19–21
[245] Acts 16:4, 5 MSG

growth. Secondly, each community incorporated small groups of Diaspora Hellenistic Jews who became the intended objectives of the three missionaries. Thirdly, that some Gentiles joined their Jewish purposes was a most joyful bonus, but also a most acceptable and legitimate godsend. Silas, Paul and Timothy took the high-priority time and pre-eminent effort required to help the recent converts sink their faith roots deeply into nutritious Gospel loam.

Paul now needed to review his maps. The three had reached boundaries that were not written in any script God had handed them. Should they travel North to Bithinya? Visas denied! Perhaps God wanted them to travel in Northwest Mysia near the Dardanelles? Denied again! How did Paul accept these roadblocks? He was somewhat frustrated but patiently learned to await the Holy Spirit's leading. However, God had not yet given them his re-worked script.

The Lord delivered his instructions in a communication of his own choosing–a vision given to the Apostle Paul. God gave the vision. Paul needed to decipher it. What Paul saw in that dream was a man dressed in Macedonian-Greek garb, inviting him to enter Europe. That would be the next locale for mission. The three men clambered down from the Galatian hills to the popular port of Troas on the Aegean Sea. Paul accommodated his schedule to adapt to God's mission locale.

After scouting the harbour for suitable ships headed to their desired destinations, they sailed in two stages, pausing at the island of Samothrace, home of many Greek mystery religions, finally landing at Neapolis in Europe.

Archaeologist James L. Kelso argues that, "The best sailing weather was from May 26 to September 14. Insurance rates on ships and cargo increased considerably if the sailings" pre-dated or post-dated those good weather parameters.[246] Thus we know the likely months that Paul, Silas, Timothy and now Luke moved from Asia to Europe.

They quickly found the Roman pre-Egnatian Way, the undeveloped military super roadway taking them right into Philippi and beyond.

---

[246] James L. Kelso. An Archaeologist Follows the Apostle Paul. p. 17

CHAPTER ELEVEN
WEAPONS: THE SWORD OF THE SPIRIT

Neapolis

One of the most significant transitions in human history took place in what we now call the 49th year of our Lord. Almost 20 years had passed since Jesus was crucified in Jerusalem. Unlike many of the significant alterations to history, this transition did not develop on the battlefront or in political upheavals. This was not a military conquest. It was no usurping of a throne. This war was begun by unarmed missionaries–except they were armed in a contrastive way. Paul himself explained the weaponry:

> *"For our struggle is not against flesh and blood, but against the rulers, against the authorities, against the powers of this dark world and against the spiritual forces of evil in the heavenly realms. Therefore put on the full armour of God, so that when the day of evil comes, you may be able to stand your ground, and after you have done everything, to stand. Stand firm then, with the belt of truth buckled around your waist, with the breastplate of righteousness in place, and with your feet fitted with the readiness that comes from the gospel of peace. In addition to all this, take up the shield of faith, with which you can extinguish all the flaming arrows of the evil one. Take the helmet of salvation and the sword of the Spirit, which is the word of God."*[247]

In that year, a mere two decades after Jesus rose from death and was resurrected in Jerusalem, Paul set out to "spread the Gospel word." Paul entered the pages of the Bible like a lightning strike. He set out as a zealot to erase the believers in Jesus from the face of the earth–*"Saul began to destroy the church."*[248] However, during his celebrated Damascus highway hike to persecute Christians, a bolt from heaven, something like lightning struck him.[249] As he humbled himself during this ego-abasing experience, he soon dropped the proud name of Saul, the first and deeply dithering dynast of Israel, and adopted a Roman name Paulus. Paulus meant "little." As we described earlier in this book, God could use Saul only after he realized he needn't act as the clone of the once proud failed King of Israel. As Mary said about her part in birthing the Saviour of the world, *"He has brought down rulers from their thrones but he has lifted up the humble."*[250]

Paul's Team journeyed by sea from the coastal city of Troas (not the nearby Troy mentioned in Homer's Iliad) in Asia Minor to Neapolis, a port in Northern Greece in Europe.[251]– His normal method of travel likely was by searching the wharf for ships about to sail in the direction he was headed. Then he and his team would pay for their voyage and settle amid the merchandise being shipped to a suitable destination.

The first transfer point was the Island of Samothrace. Samothrace was the centre of cults referred to as mystery religions. The name Samothrace probably derived from one

---

[247] Ephesians 6:11–17
[248] Acts 8:3a
[249] Acts 9:3 *ff*
[250] Luke 1:52
[251] Acts 16:11 *ff*

of the occupations of the Island. Thracians occupied the Island circa 700 BC. Inhabitants from the Island of Samos also colonized the Island, hence the name Samothrace.

The mystery religions involved secret communions between worshippers and priestesses. The cult of Magna Mater radiated out from the Island to Greek and Persian cities everywhere. This fertility cult involved the killing of a castrated bull, drinking its blood and expecting its resurrection. Paul (and companions) could hardly catch his breath at Samothrace, so instead of stopping to counter the claims of the cult, he and his companions scurried to another wharf where they could catch a different trading vessel to reach Neapolis (meaning "new city"). That entire journey took two days. The team's mission was Macedonia, not Samothrace. No one would sidetrack the four missionaries.

Paul's "commando" group, infiltrators in this pagan and Hellenistic country, landed at the Macedonian community of Neapolis, today known as Kavala. Paul knew that the city name derived from a settlement by Thassians 600 years prior to Paul's short visit. It means "new city." Paul wasted no time in scouting the city–but they were not sightseers. The four Apostles, prompted by Paul's recent vision, made speedy tracks along the improvised Roman military road–what would become the Via Egnatia–directly into Philippi. The Via Egnatia would soon be an elitist fast track Roman army route.

Romans colonized Philippi. It became a "little Rome." Neapolis had importance only as a port of Philippi some 17 kilometres Northwest of the port. Neapolis has a different kind of importance to Christians. It is now remembered as the beginning of Christian ministry to Western Europe. Today's Kavala is interesting because it provides a glimpse into the Byzantine period of the city and its water aqueduct built by emperor Suleiman the Magnificent to supply water to the city. It is a wonder of a sight.

Today's harbour, like that of ancient Neapolis, shows ships of various sizes for various purposes. The Aegean had no passenger ships as such, no ocean liners, no yachts, no cruise ships. Its fleets were used mostly for trade, sometimes for military purposes. Ships were large, small and in between. They were oar-powered or sail and wind-driven. Paul, Silas, Timothy and Luke took convenient passage on such ships to reach Europe. They went from Troas in Asia Minor–present day Turkey–to Neapolis, the new city in Macedonia, present day Greece.

Thanks to the stable Pax Romana (sometimes called the Pax Augusta), few pirate vessels plied the Mediterranean to steal goods or press-gang sailors. Sailing was still somewhat risky, with storms, navigational hazards and shifting sandbars–and a few buccaneers. Yet with Rome ruling both seas and lands, merchandise and voyagers were relatively safe from maritime mischief or sudden slavery. Within the "Roman Peace" established in 27 BC, piracy was considerably contained.

Four Slogging Missionaries

Paul had been a Pharisee, rabbi, a teacher and a scholar. He was Jewish. He was also a citizen of Rome. As previously noted, he was born in Tarsus not far from the border of present day Turkey and Syria. Rabbis were required to have a trade, so that no one could accuse them of being "so heavenly-minded that they were of no earthly good." Many a rabbi taught that, "a man who does not teach his son a trade is like teaching him to be a thief."[252]

Therefore we read that Paul was a "leather worker," also called a tentmaker. Some athletes travelling in areas supporting Olympic Games or Pan Hellenic Games, lived in tents (*sub pellibus*–under skins). Moreover, tents needed constant repair, as did sails. This was a handy trade for itinerants. "Leatherworker" meant much more that darning vestments but included sail making and sail mending as well as patch repairs for clothing worn by the military. This meant that Paul could earn his keep working with certain animal skins, likely *kosher*, because he was a maker of tents or a sail crafter or both.

As a devout, perhaps even fanatical Pharisee, Paul aka Saul once persecuted the new Jewish sect, the followers of Jesus. Paul's mentor, the renowned Pharisee Gamaliel, was less zealous, much more tolerant than Paul. Paul later learned to be more liberal in his application of Pharisees' intolerances. As he progressed in his transformed, spiritual maturity, Paul did not behave as more conservative rabbis would have. For example, a rigid Pharisee would have looked at the ground as he passed by idols of Greek deities. Paul now saw them for what they were, items of stone or wood.[253] Note that Paul said he looked "carefully" at the Athenians' objects of worship. He eyeballed the idols up close.

In those earlier days, he had been known as Saul. Now he was Saul aka Paul with a Roman name he used some many months following his marvellous conversion on the road to Damascus. Followers of Jesus were already in Damascus because the gospel spread quickly to many places within the Roman Empire. The very people whose faith he wanted to stamp out showed him a charity of acceptance, then a bond of love and ministered to him. Soon, Paul became a major leader in "The Way."

Silas, Paul's missionary companion on this European mission, came from Antioch in Syria, but if he was in that Jesus-commissioned 70, he must have travelled much. Believers within Antioch ordained and commissioned him to work with Paul. As already argued, "Silas" may be an abbreviation of Silvanus, meaning "of the forest." Did Silas translate into "Woody" the way Peter translated into "Rocky?" Perhaps. Was he Jewish? Most likely. Silas is a Greek version of the Aramaic name "Seila," which in Hebrew means Saul!

Luke likely was a Gentile.[254] He was a physician[255] with a knack of recording his observations. He demonstrated that he was familiar with case studies. He appears to have joined Paul, Silas and Timothy at Troas. The text of Acts, chapter 16, changes in verse six from "Paul and his companions" to "we" in verse 11. Luke, most assume, wrote two books, the Gospel of Luke and the Acts of the Apostles. Thus Luke provided about a quarter of the New Testament. Regrettably, Luke records much about others, yet little

---

[252] Abraham Cohen, <u>Ancient Jewish Proverbs</u> (Kid. 29); 1 Thessalonians 4:11; Genesis 3:19; 2 Thessalonians 3:7–13
[253] Acts 17:23
[254] Colossians 4:11–14 Paul does not include Luke as among the Jews
[255] Colossians 4:14

concerning himself, and still less how he learned the accounts he penned before he joined up with Paul, Silas and Timothy–or the source of his medical knowledge.

We can only speculate about Luke's background. Too much is missing. Generally, physicians, first of all, were priests. Luke (not Matthew, Mark or John) notes that fact when he relates how Jesus healed a leper. Afterwards he sent those healed to have a priest ensure they were cured and no longer required to live outside a normal community or cry out, "unclean" as they approached someone. *"When Jesus saw them* (the lepers) *he said, 'Go show yourselves to the priests.'"*[256]

Luke does not appear to have been a priest; indeed he could not have been a Jewish priest. Most other physicians in the Greek world were priests of the Greek deity Asclepius, a mythical child of the mythical Apollo. These priests were skilled in many medical specialties; with a healing centre on the Island of Cos. Mental health was studied and practised at Pergamum and Epidauros.

Luke's attitudes suggest that he understood the good principles of mental health. Ophthalmology was a specialty in Laodicea. Early priests of Asclepius, like Galen, understood hygiene and epidemiology. Did Luke train under the priests of Asclepius? Did he take the Hippocratic oath? We do not know. Perhaps not. Yet he was a physician.

Luke appears in Acts 16:10 with the word "we." "They" has changed to "we." Some "experts" surmise that Luke perhaps came from Troas, if not from Antioch–it's a guess at best. We really don't know from whence came Luke nor do we know his background except that Paul calls him a physician. That fact alone raises questions about his upbringing. His careful note-taking mirrors that of a doctor. Regrettably, Luke leaves himself out of the narrative, again a physician's case study example.

If he was a physician, where did he train? The medical people in the ancient world nearly all came from some form of priesthood. In Jesus' realm, it was the priests who declared people healthy–*"Go, show yourselves to the priests,"* declared Jesus to the lepers he healed.

Greek doctors also came from a medical priesthood with notable medical pioneers such as Hippocrates and later, Galen. They served Asclepius, the mythical god of healing. They had special healing centres where medical priests taught each other diagnoses and treatment skills. They centred their training in schools on the Island of Cos, at Epidaurus, at Pergamum (mental health) and in Laodicea (ophthalmology). Their 10-point code of medical behaviour known as the oath of Hippocrates went as follows:

"I swear by Apollo the physician, and Asclepius the surgeon, likewise Hygieia and Panacea, and call all the gods and goddesses to witness, that I will observe and keep this underwritten oath, to the utmost of my power and judgment.

"I will reverence my master who taught me the art. Equally with my parents, will I allow him things necessary for his support, and will consider his sons as brothers. I will teach them my art without reward or agreement; and I will impart all my acquirement, instructions, and whatever I know, to my master's children, as to my own; and likewise to all my pupils, who shall bind and tie themselves by a professional oath, but to none else.

---

[256] Luke 17:14

"With regard to healing the sick, I will devise and order for them the best diet, according to my judgment and means; and I will take care that they suffer no hurt or damage.

"Nor shall any man's entreaty prevail upon me to administer poison to anyone; neither will I counsel any man to do so. Moreover, I will give no sort of medicine to any pregnant woman, with a view to destroy the child.

"Further, I will comport myself and use my knowledge in a godly manner.

"I will not cut for the stone, but will commit that affair entirely to the surgeons.

"Whatsoever house I may enter, my visit shall be for the convenience and advantage of the patient; and I will willingly refrain from doing any injury or wrong from falsehood, and (in an especial manner) from acts of an amorous nature, whatever may be the rank of those who it may be my duty to cure, whether mistress or servant, bond or free.

Whatever, in the course of my practice, I may see or hear (even when not invited), whatever I may happen to obtain knowledge of, if it be not proper to repeat it, I will keep sacred and secret within my own breast.

"If I faithfully observe this oath, may I thrive and prosper in my fortune and profession, and live in the estimation of posterity; or on breach thereof, may the reverse be my fate."[257]

Did Luke learn his profession from the Greek medical establishment? Had he dallied with the priests of Asclepius? Was he Greek or Jewish? Paul excludes him from "the circumcised" in his writing to Colossae. Yet it is difficult to believe Paul would allow a non-Jewish Luke to accompany him when he insisted that Timothy should be circumcised. Is it possible that Luke was a proselyte? Maybe Luke was exempted because his role was different, or probably because Luke the uncircumcised proved to Gentiles his acceptability as a Christian without have to become a Jew.

One New Testament scholar, Dr. Robert Lindsey wrote a doctoral dissertation (Southern Baptist Seminary, Louisville KY) proposing that Luke penned his Gospel specifically for Jews and that Luke's writing preceded Mark's Gospel.[258] That perspective differs from most synoptic scholars who situate Mark's Gospel as the template for recording the life and work of Jesus related by Matthew and Luke.

Luke's Gospel quotes Jesus differently than does Matthew. The Lucan version of the Beatitudes reflects a doctor's deep concern for the poor. Luke wrote more about hunger, than did Matthew. Luke's script offers stories of banquets and feeding, more than Matthew's quotations from Jesus.

As noted, some writers suggest Luke came from Troas, or possibly Syrian Antioch. Whatever Luke's background, he was a faithful, loyal, balanced, even-tempered and encouraging mission partner of Paul. Undoubtedly he helped keep Paul relatively emotionally stable.

Of Timothy, we know a little more. Paul's letters tell us more about Timothy than they do about Luke. Timothy was a "Jesus-disciple" with whom Paul became acquainted during one of his missions in Asia. Paul *"came to Lystra where a disciple named Timothy*

[257] A. Alexandri, Kos, p. 77
[258] Robert L. Lindsey, Unlocking the Synoptic Problem: Four Keys for Better Understanding Jesus., Library, Southern Baptist Seminary, Louisville, KY

*lived, whose mother was a Jew and a believer but whose father was a Greek. The disciples at Lystra spoke well of him, and Paul wanted to take him on the journey, so he circumcised him because of the Jews who lived in that area.*²⁵⁹ Paul considered it important for Timothy to bear the scars of genital mutilation demanded by the Jewish covenant. Timothy agreed to the procedure.

At the end of his life, Paul needed Timothy to be a sounding board and confidante. Paul vented to Timothy. *"You are aware that all who are in Asia have turned away from me, including Phygelus and Hermoneges."*²⁶⁰ When Paul wrote those words from prison in Rome, he was in a slough of despair, lonely and considerably bereft of companionship. Certainly his mental state was being tested; his spiritual strength likewise appraised. Was he well physically, mentally, spiritually? Probably he was a well as he could be in all three sectors.

Paul, insisting on Timothy's circumcision, was not contradicting his carefully explained principles made in Galatians. He knew that there were some places where Timothy would be otherwise unwelcome, i.e., a synagogue and the Jerusalem Temple.

Another principle was in play here. It was understood that if a mother was Jewish, her child automatically was Jewish. One did not always know who was the child's father, so the mother determined the religion or ethnic factor of her child. That understanding was not good enough for the Temple's Sanhedrin–they demanded that the male worshiper always must have been circumcised before his being admitted to the Temple precincts.²⁶¹

Timothy became one of Paul's most reliable converts and ministry associates. He was a fellow evangelist, a teacher, a pastor, a messenger, a fixer-upper, a "gopher" and generally a "go to" missionary of Paul's choice. Since he was raised in a godly home in Lystra he was fully acquainted with the *Torah* and its teachings.

While being firm in his faith, he was neither petulant nor petty. Where Paul failed in relational situations, such as in Thessalonika, Timothy stayed behind and in a cooler way, taught and discipled Jews and Gentiles who were drawn toward Jesus. When imprisoned Paul, perhaps out-of-touch with his many friends, sensed that few associates continued with him, he confided in Timothy by venting his sense of loss.²⁶²

Some of Paul's difficulty, it seems, was that many Hellenistic Jews had become aware of his conversion to The Way, even while he had been persecuting Jewish believers. Paul carried that baggage in every stop he made, whereas Timothy was less of a bull's-eye target for Paul's critics. Timothy was not a turncoat. He seems to have been mature, firm, yet mild-mannered-–in a word, Timothy was "balanced."

Working with Silas, Timothy was able to put a surer footing among the burgeoning batch of believers of Thessalonika. When he and Silas were assured of their completed work in Thessalonika and Berea, they rejoined Paul now re-situated in Corinth.

Paul's writing includes Timothy as a co-author, as noted in several letters: 2

---

²⁵⁹ Acts 16:1–3
²⁶⁰ 2 Timothy 1:15
²⁶¹ Acts 21:27–29
²⁶² 2 Timothy 4:9–17

Corinthians, Colossians, Philemon, 1 and 2 Thessalonians and Philippians. Paul sent letters of encouragement and instruction to him as cited in the letters of 1 and 2 Timothy. The name Timothy (Timotheus) in Greek means "honouring God" or "respecting God" or "honoured by God."

Moving On

As we saw, Paul and his companions had been having a difficult time in Asia Minor. For a while, new congregations had sprouted and were growing, Having met with opposition from some Hellenist Jews in this area, Paul turned his team to the Gentiles, who, apparently, were *"overjoyed and thankfully acclaimed the word of the Lord."*[263]

Things quickly soured. Doors began closing. Acts doesn't tell us quite what happened; the Bible merely says,

> *"They were prevented from delivering the message."*[264] *"Paul and his companions travelled throughout the region of Phrygia and Galatia, having been kept by the Holy Spirit from preaching the word in the province of Asia. When they came to the border of Mysia, they tried to enter Bithynia, but the Spirit of Jesus would not allow them to. So they passed by Mysia and went down to Troas. During the night Paul had a vision of a man of Macedonia standing and begging him, 'Come over to Macedonia and help us.'"*[265]

The Holy Spirit apparently stopped them from crossing a border into Bithynia.

At the port of Troas the four seemed to have reached a dead end. What to do? Then, one night Paul had a dream–a vision. He saw a Macedonian pleading for help. That vision persuaded Paul of a new direction for their mission, and an alternative approach to doing mission.

The quartet embarked on a ship that would allow them to travel with the freight heading for Europe. They stopped overnight at the Island of Samothrace as we have noted, and transshipped on another freighter that would carry them to Macedonia, specifically to Neapolis the port of Philippi. Evidently God's instructions to Paul meant he would not linger long in Neapolis. They were focused missionaries, not tourists. The quartet immediately set out on foot–their customary means of travel.

Four men on foot would not have been an unusual sight on that multi-purpose road. Their route took them 17 kilometres West and North to the plain on which was located the Roman colony of Philippi. They walked on the precursor of the vaunted stone-based, chariot-rutted Via Egnatia, the Egnatian Way. As Paul's team strode to Philippi, the great army highway was yet unbuilt. This would become a strategic military highway designed to move troops quickly when needed for army purposes. The still visible Egnatian highway derived its name from the engineer who designed it.

Built by the Romans to secure and assert their territory, the road was intended to move troops and materiel across the top of the Greek peninsula from the Balkans to the

---

[263] Acts 13:48
[264] Acts 16:6
[265] Acts 16:6–9

Adriatic. The sea might provide better passage for the army and its weapons, yet the sea did not always accede to the requirement of smooth sailing.

Apart from army maneuvers, the pre-Via Egnatia was a general-purpose road, travelled by merchants, shoppers, tradespeople, bureaucrats and now invading missionaries. Among the travellers were the four undistinguishable evangelists. Only their purposes set them apart from others taking the same route.

CHAPTER TWELVE
QUELLING PHILIPPI

Philippi derived its name after one of the greatest soldiers of the ancient world, Philip II of Macedon, the one-eyed father of the meteoric Alexander the Great. Philip had conquered the territory to protect his other possessions and to exploit neighbouring gold mines.

The plain containing the archaeological ruins of Philippi–now laid bare for examination by history buffs and tourists alike–spreads serenely below nearby snow-capped peaks. It now contains fields of corn, tobacco and wheat. Its pastoral appearance gives little hint that the same plain once hosted a watershed battle of Roman conquest.

In 44 BC, about a century before Paul's team visit, the armies of Brutus and Cassius clashed with the forces of Octavian and Marc Antony. Brutus and Cassius were trampled, changing Roman history. Octavian survived to become Caesar Augustus–the same emperor mentioned in Luke's version of Jesus' birth story.[266]

One hundred years after this historic ruler-changing Roman conflict, the four unheralded invaders set foot in the Roman colony of Philippi. Paul the leader and strategist Gospel firebrand with co-partner compatible Silas, Timothy the convert and Luke the physician cum church reporter, silently entered the city they sought to cover with God's redemptive love. They walked unchallenged and unnoticed into the site of their first conquest.

The city's official name was Augusta Julia Philippensis. This was understandably shortened to Philippi. Octavian settled it with Latin-minded citizens to ensure Philippi's continuing loyalty to Caesar. Augustus honoured the community with the status of a privileged colony. Latin would soon replace Greek.

Luke says Philippi wore an honoured distinction of being a leading city. "*From Neapolis we travelled to Philippi, a Roman colony and the leading city of that district of Macedonia. And we stayed there several days.*"[267] Luke could have put it another way, for as a Roman colony (like Antioch in Pisidia, Lystra and Troas), Philippi was able to boast about its autonomous government.

In effect, Philippi was not only a Macedonian city, an outpost of Greek culture and civilization. It now was very much a clone of Rome. Philippi, in fact, was a colony of Rome and did everything "the Roman way." The Latin language on today's decaying monuments and stele among Philippi's ruins is so evident today in the remnants that it is difficult to find Greek script.

The First Known European Christians

Luke records that the team stayed in Philippi "several days." To this point, Paul's strategy had been similar to every community he visited. He led his team straight for the

---

[266] Luke 2:1
[267] Acts 16:12

community's synagogue where he could expect to find the people most eager to hear that the Messiah had arrived. However, Philippi apparently had no synagogue building–which suggested that fewer than 10 Jewish men lived in the city. Ten was the number of Jewish males required to form a minyan, a quorum for meeting as a synagogue. A minyan is also needed for an examination of today's *bar mitzvah*. The word minyan is related to the Aramaic word *mene*, (numbered) appearing in the writing on the palace wall in Daniel 5:25 (*mene, mene, tekel, parsin*).

The quartet knew what to do. They headed for the riverside of the Gangites River that flowed Southerly and, in spring, also swiftly at the Western edge of Philippi's (now) archaeological site. Visitors to the city could easily detect the signs of a river. From the pre-Egnatian Way where they were plodding, Paul's team saw a distant long line of leafy trees suggesting that a stream was feeding them. The quartet headed there. A group had gathered at the riverside for traditional Jewish ritual immersion (*tevilah*) as they prepared for prayer. Paul expected a worshipping group to be there.[268]

When no synagogue could meet by virtue of small number present, Jewish people commonly gathered in a riparian natural setting–"natural," in the sense of being out-of-doors! Also "natural" in the sense of being suitable for prayer, for as one of the preludes to prayer, the worshipper would submerge himself or herself in an act of ritual washing! Where the water was shallower, the penitent would lie in the stream and let the flowing water entirely cover him or her. With no apparent synagogue in Philippi, Paul anticipated a prayer gathering of a few Jews at a riverbank.

For their ritual washings Jews preferred running water to still, unflowing water. They could not use stagnant water for their rituals. Where no synagogue immersion vat (*mikveh*)[269] was available to Jews, the stream would have to do. The ritual washing also stood for death and resurrection. When Jesus spoke of "living water" to a Samaritan woman at Jacob's well[270] the Lord was probably connecting dots to this running (living) water associated with preparation for prayer and worship. Philippi's River Gangites provided "living water." Jesus added a new meaning of "living."

Jesus answered this woman, *"If you knew the gift of God and who it is who asks you for a drink, you would have asked him and he would have given you living water."*[271]

In Jerusalem and throughout the Jewish Diaspora, all Jews ritually cleansed themselves at regular intervals in immersion vats known as *mikve'ot*. One such purpose was in preparation for prayer and worship. In a Jewish building, men and women separately and unclothed would walk down into the vat a prescribed number of steps (usually seven) on the right side, self-immerse (perhaps three times) and climb steps on the left side ensuring they did not retrace their footprints on the right lest they

---

[268] Acts 16:13

[269] See my M.Th. thesis registered at McMaster University, 2001, also in book form, Jewish Ritual Washing and Christian Baptism, 2010 ChiRho Publications Toronto.

[270] John 4

[271] John 4:10

recontaminate themselves. At Qumran near the Dead Sea, this was a daily ritual; the Essenes actually performed this rite several times a day.

The Gangites River flowed rapidly and widely in the spring. In the summer, one could jump across it in places. Sometimes when water was shallow in an outdoor ceremonial washing, Jews would lie prone in a stream to let water flow over them. The water must fully cover the person. Jews considered this variant also as immersion. It symbolized the grave, which was the purpose of the *mikveh*, since it represented a ritually impure person's death and rebirth. Even during a minimal flow, the Gangites had yawning, gaping spots, with water deep enough to cover a person fully. The *mikve'ot* provided a Jewish version of being "born again."

At the river the missionaries met Lydia, "a worshiper of God." This description implied that she was a Gentile, perhaps a proselyte converted to Judaism. No explanation would have been necessary for a Jew. Lydia was a merchant, an entrepreneur, perhaps a street vendor, yet more probably a successful businesswoman and a franchised representative of her clothing guild emanating from Thyatira in Asia Minor with others working for her.

She was an agent for the clothiers-exporters who created special purple cloth created in the unique crushed snail-dye vats of that Asian city. The crushed snails provided the colour. She may have been named after her homeland. Perhaps Lydia may simply have been a nickname. Lydia possibly acquired it because of her origins. Luke wrote: *"One of those listening was a woman named Lydia, a dealer of purple cloth from the city of Thyatira, who was a worshipper of God."*[272] It is not a wild guess to suppose that Lydia's employees were Jewish, for the laws of *kashrut* (*kosher*) laws are not violated when Jewish labourers are working on textiles. Otherwise, why would they be at this riparian setting on Shabbat?

Lydia was fascinated by the exhortation of Paul, impressed enough to respond. Paul baptized her right there at the riverside, not in the Jewish model of the *mikve'ot's* ritual self-immersion, but in response to her faith in Christ. Luke wrote: *"The Lord opened her heart to respond to Paul's message. When she and the members of her household were baptized, she invited us to her home. "If you believe me to be a believer in the Lord, she said, 'come and stay at my house.'"*[273] Note that John the Baptist and the early church all practised baptism involving an agent. You can't bury yourself, so this principle continued in Christian immersions, beginning at Pentecost in Jerusalem.

Of course this was a death and new life profession of faith by Lydia. Paul explained baptism to the Romans as he must have clarified to the riverside devotees at Philippi:

> *Or don't you know that all of us who were baptized into Christ Jesus were baptized into his death? We were therefore buried with him through baptism into death in order that, just as Christ was raised from the dead through the glory of the Father, we too may live a new life.*

---

[272] Acts 16:4
[273] Acts 16:15

For if we have been united with him in a death like his, we will certainly also be united with him in a resurrection like his. For we know that our old self was crucified with him so that the body ruled by sin might be done away with, that we should no longer be slaves to sin— because anyone who has died has been set free from sin.

Now if we died with Christ, we believe that we will also live with him. For we know that since Christ was raised from the dead, he cannot die again; death no longer has mastery over him. The death he died, he died to sin once for all; but the life he lives, he lives to God. In the same way, count yourselves dead to sin but alive to God in Christ Jesus.[274]

She then challenged the four to verify their trust in her new faith by insisting that they use her villa as a base for their local ministry. Paul was gobsmacked. Stay overnight with a woman? A Greek woman? Jews would not even shake hands with a woman! A woman might be in estrus, therefore *niddah*–"ritually impure." The missionaries may have suffered a stricken Jewish conscience about accepting her hospitality, but they graciously accepted it. Moreover, they had no other accommodation. God was providing them with a place to stay in Philippi and they had not immediately noticed it.

When the four strangers, now partners-in-faith with Lydia and her employees, accepted her invitation, they may have suffered Jewish ethnic pains in co-mingling with a woman, especially given the loose conduct of many Greeks. Perhaps they anticipated a resulting controversy. Perhaps they were learning a truth that Paul later produced for Galatian believers: *"There is neither Jew nor Greek, slave nor free, male nor female, for you are all one in Christ Jesus."*[275] Lydia taught them something. As Luke wrote, *"She persuaded us."*

As result of this riverside encounter, Lydia stands in history as the first *named* European Christian. Probably, other believers emerged earlier in Rome, converted by traders who travelled in and out of Jerusalem while transacting business. In the Temple's ample courts, these merchants most assuredly came in contact with the early disciples daily gathering there for worship. Traders not only trafficked cargoes of spices, they likely absorbed the Gospel and transmitted it to Rome. Jerusalem was closer to the spices' sources and "Zion" perhaps did more commerce in this business than did Rome.

We learn even more about Paul from his letter to Philippi. It was penned from a Roman prison, about 13 years after the Paul Team invaded Europe and slogged along the prototype Via Egnatia. The letter to Philippi reveals Paul as a caring pastor, instructing the believers in that city to continue in their generosity to others, to be alert to imitation faith, to put Jesus clearly at the centre of their lives, and to rejoice in every situation.

The faith connection to this Roman colony began when Lydia the merchant accepted Jesus as her Saviour. Her influence among her servants (or described as household) and in the city allowed the Gospel to take root in Europe.

Thyatira was a commonplace, conventional community in the province of Lydia. It

---

[274] Romans 6:3–11
[275] Galatians 3:28

seems the unordinary Lydia introduced to Paul's team arriving in Philippi, used the city name to describe herself. She was a god-fearer, probably a proselyte Jew, ripe for the discovery of Jesus the Saviour.

> *"She was a worshipper of God. The Lord opened her heart to respond to Paul's message. When she and the members of her household were baptized, she invited us to her home. 'If you consider me a believer in the Lord,' she said, 'come and stay at my house.' And she persuaded us."[276]*

Lydia had luminary status in Philippi. Lydia was a high-powered seller and businesswoman, knew the populace and generously allowed (invited) Paul, Silas, Timothy and Luke to use her villa in that city. She may have employed Diaspora Jewish textile workers in the city, a possibility that from them she came to believe in one God, the God of the Hebrew people. It became the team's headquarters (HQ) during their mission in the city. Her support for the "Paul Team" was immeasurably helpful in establishing a congregational witness in that city. Her staff also believed the Gospel and were baptized.

Later, from this Philippian letter the reader also sees Paul as gentle but firm in admonishing two obstreperous church members, Euodia and Syntyche, to get their act together. How he had matured!

One would not want to be recorded in the annals of history, particularly in sacred scripture, for being argumentative. But that is what happened between two quarrelsome women from the colony of Philippi. Paul's pointing to Jesus is the key to Philippian body life, just as it is to any modern church. Jesus is the model of our behaviour, our humility. Surely Euodia and Syntyche got the message!

Paul traces how Jesus left the heavenly realms to come to earth (as a helpless baby) and be subject to death and crucifixion. God answered him by resurrecting him and then by naming him to be "the most exalted." This may have been an early Christian–Christmas-Easter-Ascension song.

> *"In your relationships with one another, have the same mindset as Christ Jesus: Who, being in very nature God, did not consider equality with God something to be used to his own advantage; rather, he made himself nothing by taking the very nature of a servant, being made in human likeness. And being found in appearance as a man, he humbled himself by becoming obedient to death — even death on a cross! Therefore God exalted him to the highest place and gave him the name that is above every name, that at the name of Jesus every knee should bow, in heaven and on earth and under the earth, and every tongue acknowledge that Jesus Christ is Lord, to the glory of God the Father."[277]*

Sometimes such church arguments like those of Euodia and Syntyche are ego driven, who's right and who's not. Some Christians always think they are correct and won't abide any other course. Pride gets in the way; so does obstinacy. In far too many churches an idea is enacted into action depending upon what person in the congregation proposes it.

That is one reason Paul wrote to Corinth to remind believers in that city,

---

[276] Acts 16:15, 16
[277] Philippians 2:5–11

"You yourselves are our letter, written on our hearts, known and read by everybody. You show that you are a letter from Christ, the result of our ministry, written not with ink but with the Spirit of the living God, not on tablets of stone but on tablets of the human heart."[278]

That comment applied not only to Corinth but especially to Philippi. Perhaps the bearer of Paul's letter to the Philippian church persuaded the two female church leaders to agree as Paul requested, even pleaded. The messenger was Epaphroditus who came to Philippi, first to thank the believers for a generous gift they had forwarded to needy believers in Jerusalem.

This New Testament saint–Epaphroditus–was regarded by Paul as vital to bringing a balm to the angst of the Philippian church. For one thing, he followed the suggested lead that the churches of Macedonia could alleviate the penury of the Jerusalem Church. So he carried a gift there. Paul commended the gift: *"They gave as much as they were able and even beyond their ability . . . they urgently pleaded with us for the privilege of sharing in this service."*[279]

Paul refers to him as an apostle (*apostēllo*=messenger) a "sent one" and also a "minister" (*leitourgos*). In the Greek civic world, minister has a double meaning, both "servant" and "public official." So he may have had an important management position in the city affairs. But somewhere in his journeys, Epaphroditus got ill, nigh unto death. Paul noted that God restored him.

Some believe that Epaphroditus and Epaphras are the same person–likely so. Epaphras seems to be the missioner who, in part, had founded the church at Colossae. His name derives from the pagan love deity, Aphrodite. When used as a common name it means "charming." In writing to Philippi, Paul makes a pun out of the messenger's name referring to Aphrodite (the deity of gambling) with Epaphroditus' "gambling" or "risking" his life for the Gospel.

Epaphroditus was the epistle's postman. In what was a double entendre, Paul wrote about the mail carrier "risking" (gambling)[280] his life for the gospel. The name derives from the goddess of love and fortune–"belonging to Aphrodite." In a way Paul was putting a smile on Epaphroditus' face and provided a light moment for his Philippian readers.

Everyone knew messenger's name derived from the goddess Aphrodite, mother of Tyche (Greek) or Fortuna (Roman). In the Roman tradition, she was "Venus Felix,"[281] the bringer of success. She was the deity used by gamblers! Greek gamblers rolled the dice only after invoking the name of Aphrodite. Casting dice with two sixes was described as "the throw of Aphrodite." The "throw of Venus" was a little different.[282] Aphrodite was the mythical deity of fecundity!

Ironically, Syntyche's name also imitated a gambler. Her name derived from the

---

[278] 2 Corinthians 3:2, 3
[279] 2 Corinthians 8:4
[280] Philippians 2:30
[281] Mark P. O. Morford and Robert J. Lenardon, op. cit., p. 515
[282] The Venus Throw was the highest roll in the ancient Roman gambling game

mythical Aphrodite's daughter. Tyche (Fortuna in Roman myth) was even more of a gambler than her mother.

Even in prison, irrepressible Paul could not resist making a pun. How essential it is for a Bible student to know the ambiences of the world in which Paul lived! How important it is to discuss the wellness of Saint Paul while noting his appealing, "captivating" sense of humour even while he was confined "in chains!" Is this not from a developed wellness? How many prisoners find amusement during their extended incarceration?

So the Apostle wrote to Philippi, "He risked (*paraboleusámenos*=gambled, acted recklessly) his life to make up for the help you yourself could not give me."[283] Yet the spiritual milieu of Paul's bizarre secular world was as alien to the Paul Team as the atmosphere of the moon was compared to that of the earth. That mission called for divine help. It also called for Paul to steer his abundant energies and his prickly personality into positive, pastoral pursuits.

Paul describes him in three ways in the scope of the Philippian letter. First (1), the Apostle terms Epaphroditus, "my brother," suggesting that the two were in spiritual accord and on the same "wavelength" in terms of faith and purpose. Secondly (2), Paul tells the Philippians that he is a "fellow worker," meaning that they both are fully linked in the same cause of sharing their faith with others. Thirdly (3), Paul calls Epaphroditus, a "fellow soldier." In other words this man was a warrior for God. He did not sit on the benches as a reservist but was a reverenced player on the A-Team.

Paul needed to call the debaters out on their deportment, the news of which adversely both infected and affected the broader church, the report even reaching into his prison cell. Paul specifically cautioned the entire church with a universal Christian principle: "*Do everything without complaining or arguing so that you may be blameless and pure, children of God without fault in a crooked and depraved generation, in which you shine like stars in the universe.*"[284]

Paul effectively told Euodia and Syntyche, "It's nice to be generous to people elsewhere, but clean up your own act at home." Paul made his criticism gently, as a pastor should. This is not a hard-nosed ex-Pharisee writing. It is a tender, friendly, pastoral admonition. Paul asked an impartial, unnamed believer dubbed ("*loyal yokefellow*") to mediate between them.[285] They were yoked, like a team of oxen, to each other and to Paul.[286][287]What Paul did not confess was his own past history of quarrelling,

---

[283] Philippians 2:30
[284] Philippians 4:14, 15
[285] Philippians 4:3
[286] see 2 Corinthians 6:14; James 3:17; Deuteronomy 22:10
[287] "I plead [*parakaleo*, to call for, entreat, beg, admonish, persuade"] with Euodia [Lydia?] and I plead with Syntyche to be of the <u>same mind</u> (*phronein*, mindset, agreement, considerate, heed] in the Lord. Yes, and I ask you, my true companion [*Syzgus*, unknown gentleman or perhaps a created name–True Yokefellow (*gnsie souzuge*) perhaps meaning the entire congregation as one person, or possibly

with Peter and with Barnabas.

A sidebar to this story is that the women had leadership responsibilities. The Apostle did not order them to *"be silent in the church,"*[288] as he did to some in the Corinthian congregation. Rather, Paul urged them to be more agreeable with each other. Paul did not argue about these women's leadership. After all, Lydia was the first convert and abetted the mission of Paul, Silas, Timothy and Luke in her adopted city of Philippi. He would not tell his first converts to effectively "shut up!" "Zip the lip!"

Thrown in Jail

Luke records two other noteworthy events of his initial European foray into Greece. The first incident led to the second. *"Once when we were going to the place of prayer, we were met by a slave girl who had a spirit by which she predicted the future. She earned a great deal of money for her owners by fortune-telling."*[289]

Paul and his companions began to tell the Good News of salvation and eternal life available to those who believed in Jesus the Messiah once crucified, and raised from the dead. Many inhabitants hardly knew what he was talking about.

One day, en route from Lydia's villa to the place of prayer at the riverside, the four were confronted by a slave girl–a junior Pythian Oracle of Delphi, Apollo's shrine. For a price she could foretell the future. Luke writes:

"She followed Paul and the rest of us, shouting, 'These men are servants of the Most High God, who are telling you the way to be saved.' She kept this up for many days. Finally Paul became so annoyed that he turned around and said to the spirit, 'In the name of Jesus Christ I command you to come out of her!' At that moment the spirit left her.'"[290_291]

Her abilities enabled her to reveal that Paul, Silas and friends had come to proclaim salvation. She may have done that by ventriloquism. The style was not uncommon. Among Greeks, this feat was attributed to Pythian Apollo, the main deity at the sacred sanctuary of Delphi, in Southwestern Greece. The snake served as a symbol of this Greek god, thus the term Pythian, as in the reptile, python.

People travelled great distances to Delphi to consult the Oracle. The Oracle, according to Greek mythology, was a consultant about the future. Lucky the slave owner who found such a person and could have money made for him by such divination! To Paul and his team, her talent was merely an evil spirit, and as such, he commanded it to "come out of her." Luke says the shock treatment worked–it did.

Epaphroditus], help these women since they have contended (pun intended) at my side in the cause of the Gospel, along with Clement and the rest of my co-workers, whose names are in the book of life." See also Ernest F. Scott, The Interpreter's Bible, Vol. 11, p. 108, and Frank Stagg, Broadman Bible Commentary, Vol. 11, p. 212.
[288] 1 Corinthians 14:34
[289] Acts 16:16
[290] Acts 16:17–19
[291] see the Chapter 15 ahead detailing Delphi and its religious rites and visitors

That successful exorcism set the stage for the next event. The slave owners, now deprived of their income by this healing, dragged Paul and Silas (not Luke and Timothy) to the agora, the market area. Once there, the angry plaintiffs demanded that the city magistrates try them. The charge was advocating illegal customs for Roman citizens to practise. The crowd, as fickle as in any city, forgot the side of law and order, the magistrates holding a quick, illegal trial and did not allow Paul or Silas to speak for themselves.

The judges ordered that Paul and Silas be stripped, beaten and thrown into jail. The jail, or a very small part of it, supported by archaeologist's assertions, survives today on a hill Northeast of the ancient city's outskirts. Because they were held under close guard, the jailer put them in the inner part of the prison–quite possibly a cell carved back into the solid rock cave of a hillside–and he fettered their feet. *"After they had been severely flogged, they were thrown into prison, and the jailer was commanded to guard them carefully–he put them in the inner cell and fastened their feet in the stocks."*[292]

That night, in the inky blackness of the crude unlit lockup, recovering from the whippings they both received, the two missionaries sang hymns. The earliest Christians sang hymns readily during their worship times. Paul emphasized that Ephesians were doing that too–note his mention to the Ephesian church: *"Be filled with the Spirit, speaking to one another with psalms, hymns, and songs from the Spirit. Sing and make music from your heart to the Lord."*[293]

During this series of events Paul (and Silas) had a sense of calm in this situation. When Luke writes that they sang hymns together, it was for more than cheering up. It was a sense of finding God's presence in adversity, a theme that Paul had learned in his Christian maturing. Perhaps three of the psalm/hymns they sang went like this:

"I trust the LORD God to save me, and I will wait for him to answer my prayer."[294] Or *"You bless all who depend on you for their strength."*[295] Or *"I depend on God alone; I put my hope in him. He alone protects and saves me; he is my defender, and I shall never be defeated. My salvation and honour depend on God; he is my strong protector; he is my shelter."*[296]

Luke reports then that an earthquake shook the foundations of the jail, liberating the incarcerated men from their shackles. The jailer nearly took his own life when he saw the prison doors fully open.

"Suddenly there was such a violent earthquake that the foundations of the prison were shaken. At once all the prison doors flew open, and everyone's chains came loose. The jailer woke up, and when he saw the prison doors open, he drew his sword and was about to kill himself because he thought the prisoners had escaped. But Paul shouted, 'Don't harm yourself! We are all here!'"[297]

Paul, like any observant Jew,[298] especially with a Pharisee's mein, could not abide

---

[292] Acts 16:23–24
[293] Ephesians 5:18, 19
[294] Micah 7:7 CEV
[295] Psalm 84:56a CEV
[296] Psalm 62:5–7
[297] Acts 16:26 *ff*

81

anyone committing suicide. *Torah* taught the importance of living.[299] *"This day I call the heavens and the earth as witnesses against you that I have set before you life and death, blessings and curses. Now choose life, so that you and your children may live."* J. Jocz (a Lithuanian Jewish Christian) comments,

> "To give sense of life [man] has to know what purpose he serves and what is the meaning of history. Without a positive answer . . . life becomes unbearable and existence is felt to be a burden. In such a case Schopenhauer's conclusion become inevitable: '. . . the best thing for man is not to have been born; world and man are something which ought not to have been' (Perga, ch. 12,.§157). "Pessimism is the inevitable answer to every immanental explanation as to the question of existence . . . The prohibition to murder [and suicide] is not sociological but theologically founded: life is by the will of God and to destroy it is an act of rebellion; is *laese majestas.*"[300]

Paul had a healthy respect for life. Paul stopped the jailor before he could harm himself, shouting that all prisoners remained inside. The warden was even more shaken by a spiritual event than by the earthquake. *"The jailer called for lights, rushed in and fell trembling before Paul and Silas. He then brought them out and asked, "Sirs, what must I do to be saved?"*[301] Now, a Jew, even a Roman, thought that "doing" was a way to eternity. But, course, it is not. The pair told the jailor, *"Believe in the Lord Jesus Christ, and you will be saved–you and your household."*[302]

Profoundly impressed by Paul and Silas,[303] the jailer asked them to explain the faith that he may have partially heard about the day before. Like Lydia, his was a speedy conversion. He shared his new-found faith with his extended family, the entire household, servants and family. They all believed the Gospel and were baptized during the night, probably across the city in the Gangites River. The jailor then fed the prisoners in his own residence, housed them for the rest of the night and ministered to their lash-wounds.

Either the town had calmed down or the earthquake had distracted attention from Paul and Silas. At dawn the magistrates sent a message to say that the two prisoners could leave the city, and good riddance. For Paul that was not good enough. In yielding to a mob, the magistrates themselves had broken the law. They had flogged and jailed a Roman citizen without a fair trial or a guilty verdict. Paul was not a "doormat for Jesus." Had Paul been wearing a toga, the sign of a Roman citizen,[304] the magistrates and the jailer might have acted differently.

While he did not seek retribution upon those who treated them unjustly, Paul insisted that the magistrates themselves accept responsibility for wronging them. He did

---

[298] Jakob Jocz, The Spiritual History of Israel, pp., 228, 229
[299] Deuteronomy 30:9
[300] Jakob Jocz, op. cit., pp. 222, 223
[301] Acts 16:29, 30
[302] Acts 16:11
[303] William M. Ramsay, St. Paul the Traveller and Roman Citizen, p. 176. Ramsay argues that by inference, Silas was also a Roman citizen, Acts 16:37
[304] Bruce Chilton, op. cit., p. 25

not take them to court. Paul required the city leaders to come in person to release him from prison. They did–and then begged them to "please leave the city."[305] In their dealing with this untoward situation, the spiritual maturity of both Paul and Silas is noteworthy.

Paul and Silas complied, but took their time. First, they visited Lydia's villa to say farewell. Let the magistrates wait! By this time, while Paul and Silas lingered in prison, Timothy and Luke had busied themselves winning some Philippians for Christ. The church at Philippi was now firmly established and growing. At Lydia's home they "*met with the brothers (adelphoi=brothers and sisters) and encouraged them." "After Paul and Silas came out of the prison, they went to Lydia's house where they met with the brothers and encouraged them. Then they left.*"[306]

This last phrase suggests the immediate success of their first mission into Europe. When the four entered Philippi, apart from the handful of riverside prayer people, it was virtually a pagan city. When they departed, it was a community with a caring church. It was, apparently–perhaps, apart from Rome–the very first congregation in all of Europe.

The trek had been arduous for Paul and his team members. Considering where the Apostle Paul came from–his long journey from being a fire-breathing Pharisee bent on rooting out The Way–it was a dragged-out distance indeed. Paul was sustained by the Lord in his labour but also by his reliance on the word of God as he suffered beating and incarceration in a Philippian jail. "*The LORD is close to the brokenhearted, and he saves those whose spirits have been crushed.*"[307] Paul was demonstrating his spiritual and mental "wellness."

Philippi Today

Philippi's present archaeology site is quite extensive. The remaining partial ruin of the prison, probably authentic, lies on the Northeast side of the modern highway. Farther East and South is the ancient amphitheatre that might have been used by Paul. It was built in the Fourth Century BC. The major archeological site is well-preserved and is located on the Western side of the present highway. The entrance of an uncompleted foremost basilica overshadows the remainder of derelict ruined buildings in the city. When Rome occupied the city, officials also turned the theatre into an arena for those who liked blood sports involving gladiators and animals.

The much larger archeological site is situated on the West side of the highway from Kavala to Drama. Most of the Roman forum was constructed a century after Paul's visit to Philippi. Certainly, both the Greek market/agora were there for Paul to use. The magnificent basilica, apparently begun in the Sixth Century AD was never finished. Two large baptisteries used for immersion are visible, as well as indications of a bishop's chair or throne. Behind the basilica and markets are public toilets, complete with drainage.

If one walks West and South one will arrive at the river where the God-fearers met.

---

[305] Acts 16:9
[306] Acts 16:40
[307] Psalm 34:18

A Greek Orthodox chapel now marks the supposed location where Paul and Silas were presumed to have immersed Lydia, her household believers, and probably the jailer and family in the fast-flowing stream. The Orthodox-suggested site may not exactly show the very place of baptisms but it must be reasonably close, maybe within a hundred meters.

Luke writes that from Philippi, the four apostles continued West, passing through but evidently not stopping except for victuals and accommodation. These were Amphipolis and Apollonia (named after a Greek deity, Apollon). In doing so, they passed by Mount Pangaion, the holy mountain of the Greek cult of Dionysos. Amphipolis was an important stopping point on the proto-Via Egnatia, running across to the Adriatic.

A large marble lion (Fourth Century BC) stands by the River Strymon (Stremones) near Amphipolis. It probably dates from the time of Alexander the Great. Alas, it was destroyed. The present lion is a replica for today's visitors to contemplate.

CHAPTER THIRTEEN
A STORM IN THESSALONICA; A CALM IN BEREA

The quartet's ministry in Thessalonica didn't last much longer than the mission in Philippi. The apostles' time in Philippi was "several days." Their stay in Thessalonica was "three Sabbath days."[308] *"As his custom was, Paul went to the synagogue, and on three Sabbath days, he reasoned with them from the Scriptures, explaining and proving that the Christ had to suffer and rise from the dead."*[309]

Paul and Luke were there for 21 blustery days. But Timothy remained somewhat longer, long enough to form the fragile fellowship into a believing force for mission.

One must marvel at the success of church planting achieved in such a short time. However, it is wrong to say that Paul and his companions set out to plant a church. They did not! In the face of noisy and virulent opposition, they planted faith, not a church. They set out to share their faith and to lead those interested in receiving eternal life. The success—let modern missionaries note—stemmed from their well-defined purpose, not to plant churches but to lead people to faith in the Saviour. Paul's mission was to plant faith; churches sprouted from that faith.

This is no secret at all. First (1), Paul demonstrated a clear leaning on the direction from the Lord—however he discerned that direction. Second (2), he worked in a team ministry, with each member providing resources and insights that no other member of the four provided. He was the leader but he was not a lone ranger. Third (3), the partners sought the synagogue or "faith people" as their starting point in most instances.

The strategy of starting at a synagogue ensured that the missionaries would find a group of people who already knew the Scriptures. These Jews, he thought, would be keenly interested in hearing about the long-awaited Messiah and his prayed-for arrival.

Paul was a "fisher of men"[310] as Jesus commissioned his disciples. So he cast his net where he thought the fish would be–at the synagogue. Paul saw some satisfactory outcomes. To bring on board new Christians of Jewish background was immeasurably more productive than to reach and educate those connected to Greek mythology who had no biblical roots.

Many Jews in Thessalonica, however, were stuck in the cemented past and seemed little interested in hearing that the Messiah of whom Paul spoke was the long-awaited Saviour of mankind. The God in whom those Jews believed was legalistic, apparently. Many of them were among the faithful who no longer looked anywhere for a Saviour except through their own warped interpretation of the *Torah* and other sacred writings.

Thessalonica, like Antioch, was a cosmopolitan city, quite unlike the lesser-populated Philippi. Worship of the divine Caesar was imposed by the emperor cult. This was a reality in Thessalonica although the imperial cult would fine-tune this matter in

---

[308] Acts 17:2
[309] Acts 17:2, 3
[310] Luke 5:10

following decades. Many other deities abounded in this city as well, and anticipated that devotees would honour their divine nature out of deference or financial support. Paul's team had much to counter.

The city had its usual share of the typical fertility cults that exemplified Greek mythology. One of these sects followed Dionysos, the "dying and rising" god, whose holy mountain Pangaion the four had passed while travelling the pre-Via Egnatia. Another sect proclaimed Orpheus, also a part of the Dionysian dynasty. There was also the primitive cult of Cabriri. Today we use the term "Mystery Religions" to describe these cults in general because of the extreme secrecy involved in their initiation rites.

Their behaviour encouraged what we understand as immorality. They considered promiscuity to be natural and normal. They developed a "Tom cat" morality. Sexuality was an essential aspect of "communion" with their god; temples dedicated this communion by providing cultic prostitutes such as in Corinth on the Acrocorinth.

Thessalonica, a key city on the Via Egnatia, was founded by Cassander about 315 BC, and named after his wife, the sister of Alexander the Great. A small number of Jews moved here during periods of the Diaspora–thus the existence of a synagogue. A couple of centuries after Paul, especially during the reign of Galerius, the Christian community was severely persecuted here. Galerius admitted, toward the end of his life, that he was unable to destroy Christianity. Persecution stopped two years before he died. The achievements of Galerius are recorded on friezes in the present city, now known as Thessaloniki.

Supporters built a Rotunda in Thessaloniki to honour Galerius. However, he was buried in Serbia. The new Emperor Constantine dictated that the Rotunda become a church building and it was so until the Ottomans attacked in 1590 AD when it became a mosque. When the Ottoman Empire ceased to exist in 1912 AD, Greeks returned it to an Orthodox building for worship, as it remains a century later.

Persecutions of believers began when Paul attempted to preach in a synagogue of that city. For three Sabbaths Paul went to the synagogue and as a legitimate worshipper/teacher he was allowed to read and exegete the Scriptures during the allocated teaching period. Following the custom, he started with the known, the content of the Hebrew scripture. From that point, he argued, persuaded and inspired his Jewish audience towards the unknown. He had some success in this method. Luke writes about a number of members of a new congregation gathering in the house of someone named Jason. Like a church, a synagogue was not a building but a "people."

Trouble developed quickly.

"Other Jews were jealous; so they rounded up some bad characters from the marketplace, formed a mob and started a riot in the city. They rushed to Jason's house in search of Paul and Silas in order to bring them out to the crowd. But when they did not find them, they dragged Jason and some other believers before the city officials, shouting: 'These men who have caused trouble all over the world have now come here, and Jason has welcomed them into his house. They are all defying Caesar's decrees, saying that there is another king, one called Jesus.' When they heard this, the crowd and the city officials were thrown into turmoil. Then they made Jason and the others post bond and let them go."[311]

As in Philippi, an interrupting mob took over. They stormed Jason's house looking for Paul and Silas. Apparently, Luke and Timothy were absent from the fray. When the instigators could not find Paul and Silas they dragged Jason and other converts to the magistrates. Jason had to post a bond to keep the peace and the authorities set him free.

The posse's charges are interesting. They described the missionaries and converts as troublemakers. *"These men who have caused trouble all over the world have now come here."* This was outright hyperbole. Then, like the charges made to Pilate by the Jerusalem Sanhedrin, the mob leaders raised the specter of Roman retaliation: *"They are defying Caesar's decree, saying the 'there is another king, one called Jesus.'"*[312]

By one tradition the synagogue in which Paul and Silas preached is now marked by the Church of Saint Paul. If this information is correct, the existing site is on a hillside hovering over the city. It is situated part way between the harbour and the ancient acropolis. Nothing remains of the synagogue building that once occupied the location.

The Greek Orthodox Church of Saint Paul displays four icons, which Orthodox believers consider windows into the mysteries of God. Since Paul is the Patron Saint of the congregation, his icon is displayed second from the left. The other three icons represent Saint John the Baptist, Jesus, and his mother, Mary.

Causes of Conflict

It is not clear whether the uproar resulted directly from the missionaries' work in Thessalonica. Negative reports about the apostles' earlier preaching in Asia Minor may have already arrived through the very active Hellenist Jewish pipeline. *"At Iconium Paul and Barnabas went as usual to the synagogue. There they spoke so effectively that a great number of Jews and Gentiles believed. But the Jews who refused to believe stirred up the Gentiles and poisoned their minds against the brothers."*[313] Quite possibly, the stricter local Jews may have been outraged when the new community of faith included not only Jewish converts but also Gentile men and women.

Perhaps the Thessalonian Jews also had heard of controversies in Rome centring in this new Jewish sect. The controversies led to the Emperor Claudius expelling–for the time being–all Jews (including Christian Jews Aquila and Priscilla) from Rome. That decree, in itself, indicates that Christians lived in Rome long before Paul visited the Roman Empire's capital. Unfortunately little record exists of all their names or how they came to faith. Could Rome, not Philippi, actually be the first church in Europe?

Whatever the cause of this unrest in Thessalonica the disturbance effectively ended Paul's current mission in that city. It did not end Paul's ministry to Thessalonica because that continued in letter-writing form and through his many like-minded Christian friends. New friends spirited Paul and Silas to Berea, further West along the Via Egnatia under cover of darkness. *"As soon as it was night, the brothers sent Paul and Silas away to*

[311] Acts 17:59
[312] John 18:12, 15
[313] Acts 14:12

Berea."[314]

Paul also had to encourage a radically redirected lifestyle for the new Christian community. He also rejoiced in those who found redemption and new life in Jesus. God had new trophies in that city in whom to glory.

> *"We ought always to thank God for you, brothers loved by the Lord, because from the beginning God chose you to be saved through the sanctifying work of the Spirit and through belief in him in the truth. He called you to this through the gospel, that you might share in the glory of our Lord Jesus Christ! So then, brothers and sisters stand firm and hold to the teaching passed on to you, whether by word of mouth, or by letter."*[315]

The Apostle Paul needed to set straight the work ethic of the Thessalonians. He had to teach an appropriate attitude towards the return of the Lord. He needed to construct an authoritative theology of end times. With purpose-driven Paul, steady Silas and note-taker Luke sent packing to Berea by Jewish troublemakers, the quieter, loyal Timothy remained in Thessalonica for a short sojourn to disciple the early believers of that city.

Berea

The city that the Bible calls Berea retains a similar name today–Veria. It is not a large centre. It is pleasantly located. To the North and West lie the snowcapped mountains of today's Yugoslavia and Albania. To the South is the "sacred" mountain of Olympus. On a clear day, the view is impressive. Berea is located on a plain and today's Veria is also an active, productive, agricultural centre.

In Paul's time, circa 49 AD (likely) or 50 AD (possibly), Berea was relatively unimportant, being situated just South of the proposed Via Egnatia, the multi-use autobahn of the time. Berea was not a normal stopping point for military travellers or traders.

We can only speculate why Paul was transported to Berea. Perhaps his conductors on the escape route from Thessalonica knew that the Jews in Berea were less hardliners and more receptive to add to their knowledge of the *Torah*, Wisdom literature and historical books that we now call "The Old or First Testament." Luke fails in offering any valid reason for spiritual friends whisking them away to Berea. Luke does not even suggest that the Holy Spirit directed this escape, but of course he did.

Perhaps some residents of Berea had been in Thessalonica when Paul was "holding forth" in the synagogue for three Sabbaths. Maybe some Bereans had met one or more of the missionaries in the market place or wherever. Perhaps the sympathetic new believers in Thessalonica suggested that the people of Berea were more open, more receptive to the truths of Scripture. Or, perhaps it was deemed that Berea was far enough off the beaten path of the Via Egnatia and offered a safe asylum for the missionaries.

There may yet be another reason, one that the predominately patriarchal males of

---

[314] Acts 17:10

[315] 2 Thessalonians 2:13–15

the Old Testament might not even have recognized. Macedonian women took more community leadership, it seems, than did women elsewhere in the Roman Empire–or even in the Southern areas of Greece. That seems evident with Lydia, the agent for selling Thyatira's special purple cloth in Philippi.

Apparently, this situation was also true in Berea. The men may have had the upper hand in debating the nuances of the *Torah* in the synagogues, yet the women ruled the community in generous hospitality. The men may have been "heads" but the Berean women were the necks who turned the heads! Perhaps the women had a working network that helped to spirit Paul and Silas from their tribulations in Thessalonica into the relative refuge of Berea. Luke writes:

> "*On arriving there Paul and Silas directly attended the Jewish synagogue to share the Scriptures. They were effective in opening the minds of both men and women. Now the Bereans were of more noble character than the Thessalonians, for they received the message with great eagerness and examined the Scriptures every day to see if what Paul said was true. Many of the Jews believed, as did a number of prominent Greek women and many Greek men.*"[316]

The Berean mission was somewhat successful. Paul and Silas journeyed to the synagogue to share their faith with the synagogue leaders. They were effective in opening the minds of both men and women, people of long standing in the community as well as synagogue leaders. Bereans seemed to have been eager to hear the word brought to them by the disciples. Luke gives readers the impression of a real "chemistry" between the apostles and the people of Berea.

Alongside a mosque in modern Veria are three steps, said to be the surviving remnants of the synagogue where Paul once preached. A contemporary portrait in the form of a mosaic is also there (see the book cover). It is protected by an arch and iron bars. The representation reflects a description of the Apostle written by the Seventh Century monk John of Antioch (a similar description is found in The Acts of Paul and Thecla). It describes the Apostle as: "*a man small in size, baldheaded, bow-legged, well-built, with eyebrows meeting, aquiline (hooked) nose, full of grace. For sometimes he seemed like a man, and sometimes he had the countenance of an angel.*"[317]

The other version is much like it: "*Paul was a person round-shouldered with a sprinkling of grey on his head and beard, with aquiline nose, greyish eyes, meeting eyebrows, a mixture of pale and red in his complexion, and an ample beard.*"

Once again Paul needed to depart in a hurry. Berea may have been off the beaten track but it was still far too close to Thessalonica. Paul's detractors in Thessalonica tracked him down and started their rabble-rousing again. "*When the Jews in Thessalonica learned that Paul was preaching the word of God in Berea they went there too, agitating the crowds and stirring them up.*"[318] The peace disturbers did not chase Silas, however.

Fortunately, Paul had developed associated allies in Berea, so much so that they helped him leave the city safely to ensure his sheltered arrival at his next mission point.

---

[316] Acts 17:10–13
[317] Ante-Nicene Fathers, Volume 8, p. 487
[318] Acts 17:13

THE WELLNESS OF SAINT PAUL

Why Athens? Maybe the Bereans, prodded by the Holy Spirit, advised him to go there. Perhaps–probably, likely–the Hellenistic Jewish network had little influence in Athens.

Silas and Timothy remained to continue a ministry among the Bereans until Paul summoned the two to join him in Southern Greece. Luke summarized what followed: *"The men who accompanied Paul and brought him to Athens and then left with instructions for Silas and Timothy to join him as soon as possible."*[319]

---

[319] Acts 17:15

PART THREE: A CROSS-CULTURAL MISSION

CHAPTER FOURTEEN
MISSION MEETS MINDSET

Vergina

On their hasty exit from Berea, Paul, Luke and their friends would have passed by Pella, only 15 kilometres away and on the route South to the coast. Pella is not mentioned in the Bible nor is Vergina. The travellers would have paid little heed to Pella. At the time of Paul's lam to a safer haven, Pella would be deemed inconsequential. A few local people might have reminded passersby that this once was the location of the great palace of King Philip II of Macedon, father of the whirlwind conqueror, Alexander the Greek. But Pella is not inconsequential.

We know about Pella today because in 1861, a French archaeologist, Leon Heuzey, began excavations at this site practically a hop, skip and jump from where Paul, Luke and a few Bereans were hasting to a ship heading to Athens. Heuzey uncovered Philip II's humungous palace.

The archaeologist concluded that Pella, near the modern community of Vergina, was the place where someone murdered an inebriated Philip in 336 BC, immediately following the marriage of his daughter. That was four centuries before Paul trekked by. At that point, Paul and Luke had other more important matters on this mind. He strategized how he could lead people to know that Jesus Christ was the Saviour of the world.

In 1937, Professor Konstantine Rhomaios made further excavations–and another major discovery. He uncovered evidence of a royal burial place. One of Rhomaios' students, Professor Manolis Andronicos, returned to the site to dig several times. On 08 November 1977–at 3:00 in the afternoon–his diligence paid off. He found what he believed to be the skeleton and the treasury of Philip II of Macedon.[320]

The treasury of Philip is now displayed in the Thessaloniki Museum. The skeleton of Philip is laid out for all to see; the bones found in a gold sarcophagus are also on display. On the coffin's lid is a star, the emblem of the Macedonian dynasty. The excavators unearthed an oak wreath in the chamber of the great tomb, the oak being the sacred tree of Zeus, Greek mythology's top and often capricious god.

Even the breastplate worn by the king is on display, although somewhat corroded, the decoration is impressive. This iron artifact is ornamented with gold. Philip's great shield, decorated with ivory, is splendidly featured in a glass display case. Philip's helmet, showing the deity Athena as an emblem of power and victory, is fairly intact. His sword, also encrusted and oxidized, is similarly trimmed with gold.[321]

---

[320] Manolis Andronicos, Regal Treasures from a Macedonian Tomb, National Geographic Magazine, July 1978, pp. 55–76
[321] Manolis Andronicos, Thessaloniki Museum, p. 9

Why is this important to this flight of Paul's troupe en route to Athens? In a way, it is not obvious to the Paul story. However, it is Philip II's heritage to the world, to make the Greek language the lingua franca of the Mediterranean world. It now was Paul's language. The Greek Bible took form through the wildfire growth of Philip II and Alexander the Great as they subjugated the Mediterranean and Mideastern world and promoted Greek culture.

Would Paul have been impressed by Philip? Not likely. Paul had no special political concerns–except that believers pray for leaders and that they hear the Good News he had brought to Greece. Philip's burial place would likely never occurred to him. The Apostle was more interested persuading those living to learn to love God as much as God loved them. Yet Philip II provided the biblical, writing and preaching medium Paul used to tell his Gospel story.

Philip first began to control the city-states of Greece and then to unify them. After Philip II's demise, his son Alexander the Great conquered most of the known world as far east as the Hindu Kush in Afghanistan and Northern Africa including Egypt. Alexander and his successors disseminated the Greek language and culture wherever they went, Because of the conquests by Philip II and Alexander, the New Testament came to be written in Greek and not in some other language. Moreover, Jewish scholars in Alexandria translated the Old Testament into Greek. That translation was the one Paul used–the Septuagint.

Had it not been for the Greek language, the spread of the gospel which Paul and Silas, Timothy and Luke proclaimed would have required translation into hundreds of tongues and myriads of dialects. The Greek language and culture became the vital link, the vehicle for proclaiming the Good News of salvation through Jesus, crucified, risen, ascended into heaven and Saviour of the world.

Jesus said that the *"meek will inherit the earth"* (Matthew 5:4). He knew that Paul's quiet revolution depended on a different conquering style than that of Philip and Alexander. As Paul wrote: *"When I came to you brothers, I did not come with eloquence or superior wisdom. I proclaimed to you the testimony about God. For I resolved to know nothing while I was with you except Jesus Christ and him crucified."*[322]

---

[322] 1 Corinthians 2:1, 2

CHAPTER FIFTEEN
DELPHI

With their voyage South to Athens, Paul and Luke began a new phase of their missionary work. They were coming face-to-face with imbedded Greek culture. It was not like Hebrew thinking. Jews and Greeks differed on many fronts such as ideals of perfection, creation, spiritual realities and an understanding of monotheism.

Greek deities were made in the image of man; Jews held that man was created in the image of God. That was only one of several challenges for Paul. Fortunately for the Apostle, he had spent his early youth in Tarsus that would have introduced him to much of Greek intellectualism, art, literature and humanities.

Until their expulsion from Northern Greece, the four missionaries preached to Jews and Gentiles converted to Judaism. Their main emphasis had been to plant seeds of faith where the ground had already been tilled. That is, they spoke first to Jews in synagogues. Jews already knew from Scriptures that God had promised a Messiah and presumably, would be eager to learn that Messiah had arrived. Jews who heeded the Pharisees' teachings in their synagogues would have accepted the theology of resurrection.

The Jewish context also provided a framework for the behaviour of new converts, which was often in great contrast to the morality of the surrounding Greek culture. Paul's teaching made no attempt to accommodate to that culture. He simply rejected their morality.

Starting with Athens, something new happened. Paul discovered a basic truth that still applies to missionaries–in a new culture you must start from where the people are. Then you can weave your own story into the design.

In Canadian history, for example, in early French Canada the Jesuit missionary martyr Father Brébeuf attempted to explain Jesus' birth in an aboriginal, indigenous context. Note his Christmas hymn, "'Twas in the moon of wintertime, when all the birds had fled, that Mighty Gitchi Manitou sent angel choirs instead; before their light the stars grew dim, and wondering hunters heard their hymn: Jesus your king is born, Jesus is born, in excelsis gloria."[323]

In Greece, the people did not lack religion. If anything, they were overwhelmed by their mythical deities. Greek gods, according to mythology ensconced themselves in the mountains, the meadows and the seas. Some mountains, most of them, in fact, were considered as sacred.

To mention a few we should include Mount Ossa, North of Mount Olympus, Olympus itself and Mount Parnassus. Olympus was the home of the gods. Parnassus was Apollo's mountain.

A significant exception to the mountain rule was Poseidon–adopted by the Romans as Neptune–who lived in the sea. On their journey South to Athens, Paul and Luke sailed around Cape Sounion, site of the prepossessing temple dedicated to Poseidon. They also sailed under the shadow of Mount Olympus, snowcapped much of the year, the sacred

---

[323] known as the Huron Carol, and in many Canadian hymnals

mountain abode of the mythical Greek deities.

The Hellenistic Cultural Centre

Another mountain rises South and West of Athens. It is Mount Parnassus, second to Olympus in importance but in reality, Parnassus was more precious to most Greeks. Mount Parnassus overlooks a Northern inlet of the Gulf of Corinth and shelters the impressive sanctuary of Delphi on its slopes.

Neither Paul nor Silas, neither Timothy nor Luke visited Delphi as far as we know. Yet their Athenian arrival, first of Paul and Luke, later in Corinth of Silas and Timothy rang the death knell for the practice of legendary Greek mythological tradition. Within 300 years both Greek mythology and its Roman derivatives were dead and all but buried. The legends lived on in literature, yet no longer in human hearts. The faith brought to Europe by Paul's team of missionaries had taken over the minds and hearts of the Europeans. Renowned historian Arnold J. Toynbee noted:

> "Ancient Greek or Hellenistic thought began at the moment when the first rudiments of the poetry of Homer shaped themselves in Greek minds. It came to an end when Homer yielded precedence to the Bible as the sacred book of the Greek-speaking and Greek-writing *intelligentzia*."[324]

Yet, at the time, the religions represented by Delphi remained a powerful force in Greece. Paul did not need to visit Delphi to know what went on there. The slave-girl he once met in far-off Philippi was a byproduct of Delphi's religious activities. She was a vintage "python person," doing what devotees of Pythian Apollo did–soothsaying and ventriloquism. *"Once when we were going to a place of prayer, we were met by a slave girl who had a spirit which she predicted the future. She earned a great deal of money for her owners by foretelling."*[325] Paul knew this story and it tested his mood.

Greeks visiting Delphi engaged in something of a mystical experience. Greeks considered Delphi to be the centre of the earth. The "navel of the earth" is marked by a cone-shaped large, smoothed, rounded rock located at Delphi's sacred way. It symbolizes the tradition that Delphi is the centre of the earth. Greek tradition holds that two eagles met in the air above Delphi. Zeus ordered them to fly in opposite directions so they could show where the centre of the earth was located.

Apollo, the mythical offspring of Zeus and the god of reason became the main objective of most pilgrims' devotions. Apollo, also the deity of law, music and art, was an object of adoration. With the flowering of Greek culture and civilization, Apollo naturally became the dominant god of the pantheon.

Greeks believed that Apollo endowed people with the ability to prophesy. The priests and priestesses of the sanctuary at Delphi were believed to possess the gift of prophetic utterance. Perhaps that is why Paul told the Corinthians that if anyone spoke in tongues at a church gathering, an interpreter must explain what was said.[326]

---

[324] Arnold J. Toynbee, <u>Greek Historical Thought</u>, p. ix
[325] Acts 16:16

Geo, the Earth goddess also was worshipped at Delphi, as was her mythical son Python who guarded the Oracle. A myth told of a struggle between Apollo and Python resulting in the creation of a new god, Pythias. Pythias, through the priestess Pythia, revealed the prophecies. Hence the cult of Pythian Apollo which claimed the slave girl in Philippi!

At Delphi the rigmarole involved much more than shouted predictions in the street by slave girls. The main sanctuary at Delphi was constructed over a fissure in the earth. Sulphurous vapours emerged from the fissure–sometimes enhanced by the smoke of smouldering laurel leaves.

The Pythia, the Oracle's priestesses, sat among the vapours, hallucinating and uttering sounds that only the temple priests could pretend to interpret. Usually the deciphered messages were vague; many a prophecy-seeker deduced the wrong meaning from the Oracle's usually ambiguous pronouncements. Paul was more specific in writing to the Corinthian church:

> *"If I speak in tongues of men and angels but have not love, I am only a resounding gong or a clanging cymbal. If I have the gift of prophecy and can fathom all mysteries and all knowledge, if I have a faith that can move mountains but have not love, I am nothing . . . Love never fails. But where there are prophecies, they will cease; where there are tongues, they will be stilled; where there is knowledge, it will fade away."*[327]

Symbolically, Delphi was so important that it became the objective of most military planning in Greece. Philip II of Macedon was among those seeking Delphi as a prize. Whoever controlled knowledge of the future also, according to the wisdom of the time, controlled the future itself. Such persons were a force to be reckoned with, be they slave-owners in Philippi or would-be conquerors pending on Delphi's oracles.

The ruins today show that Delphi extended over a wide area. It was built on three levels. The lowest level contained, among many spectacular buildings, a beautiful rounded structure called a tholos that was dedicated to Athena Pronaia. Slightly higher in elevation was the gymnasium. Every four years the Pythian Games, beginning in 582 BC, were held here, drawing contestants and spectators from cities allied with Delphi.[328]

The highest part of the sanctuary revered Apollo. It featured a magnificent temple, replete with the deity's giant statue. The sacred way winding up to the temple was lined with statues and treasuries (temple buildings) given by a variety of city-states as tokens for favours received from the Pythia.

Above the temple of Apollo itself was an outstanding amphitheatre, used for drama, often dedicated to the Oracle. It offered a spectacular panoramic vista over the broad valley far below, and the visible arm of the Gulf of Corinth, far beyond.

A Similar Ritual

---

[326] 1 Corinthians 14:13–19
[327] 1 Corinthians 13:1–8
[328] Basil Petrakos. <u>Delphi</u>. p. 34

Between the upper temple and the gymnasium area lay the Castalian Spring. And while Paul and his companions rejected the rites of the upper temple outright, they found themselves about something in common with the Castalian Spring. What happened here illustrates a facet of Greek worship and links it to the practices of Jewish and Christian belief–immersion. "The water of the Castalia spring conferred prophetic and poetic powers."[329]

Apparently both the priests and pilgrims coming to the shrine cleansed themselves in the water. Those who received this sanctified sprinkling[330] or sometimes "immersion-purification" were understood to have special powers. Pilgrims gasping for air in climbing up the steep mountainside from the valley below, on their way to the Oracle itself actually washed themselves several times on their route. This was a form of ablution (not the same as Christian baptism) much like that of the Jewish *mikveh* that was already noted in the account of Lydia's several friends at the riverside prior to their prayers at Philippi.[331] The Greek historian Euripides wrote that water from the Castalian Spring was sprinkled on parts of the temple of Apollo.

This use of water reflects that ancients understood water to be cleansing and life changing. Water figures into many acts of spiritual change and healing. *"So Naaman went with his horses and chariots and stopped at the door of Elisha's house. Elisha sent a messenger to say to him, 'Go, wash yourself seven times in the Jordan, and your flesh will be restored and you will be cleansed.'"[332]*

That idea is somewhat different in the Christian practice of baptism. Baptism in itself does not forgive sin. Nor does it in itself purify a penitent. In Greek culture, one entered the mysteries only by experiencing initiation. In the Christian faith, belief comes first and baptism follows it. Baptism is a symbol of one's spiritual change (and a message of Jesus' death and resurrection). *"John the Baptist came, preaching in the desert of Judea . . . People went out to him from Jerusalem and all Judea and the whole region of the Jordan. Confessing their sins, they were baptized by him in the Jordan River.[333]* – Jesus' baptism was his means of connecting with sinful people. He was not above joining them in their act of repentance clearly demonstrated by their willingness to confess their sins at their submission to John's baptism. Hear David Watson:

> "Jesus later identified himself with sinners in the fullest and most profound sense possible when on the cross he 'became sin' for us; and it is worth noting that on two occasions Jesus spoke about his coming death in terms of baptism: 'I have a baptism to be baptized with.' It was through the baptism of suffering on the cross, when he took upon himself the full consequences of our sin, that forgiveness was made possible. Moreover, that forgiveness symbolized by water baptism, could only be received through repentance and faith."[334]

---

[329] ibid.

[330] ibid.

[331] Acts 16

[332] 2 Kings 5:9, 10

[333] Matthew 3:1, 5–6

[334] David Watson, op. cit., pp. 227, 228

John Calvin has a view of baptism with which many Christians will mostly agree. Others may not fully assent to his analysis. In his <u>Institutes of Christian Religion</u>, he states:

> "Baptism serves as our confession before men, inasmuch as it is a mark by which we openly declare that we wish to be ranked among the people of God, by which we testify that we concur with all Christians in the worship of one God, and in one religion; by which, in short, we publicly assert our faith, so that not only do our hearts breathe, but our tongues also, and all the members of our body, in every way they can, proclaim the praise of God. In this way, as is meet, everything we have is made subservient to the glory of God, which ought everywhere to be displayed, and others are stimulated by our example to the same course. To this Paul referred when he asked the Corinthians whether or not they had been baptized in the name of Christ (1 Cor. 1:13); intimating, that by the very circumstance of having been baptized in his name, they had devoted themselves to him, had sworn and bound themselves in allegiance to him before men, so that they could no longer confess any other than Christ alone, unless they would abjure the confession which they had made in baptism."[335]

Calvin, however, links baptism with Abraham's rite of circumcision, i.e., a covenant. But Calvin's view does not necessarily link baptism with the *faith* of Abraham. Thus he does not repudiate paedobaptism. In both circumcision and paedobaptism, it is not the faith of the person but of a proxy, i.e., a parent. This does not seem square with Paul's teaching, for every time Paul records a baptism–immersion–it is always preceded by a faith decision. Moreover, Calvin more strongly associates baptism with repentance. Truly baptism *is* connected to a believer's repentance. But the baptismal symbol is even more connected to Jesus' death, the water being the grave. Karl Barth clarifies: "Dying with Christ is the vast negation beyond which by grace we stand."[336]

Now consider what pilgrims to Delphi practised in preparation for their "worship." While the Castalian Spring received its greatest importance during the Hellenistic and Roman periods, the practice of ablution went far back into Greek worship experiences. As noted, as far back as 1,500 BC, for example, forms of ritual immersion were recorded at Knossos in Crete and also at Phaistos[337] further West in Crete. These "purity" immersions were required for anyone coming into a king's presence for he was considered to be a god. In Phaistos, someone wanting an appointment with the king, needed to ritually immerse himself prior to the conclave. It had nothing to do with confession of sin. This rite was merely perfunctory.

Greeks provided our word "baptism." It literally means, "dipping," and was associated with the immersion process of dyeing cloth. As late as the New Testament book of Revelation, a form of the Greek verb "to baptize" is used as a synonym of "to dye." It described changing the colour of cloth: *"He is dressed in a robe dipped in blood and his name is the Son of God."*[338] Dipping in the Castalian Spring was a way of

---

335 John Calvin, <u>The Institutes of Christian Religion</u>, Chapter 15, Section 1, paragraph 2513
336 Karl Barth, <u>The Epistle to the Romans</u>, p. 201
337 Despina Hadzi-Vallianou, <u>Phaistos</u>, p. 31

changing one's colours: enter ritually impure, exit ritually pure, or so the Greeks thought.

Christian baptism is different again. It is not self-administered. John understood that. Jesus commanded it. Paul practised and taught it. Christian baptism requires an agent. (who can bury himself?). It is a personal profession of one's confession, faith, and commitment to the Lord's service. Moreover, it is a submissive act.

"As they (Philip and an Ethiopian dignitary) travelled along the road, they came to some water and the Ethiopian eunuch said, 'Look, here is water, why shouldn't I be baptized?' And he ordered the chariot to stop. Then both Philip and the eunuch went down into the water and Philip baptized him."[339]

The Apostles who were a vanguard, a beachhead for The Way, faced cultural elements that were at once common to their own traditions, and also directly opposed to what the Gospel stood for. They could neither embrace them nor completely reject them.

And so, in Athens, Paul began to build upon what was common in Hellenistic culture, Greek mythology, Jewish convictions, philosophies of the Sophists, Stoics and Epicureans–to create and celebrate a faith in Jesus, God's Son, the Messiah. The four missionaries found themselves very much in a cross-cultural mission.

Sounion

When Paul, Luke and their helping friends from Berea sailed South and West to Athens, they had to round Cape Sounion. Strategically located on the promontory of the cape–since sailors heading in almost any direction passed by it–stood a temple dedicated to Poseidon, the supposed Greek lord of the sea. Anyone travelling on the open water could see it. A statue of Poseidon, trident spear and all, was both in the temple, yet significantly sunk in the sea nearby another temple further North. All concerned considered it wise to please and appease Poseidon who ruled the waves.

The Sounion temple and its other statues were signals to Paul and Luke of things to come. They could travel nowhere without seeing the idols of such mythical deities.

They had not forgotten Silas and Timothy. The other two would meet them in good time, perhaps after those Berean helpers returned to their city and reported that Paul and Luke had arrived safely in Athens. Paul and Luke did not forget them. *"The men who accompanied Paul brought him to Athens and then left with instructions for Silas and Timothy to join him as soon as possible."*[340]

The Sounion temple served to remind the Apostles that Greeks had different attitudes towards divinity than did Jews. Greeks saw perfection in the beauty of the human form, as is testified by the idol of Poseidon now sensually displayed in the Athens National Museum. They saw beauty in muscles properly functioning, in athletic and military prowess. Perfection for Jews was altogether different. It was crystallized in justice and righteousness, spiritual values less easily measured or defined than in Greek ideals.

---

[338] Revelation 19:13
[339] Acts 8:36–38
[340] Acts 17:15

One of the finest examples of this Greek ideal, a god made in the form of man, is found in the aforesaid statue of Poseidon. It is a fully formed oversized bronze statue of Poseidon of Artemision, sans trident. The statue dates from circa 460 BC and was found under the sea near Euboea. It shows a naked, hollow-eyed Poseidon poised as hurling the trident. Some archaeologists surmise that the statue was fashioned and dedicated after the Athenian sea victory against the Persians at Salamis.

Paul, sharp as he was about biblical teaching, must have reminded himself of the psalmist's advice. *"Those who make them* (idols) *have become just like them. Have become just like the gods they trust."*[341]

From Sounion to the port at Athens is less than a day's sail. Shortly, Paul and company would see idols like Poseidon's multiplied by the thousands. This sight would challenge them. They knew the *Torah's* teachings: *"You shall not make yourself an idol in the form of anything in heaven above or on the earth beneath or in the waters below."*[342]

[341] Psalm 115:5 MSG
[342] Exodus 20:4

CHAPTER SIXTEEN
PAUL MEETS ATHENA

Athens today is a contradiction. It's a modern, bustling metropolis of five million; yet the dominant attraction is its past. Cars and trucks lurch in the penetrating smog through congested streets; yet the impaired and time-battered Parthenon, atop the Acropolis, soars in serene but sorry solitude. Athens' university buzzes with the pursuit of knowledge and wisdom; the greatness of its most honoured teachers–Socrates, Plato and Aristotle–who lived centuries before Christ, the greatest teacher of all time.

Messy pigeons fly in and out of the squares around the parliament building; children chase them, tourists feed them. One senses that their ornithological ancestors may have been similarly scattered by youths who once gathered around Socrates, and their feathered forebears may have been nourished by crumbs flicked by Plato and Aristotle, by Aristophanes and Euripedes, by Homer and Sophocles.

Visitors in today's Athens often receive the impression it was always the most influential city in Greece–but that is not necessarily so. Athens surely had influence. However, it was already half a millennium past its prime when Paul's troupe entered the Panathenaic Way leading him into the agora. Paul visited Athens when it was already well on the way to sinking into obscurity. Modern Athens, now resuscitated, is without doubt, the chief city of Greece, judged by any measurement but it had slackened status when Paul and Luke reached there.

Having sunk for a time into that relative obscurity, Athens is once again a city of poetry and art. There is a difference, however. The Greek goddess Athena, from whom Athens derives its name, is a powerless object of art, not of civic or religious devotion. Yet Athens represented the heart of Greekness. Athens exhibited platinum Grecian culture.

A City of Idols

When Paul entered Athens, he did not find anything like the metropolis of today. In the Apostle's day the population was more like 20,000 souls. Even in terms of population at that time, Athens was overshadowed by Corinth, not many kilometres West. Athens was long past its golden age when 10 times that number populated its houses and streets. Yet something very important happened in Athens, a kind of "changing of the guard."

At the Greek Tomb of the Unknown Soldier evzones enact a daily ritual. It is purely a theatrical endeavour, on a par with the Changing of the Guard, say at Buckingham Palace. Neither the parliament building nor its ceremony nor the guarding evzones existed when Paul and Luke arrived at the market (agora) of Athens. Yet the events they set in motion truly marked a Changing of the Guard in Greece. The ancient mythological deities who watched over the affairs of mortals in the civilization were about to be unemployed rather quickly.

Watching those evzones guards slow-step in front of the Monument to the Unknown Soldier is like viewing the scene in a time warp, as if one were looking through a window onto a previous century. The grind of their steel-soled boots, their dated costumes, their tasseled toques, and the painfully slow motion of their march carry one back at least a century. Yet one feels that Paul could speak to Athenians right now in this present time frame. Paul was, for one thing, a sports lover; Athens abounds in ovals, arenas, stadia and tracks.

He spoke of the Olympic competition of boxing, of pommelling the air, or races, pressing on to the goal, persistence forward to the prize, which is Christ's high calling, of physical exercise which is good, but of spiritual exercise which is better.[343] He advocated discipline as a key way to life. *"Do you not know that in a race all the runners run but only one gets the prize? Everyone who competes in the games goes into strict training. They do it to get a crown that will not last; but we do it to get a crown that will last forever."*[344] This fleeting crown is the Greek *stephanos*, a brow wreath of laurel leaves awarded to a victorious champion.

Paul, according to Luke's record, was at home with almost any audience. He could discuss philosophy with the Stoics, physical enjoyment with the Epicureans, literature with the poets, theology with the divines, attitudes with the Sophists, politics with the city leaders and war with the soldiers. In Athens he had opportunity to do most of these.

The Sophists also had a loud voice in forming Athenian philosophies. A Sophist named Protagoras (from Abdera) dating from 400 years before Paul and Luke proclaimed that, "Man is the measure of all things." This conviction collided with Paul's Hebraic understanding. God, not man, was the standard of every measurement. The psalmist wrote, *"His* [God's] *pleasure is not in the strength of the horse, nor his delight in the legs of the warrior."*[345] YAWEH's view of humanity is illustrated by his word to Samuel when Israel needed a new king. *"The LORD said to Samuel, "'Do not consider his appearance or his height, for I have rejected him. The LORD does not look at the things people look at. People look at the outward appearance, but the LORD looks at the heart.'"*[346] Hebrew and Greek theologies were on a collision course.

The spiritual milieu of Paul's bizarre secular world was as alien to the Paul Team as the atmosphere of the moon was compared to that of the earth. That mission evoked divine help. It also called for Paul to steer his abundant energies and his prickly personality into positive, pastoral pursuits in order to countermand the indelible, instilled imprint of Greek mythology. What a daunting task!

Paul was stymied with Athens despite his pre-teen background in Hellenist Tarsus. He was gobsmacked again, just as in Philippi! As Keith Hopkins, a Cambridge professor records, "Pagan idol-worship was foolish and illusionary, pagan myths were immoral, their religious and domestic practices were disgusting."[347] For the number of deities, Athens made Tarsus pale into insignificance. His dismay stemmed from seeing such a

---

[343] 1 Timothy 4:7, 8
[344] 1 Corinthians 9:24, 25
[345] Psalm 147:10
[346] 1 Samuel 6:7
[347] Keith Hopkins, A World Full of Gods, p. 81

surfeit of idols. Indeed, how could he avoid seeing them? Any Pharisee would be abashed at such a sight. In Jerusalem, the Pharisees and other Hasidic-type Jews would even close their eyes in walking by any forms of idolatry. Blinded for a few moments, some of them bumped into objects in their way. That led to injuries. Less impressed Jews teased them as "bruised and bleeding rabbis."

Paul, even as a practising Pharisee, was never attracted to this ultra strict spirituality; nonetheless he was much offended by what he faced starkly. *"While Paul was in Athens, he was greatly distressed to see that the city was full of idols."*[348] The distress was not in the idols themselves but in the deluded Athenians who understood that their deities could enrich them with truth and save them from their follies and sins.

When Paul via Luke described Athens as "full" of idols he was accurate. Idols abounded everywhere, on the Acropolis, in the agora and anywhere someone walked. Idols smothered the city. The most obvious aspect of idolatry was on the Acropolis. "Acropolis" is a Greek word meaning "on top of the city." It simply means, "the upper city." An acropolis was generally the city's stronghold, for it was the city's most defensible place. On the Acropolis of Athens a large cluster of temples existed dedicated to the myriad gods revered and worshipped by the Greek people.

Central to this acropolis was–and is–the Parthenon, now in partial ruins, but being restored. In Paul's time it was not only a model of flawless temple architecture yet it was also an attempt to show Doric-styled rectangular perfection in its mathematical design.

It is a design thought to be ideal beauty in mathematical form, about 111 feet (30.9 m.) by 228 feet (69.5 m.).[349] To reach the Parthenon one must climb a great number of stairs, pass by a series of shrines such as the temple of Athene Nike, and ascend to the highest point of the acropolis where the Parthenon dominates everything surrounding it.

Construction on the Parthenon began about 448 BC. When Paul, Luke and their Berean travellers arrived (and returned, leaving Paul and Luke in Athens), the marble shrine had been completed by 500 years. In the heart of the Parthenon stood a 40-foot (12 meter), gold, silver, bronze and ivory ornate wooden-cored stature of Athena, the civic deity and goddess of wisdom.

The mini-model on display in the National Museum may not be an accurate copy. It is close enough to the original to accurately guess what the first statue looked like. It features griffons on her helmet, a spear in her right hand and a shield at her feet. Somewhere, as part of the idol, it was also emblemized. Athenians deemed Athena to be all-powerful and all-wise.

Could Athenians harbour any doubt, when she answered the prayers of the people time and again? When the city was matched against many enemies, did she not win? Did not Athens grow rich and powerful? Was not her name known and respected around the world? For a full century, during the city's golden years Athenians were convinced that their prayers were effective.

The friezes and art decorating the Parthenon celebrated the victories of Athens–and

---

[348] Acts 17:15
[349] Manolis Andronicos. The Acropolis. pp. 25–34

Athena–over the Persians and other Greek city-states like Sparta. The Athenians not only subdued their enemies, but they also mastered art and architecture, poetry and drama, philosophy, education, political organization and theory. Athenians had much to celebrate. Who could build a future better than the leaders and people of Athens? Paul saw such statues as impotent.

Place those questions along side the *Torah* teachings. *"If you pay attention to these laws and are careful to follow them, then the Lord your God will . . . love you and bless you and increase your numbers . . . You will be blessed more than any other people . . . the Lord your God will drive out those nations before you . . ."*[350]

Other temples reflected other myths and accepted beliefs. Alongside the Parthenon stood yet another temple, the Erechtheion. In Greek mythology, Erichthonius, the grandson, so to speak, of Athena, was half-man, half-serpent. He was one of the founders of Athens, or so goes the legend. It was he that destroyed an enemy monarch, who unfortunately turned out to be the son of Poseidon. In turn, Poseidon slew Erichthonius with a thunderbolt. The statued Caryatides who hold up the porch of the Erechtheion also figure in the myths about the Athena cult.

Exasperated

To a Jew like Paul for whom all graven images were strictly forbidden, this abundance of idols must have been infuriating. So must have been the complacency–the spiritual ignorance–of the Greeks' unique place in God's plan for them. Luke reports (NEB) that Paul was "exasperated." Any Jew would have been. The first commandment stated bluntly: *"You shall have no other god before me."* *"Do not follow other gods of the peoples around you; for the Lord your God, who is among you, is a jealous God and his anger will burn against you, and he will destroy you from the face of the land."*[351]

To see such a significant city so saturated with statues was for a Jew akin to the proverbial bull seeing red. An ordinary Jew would walk in any deflectable, circuitous way to avoid casting his eyes on such sights. He would attempt to avert his eye so that he would miss even a stray glance at a carved image.

In Athens that was next to impossible. It may explain why only a handful of Jews dwelt in the city. Most Jews walked great distances to avoid paths containing temples and their images. How could they do that in pagan deity-honouring Athens?

Paul with Luke–and who knows, perhaps the Bereans with friendly connections there–went quickly to what possibly may have been the only synagogue in Athens. In this instance Paul slightly varied his usual strategy. His first impulse was to bring the Jews onside by sharing with them his annoyance at seeing so many images of gods throughout the city. What could Jews do about it? They didn't even try.

This was an impossible avoidance in most Greek communities–especially in Athens. Luke writes that the city was "full of idols."

---

[350] Deuteronomy 7:12–14, 22
[351] Deuteronomy 6:14–15

Or so it seemed. Luke may not have been exaggerating, for even modest archaeological remnants visible in today's Athens have stone deities of every sort adorning walls, pillars, friezes and monuments in the excavations.

Paul raised questions about this surfeit of deities in the city squares–perhaps surrounded by scruffy-feathered pigeons and transient passersby. Inevitably, his standpoint drew attention. Eventually, he was hauled before the equivalent of a city council and was asked to explain himself. Paul was seldom lost for words. *"Then they brought him to a meeting of the Areopagus, where they said to him, 'May we know what this new teaching is that you are presenting?'"*[352]

The Great Defence

The city fathers' subpoena was a propaedeutic proposition for Paul. He relished talking about Jesus, his resurrection and lecturing about his personal Christian faith. In describing Paul as "exasperated," Luke tells us several things about the Apostle. First (1), evidently Paul was one Jew who was unafraid to look upon figures that represented deities. That would make him something of a liberal among the Jews of his time. That description spoke of his improving "wellness."

Secondly (2), Paul saw the idols for what they were–merely figures or items of carved wood or chiseled stone. He likely recalled the attitude of an Old Testament prophet:

> *(The wood) "is a man's fuel for burning; some of it he takes and warms himself, he kindles a fire and bakes bread. But he also fashions a god and worships it; he makes an idol and bows down to it. Half of the wood he burns on the fire; over it he prepares his meal, he roasts his meat and eats his fill. He also warms himself and says, 'Ah! I am warm; I see the fire.' From the rest he makes a god his idol; he bows down to it and worships. He prays to it and says, 'Save me; you are my god.' They know nothing. They understand nothing."*[353]

Idols represented nothing to Paul. Probably, his exasperation centred on the ignorance of seeing people treating stone and art forms as exalted spiritual references.

Thirdly (3), Luke indicates that Paul held his temper in this situation. While inwardly riled, he remained externally calm. He took his argument for proclaiming Christ crucified and risen from death, from the example of the idols themselves.

Fourthly (4), perhaps other reasons existed for Paul to keep his private angst in check. In all likelihood Athens' laws would protect the honour of the deities.

The Jews themselves had such a law–the commandment that the Lord's name must never be taken "in vain," i.e., never misused for improper purposes. Luke proposed further evidence of such a law in his own account. Later, when Paul journeyed to Ephesus, a mob seized his current travelling companions, Gaius and Aristarchus for their preaching efforts. The Ephesus city clerk: *"You have brought these men here though they have neither robbed temples nor blasphemed our goddess."*[354]

---

[352] Acts 17:19
[353] Isaiah 44:15–18

Other Ephesian Christians constrained Paul from speaking out on their behalf. When Paul moved on, they had to live with the consequences of any impropriety of his. The Ephesian city clerk, in dismissing the case, stated that there were no charges against them for defacing or *"robbing a temple, or blaspheming the name of Artemis."*

Whether law, prudence or the proverbial advice of Scripture[355] (*"A hot-tempered man . . . gets into all kinds of trouble"*) caused Paul to contain his temper, Paul understood an important strategy in reaching people of a different culture.

Paul did not bash his audience. He didn't put them down. Rather, he used their own culture and experiences as a starting point. He found in their own idols the references upon which he could build his case of the living God.

Paul had examined these idols up close. Few Pharisees would even think of doing that! He noted one of the totems as dedicated to an "unknown god." Such statues, even temples were common in many Greek communities.

Wrote Luke, *"Paul then stood up in the Areopagus and said: 'Men of Athens! I see that in every way you are very religious."*[356] Perhaps, in seeking favour with the gods, the Athenians simply wanted to ensure that they had covered all their bases even with the deities they didn't know about! Instead, Paul used that idol as a means of revealing the known God who previously was unknown to the Greeks. Paul wanted the Athenians to meet and experience his God.

Paul's speech, recorded by Luke in Acts 17:22– 28, without doubt is one of the greatest theological presentations in human history. It was delivered to the Athenians, not on its Acropolis, but in the Areopagus adjacent to the agora (market) area. The city council honoured Ares, god of war, in the name of its meeting place nearby what is often called Mars Hill. Mars is the Roman equivalent for the Greek deity Ares. Paul said:

"Men of Athens: I see that in every way you are very religious. For as I walked around and observed your objects of worship, I even found an altar with this inscription: 'To An Unknown God.' Now what you worship as something unknown I am going to proclaim to you. " . . . The God who made the world and everything in it does not live in temples made by hands. And he is not served by human hands as if he needed anything, because he himself gives all men life and breath and everything else.

"From one man he made every nation of men, that they should inhabit the whole earth; and he determined the times set for them and the exact places where they should live. God did this so that men would seek him and perhaps reach out to him and find him though he is not far away from each one of us, for in him we live and move and have our being. As some of your own poets have said, 'We are his offspring.'"[357]

Paul's cross-cultural speech received mixed reviews from the Athenians. Yet it showed that Paul could address the politicians or deal with the philosophers on equal

---

[354] Acts 19:37
[355] Proverbs 29:22 NEB
[356] Acts 17:22
[357] Acts 17:22–28

terms, using their own idioms and not just Jewish scripture.

A Sparrow in the Market

Probably Paul and Luke, later Silas and Timothy wandered the streets of the social gathering centre and marketplace known as the agora. The agora was a more-or-less triangular-shaped (or maybe keystone shaped) area below the acropolis. It spread between the Stoa of Attilus (now fully restored by archaeologists) and the Thesseum, a miniature version of the Parthenon built in the Fifth Century BC. The Acts record: Paul *"reasoned . . . in the marketplace day by day with those who happened to be there . . . preaching the Good News about Jesus and the resurrection."*[358]

The Thesseum was built at the same time as the Parthenon and was dedicated, in part, to Athena but mainly to the mythic god Hephaestus. Later, in Christian times, this Doric Temple became known as the Church of Saint George. The Greek market in which Paul mingled is not to be confused with a Roman market (forum) a few short blocks away in which is situated the Tower of the Winds.

The agora contributed to making Athens a community. Here, items for sale were laid out in bins or on tables for customers to examine. It was more than a market of sellers and buyers. The agora was an area for mutual exchange of ideas and socializing. One can almost see Paul buttonholing people as they gathered in groups of twos or threes, telling them about the Lord Jesus who had died, been buried and had risen from death. Paul's foray into the market dismayed some vendors and shoppers. *"Some of them asked, 'what is this babbler saying to us?'"*[359]

His behaviour caused people to talk about him. Luke, recording both what Paul said and did, and what others said of him, tells that some Greeks described him as a *spermologos*, literally, a "seed picker." Some translations have them calling Paul a "babbler," a "charlatan," or a "propagandist."

J. B. Phillips, in his translation/paraphrase of Acts, turns "seed-picker" into "cock-sparrow," and in doing so catches the imagery of the original word–an excited little bird, a sparrow, hopping along the earth and the stone pavement in the agora picking up seeds here, there and everywhere. He was meeting people everywhere, starting up conversations about Jesus and his resurrection. Then he moved on to meet someone else.

Multiple Meanings

The description of Paul as a seed-picker suggests that the Athenians thought he had picked up strange ideas everywhere he travelled. At the heart of this seed-picking, we can be sure, was the concept of Jesus and the resurrection. It was a belief common to all Pharisees yet alien to most Greek minds. Yet it was central to all of Paul's discussions. Luke records: *"Others remarked, 'He seems to be advocating foreign gods' They said this because Paul was preaching the Good News about Jesus and the resurrection.'"*[360]

---

[358] Acts 17:17, 18
[359] Acts 17:18

The Greek word for resurrection caused some confusion among the Athenians. *Anastasis* (*ana*=again; *stasis*=to stand) is a Greek word meaning resurrection. It is also a woman's name. Some of the Athenian philosophers thought Paul meant a god with a consort, i.e., like Isis and Osiris of Egyptian mythology for whom Athenians consecrated a temple. They misunderstood Paul. He was not talking about Jesus (a god) and Anastasis (his consort). Paul continued preaching. They gradually realized that Paul was talking, not about Jesus' goddess consort, but about life after death. Many Greeks rejected that notion out-of-hand.

Two groups of philosophers especially were mystified equally by what Paul had to say. The Epicureans believed that life was contained in the present; they held no view of the afterlife. Epicureans lived for now, not tomorrow! The Stoics, on the other hand understood that only the soul was immortal. That did not include a bodily resurrection. Paul's statements about the resurrection of the body were incomprehensible to both groups.[361]

There were a few converts. One was Dionysius, a member of the Areopagus, a city father. Church history records that the first bishop of Athens was a man named Dionysius. Tradition also says that Damaris, a woman who believed Paul, wed Dionysius. These traditions imply believable truths that Paul's success in Athens had been achieved. *"A few men became followers of Paul and believed. Among them was Dionysius, a member of the Areopagus, also a woman named Damaris, and a number of others."*[362]

Paul's approach in Athens began much the same as in previous missions. As usual, he began with the synagogue. Then he took his message to the streets. He wasn't run out-of-town this time, yet we have no idea how big a community of Christians he left behind. There is no "Epistle to the Athenians." If there were any letters to the church in Athens, they have been lost.

Luke suggests three categories of responders to Paul's message. Some mocked. Others wanted to hear him again–they liked never-ending buzz groups. The third group believed, including Dionysius and Damaris.[363]

The real significance of this time in Athens is not in the numbers but the strategy. Paul's efforts marked the beginning of a mission strategy used by the modern church. Simply stated: "Find a point of common interest and start from there. Stand where I stand and see if you can see what I see."

Paul found the statue of an unknown god and built upon that common idea to engage his listeners. The spiritual old guard in Greece began to change when a church was born at Athens in 49 or 50 AD.

---

[360] Acts 17:18
[361] For a worthwhile discussion on the impact of Stoic and Epicurean philosophies on St. Paul and modern Christian culture, look to Professor Samuel J. Mikolaski's 2015 book, St. Paul and Free Speech: Then and Now.
[362] Acts 17:34
[363] Acts 17:34

PART FOUR: IN THE FULLNESS OF TIME

CHAPTER SEVENTEEN
CORINTH'S CANAL

What prompted Paul and Luke to leave Athens is unclear. The two apparently awaited Silas and Timothy who stayed behind to instruct the new churches of Berea and Thessalonika in Macedonia. Perhaps they were delayed too long for an anxious Paul more than eager to set out for his next mission elsewhere. Or else, the political climate in Athens was unhealthy for Paul to remain there. Again, Paul, despite his transformation in Damascus, had an annoying approach of alienating himself from others, leaving his companions to smooth over the controversies he created. Luke succinctly wrote: *"After this Paul left Athens and went to Corinth."*[364]

Initially, Luke and Paul would have set sail for Corinth. It was most unlikely that they walked that distance. Greece was a seagoing nation. Its water transport was both plentiful and inexpensive. They would have walked to Athens' port, Piraeus, then likely sought passage on one of the port's many vessels carrying goods to Corinth.

Modern travellers going from Athens to Corinth will experience at least one thing unknown to the two missionaries. If they travelled by land to Corinth they will cross, by road or train over the modern Corinthian canal. On a small cruise ship they can sail through the six kilometres of the canal, cut out of solid rock to the modern city of Corinth on the Gulf of Corinth.

A canal to link the Aegean Sea with the Gulf of Corinth was first proposed during the reign of Julius Caesar, about a century before Paul's journey. Then Emperor Nero decided to excavate the canal–to his own personal glory, of course. Nero visited the canal himself, and then set several thousand slaves to work at digging the canal. They started at both ends at the same time, a favourite method of engineering in the ancient world. They would meet at the centre. A few weeks later when Nero died, so did the project. In 1881 AD, the canal construction resumed, and by 1883, it was completed.

Paul's journey preceded Nero's efforts. When Paul and Luke crossed the Isthmus of Corinth, no canal existed. A few of Nero's excavators began to dig the canal a decade after Paul's visit. They only made a depression at one end. In 50 AD the standard way of transshipping vessels from one side to the other, that is from the Aegean to the Corinthian Gulf, was to use the ancient route called the diolkos, from the Greek verb *dielko*, meaning "to haul across."

Before the canal was built, ships wanting to reach Corinth on the Western shores of Greece either had to sail around the Southern tip of the long peninsula of Greece called the Peloponnese–which could be especially treacherous during winter storms–or they had to be hauled across the land mass on rollers or carts.[365]

Small ships were raised onto carts with wheels and then dragged across the

---

[364] Acts 18:1
[365] Nicos Papahatzis, <u>Ancient Corinth</u>.

cobbled roadway known as the diolkos. The alternative Southern sea route was a graveyard for many a mariner and the voyage took much longer. For military purposes especially, the diolkos proved valuable–troops and supplies moved quickly using this land route.

The diolkos was rediscovered and excavated only in the previous century. In 1956 Archaeologist Ephor N. Verdelis uncovered the ancient diolkos and traced its route. While it approximates the present canal's path, the diolkos wanders from the present canal at several points.

Visitors obtain their best view of it at the Western end, at the Southern rim of the canal. Chances are that Paul's ship unloaded its cargo and passengers at the Eastern port of Isthmia or Cenchrea and reloaded with a shipment for elsewhere in the Aegean or Adriatic Seas.

CHAPTER EIGHTEEN
CENCHREA

Because of the apparent inconvenience of the diolkos for very large vessels, Corinth needed two ports. One harbour, on the Southeast coast, was the port of Cenchrea. Corinth's second port, Lechaion, on the Northwest shore along the Gulf of Corinth was at the other end.

Paul almost certainly landed at Cenchrea when he disembarked for Corinth. The port is scarcely mentioned in the Bible. Luke refers to it when Paul insisted on a haircut (connected to a pledge). *"Before Paul sailed, he had his hair cut off at Cenchrea because of a vow."*[366]

Again Paul cites the location in his letter to the Romans and commends the leader of the church established there. *"I commend to you Phoebe, a servant (diakonos) of the church in Cenchrea."* Paul continued, *"I ask you to receive her in the Lord in a way worthy of the saints and to give her any help she may need from you, for she has been a great help to many people, including me."*[367]

So we know he was there. Moreover, Phoebe could have welcomed him. We know that a young church had begun there, possibly started by sailors or traders, or less possibly by Paul, Silas, Luke and Timothy–but perhaps by Aquila and Priscilla, or other lay members of the Corinthian church.

Today Cenchrea is uninhabited but the ruins of Cenchrea are plainly visible. Only recently have some of the ruins been protected by a wire mesh fence to keep out vandals, relic-seeker and scavengers. In its time the horseshoe shaped harbour must have provided the city with a protective haven. Warehouses stretched along the Southern arm (mole) of the horseshoe; they now rest slightly below the water level.

Cenchrea housed a Christian community, a family of faith. Ruins of its ancient basilica sit partially in the seawater near the closed end of the horseshoe. At the Northern mole's landward end are the remnants of houses and shops on the side of the hill. The site was excavated in 1963; some of the discoveries rest as exhibits in the museum at Isthmia.

Never Given Its Due

Cenchrea has never been given its due–neither for its importance to communications and transportation nor its importance in the history of the church. Archaeologist Nicos Papahatzis wrote that, "The harbour of Cenchraei (sic) is seldom referred to by ancient authors, despite the fact it was of some importance to Corinthians; communications with the East and West Islands."

"The Apostle Paul makes mention of a very early Christian community at Cenchreai (sic) in his Epistle to the Romans. In this same Epistle he introduces a deaconess to the Christians in Rome. The deaconess, whose name was Phoebe,

---

[366] Acts 18:18
[367] Romans 16:1, 2

received a letter from Paul himself at Corinth or at Cenchreai in the winter of AD 52–53, and took it with her to Rome. In the spring of this year (AD 53) Paul and his companions took a ship in the harbour of Cenchreai with his companions and left for Ephesos (sic)."[368]

From the epistle that Paul wrote to Rome we learn that this young church had a leader named Phoebe. The Greek noun that Paul uses, describes her as a deacon (Gr. *diakonos*) to that various renditions have translated variously as deaconess, servant, officer and leader. There appears little reason the translation should not be simply, "deacon." Deaconess is a politically correct paraphrase. "Officer" sounds elitist.

What is significant about this description? Simply that Paul openly endorsed a female leader in a church within view of Corinth! It was to Corinth that Paul wrote a dictum that probably is as much misused as it is widely known: *"Women should be silent in the church. They are not allowed to speak . . ."*[369]

That Phoebe was a leader was not surprising. Other women also took leading roles–such as Lydia in Philippi and the Berean women. If Paul's instructions were to apply universally, is it not surprising to find a woman as a deacon in the community neighbouring Corinth? Not to mention that a leader in the Corinthian church, the leader/teacher (Priscilla) served the Lord and worked with Paul in neighbouring Corinth?

Paul's letter to Timothy is much more troubling with respect for women. Again, no one quite knows the circumstances or the occasion for Paul's comments. The modesty of clothing and jewellery a woman wore is understandably significant in the Roman and Greek cultures and may have been a contributing factor. Paul states:

A woman (wife) *should learn in quietness and full submission. I do not permit a woman* (Gr. *gunaika*=wife) *to teach or to assume authority over a man; she must be quiet. For Adam was formed first, then Eve. And Adam was not the one deceived; it was the woman who was deceived and became a sinner. But women* (Gr. *gegonen*=wives) *will be saved through childbearing–if they continue in faith, love and holiness with propriety."*[370]

This surely is an arcane Pharisaic argument and neither comparable nor consistent with Paul's insistence that salvation comes through faith, not deeds. Saved by giving birth? Nor is the argument consistent with his joy of women who give leadership, i.e., The Bereans, Lydia, Priscilla, and Phoebe. Moreover, Priscilla taught a man–Apollos–who needed correction in his basic theology about Jesus and the meaning of baptism! This text implies misogyny.

Much conjecture could be generated on this subject and to a degree it connects to Paul's developing attitudes. Paul could never be described as a misogynist. Suffice it to say that Paul's instructions for some women in Corinth–this where Aphrodite's notorious shrine atop the Acrocorinth employed 1,000 cultic prostitutes–and perhaps to Timothy, had something to do with the general reputation of some females in that city or where Timothy was currently living. We simply do not know. Paul was often ambivalent about

---

[368] Nicos Papahatzis, Ancient Corinth, p. 41
[369] 1 Corinthians 14:34
[370] 1 Timothy 2:11–15

THE WELLNESS OF SAINT PAUL

his instructions. Some dicta were inalterable commands; others vary in their applications, depending upon circumstances.

> *"Now about food sacrificed to idols: We know that 'We all possess knowledge.' But knowledge puffs up while love builds up. Those who think they know something do not yet know as they ought to know. But whoever loves God is known by God.*
> *So then, about eating food sacrificed to idols: We know that, 'An idol is nothing at all in the world' and that 'There is no God but one' . . . Some people are still so accustomed to idols that when they eat sacrificial food they think of it as having been sacrificed to a god, and since their conscience is weak, it is defiled. But food does not bring us near to God; we are no worse if we do not eat, and no better if we do."*

Paul added, *"Be careful, however, that the exercise of your rights does not become a stumbling block to the weak."*[371]

At regular (usually dictated by the phase of the moon) gatherings of guilds (a form of unions or brotherhoods) guild members were expected to offer an ablution of wine and meat to the guild's patron deity. An orgy often followed. This likely was the sacrifice to which Paul referred. Luke references the guilds in his Acts account of the Ephesian uproar made by the silversmiths and related trades in Ephesus.

> *"About that time there arose a great disturbance about the Way. A silversmith named Demetrius, who made silver shrines of Artemis, brought in a lot of business for the craftsmen there. He called them together, along with the workers in related trades, and said: 'You know, my friends, that we receive a good income from this business. And you see and hear how this fellow Paul has convinced and led astray large numbers of people here in Ephesus and in practically the whole province of Asia. He says that gods made by human hands are no gods at all. There is danger not only that our trade will lose its good name, but also that the temple of the great goddess Artemis will be discredited; and the goddess herself, who is worshiped throughout the province of Asia and the world, will be robbed of her divine majesty.'*
> *When they heard this, they were furious and began shouting: "Great is Artemis of the Ephesians!" Soon the whole city was in an uproar."*[372]

Eating meat that was offered as a sacrifice to an idol was relatively unimportant to Paul. It was just meat! Was this a contradiction to the edict issued by the Jerusalem church to Antioch? *"You are to abstain from food sacrificed to idols, from blood, from meat of strangled animals and from sexual immorality. You will do well to avoid these things."*[373] Paul thought it was not a contradiction, Or, is there a hidden implication here?

Bruce Chilton gives the reader a clue. Meat sacrificed to idols may not mean that meat was used in the monthly guild meeting honouring the community's or trade's patron deities. Chilton points out that, *"In a bustling market ordinary meat might appear under the icon of a god or goddess to whom it was nationally sacrificed at the moment of slaughter."*[374] In other words, such market meats may not have been sacrificed at all.

---

[371] 1 Corinthians 8:4–9
[372] Acts 19:2–29
[373] Acts 15:29
[374] Bruce Chilton, op. cit., p. 15

Paul disagreed that Gentile men needed to be circumcised. Whether to marry or not was an option for Christians, although Paul expressed his own opinion and preference. The matter of a woman's silence in the church at Corinth versus a woman's leadership in Cenchrea and elsewhere must be explained by local needs and challenges.

Paul has much to explain if his words are taken at face value. He does say at times that his dicta may only be his private opinion. His view of Christian marriage is fuzzy. In his first letter to Corinth, he wrote:

> *"And if a woman has a husband who is not a believer and he is willing to live with her, she must not divorce him. For the unbelieving husband has been sanctified through his wife, and the unbelieving wife has been sanctified through her believing husband. Otherwise your children would be unclean, but as it is, they are holy."*[375]

In his second letter to the same church he wrote: *"Do not be yoked together with unbelievers. For what do righteousness and wickedness have in common? Or what fellowship can light have with darkness?"*[376]

Is Paul confused? Perhaps the Apostle was addressing different situations. Nonetheless, the reader is puzzled. Or did some editor play with Paul's writing?

---

[375] 1 Corinthians 7:13, 14
[376] 2 Corinthians 6:14

CHAPTER NINETEEN

CORINTH

Ancient Corinth is some six kilometres Southwest from the modern city that continues the same name. From a biblical perspective, we know a great deal about the church at Corinth–perhaps more than any other early church. Luke leaves his readers one account of it in Acts (18, 19). Paul himself wrote at least two extensive letters to Corinthians. He may actually have written a third letter, of which parts have survived as the last four chapters of 2 Corinthians.

This book will not attempt to dissect the details of those letters nor their epistemology. By the time Paul had moved on from a ministry of 18 months in Corinth, the church was viable, yet full of challenges. Some of these trials were unique to Corinth; others simply reflected spiritual immaturity.

As usual, there was much opposition to Paul's leadership, with others making claims to superiority of their apostleship. The converts had not yet learned the joy of liberal giving. Women in the church were acting out of proportion to their numbers or status. People had formed cliques. The interpretation of the resurrection was in dispute. And so it went. Corinth could have given Paul a migraine; instead he saw the strife as an incredible opportunity to further interpret the implications of the Gospel, the Good News. Thus he provided two epistles to guide the fledgling followers of Jesus to exert their faith more fervently and forcefully.

Such problems, however, reflect not the weakness of the Corinthian church but its phenomenal success. It had grown so quickly and so diversely that it suffered enormous growing pains. The Corinthian Christians may have created challenges for Paul and his co-workers, but what a church growth it must have been!

No Delusions

When Luke, Paul with their companions Silas and Timothy disembarked from their ship at the port of Cenchrea they could see the acropolis of Corinth directly ahead of them. It was dubbed the Acrocorinth, rising 575 meters above the city of Corinth.[377] The gleaming shrines atop the Acropolis were multitudinous yet hardly competed with the number of sacred shrines that filled Athens' striking skyline. The white marble sanctuaries on the Acrocorinth were clearly visible from Cenchrea's wharves. The temples were, as eagles fly, some 16 kilometres distant from the port of Cenchrea.

Paul and the others had no delusions about what awaited them in Corinth. The city's immorality was legendary. It was also renowned as an educational centre. Its trading reputation was the talk of every sailor who had watched his ship drawn across the diolkos. Corinth was immoral, indulgent, wealthy, sophisticated, and erudite–and like

---

[377] Nicos Papahatziz. Ancient Corinth. p. 64

Athens, it was very religious. It was however unlike Athens in size; Corinth was 10 times larger.

About 200 years before Paul's visit, in 146 BC, Roman armies had levelled Corinth. For a century Corinth lay in ruins until Julius Caesar revitalized it in 44 BC. Caesar not only rebuilt Corinth, he sent officials as colonizers to create a "loyal" city.

Paul said little of Corinth's immortality while he was in the city. He had much to say about Corinth' behaviours in his letters. No doubt the deportment of the people he observed brought to mind his own unbending moral and spiritual training. We can see that in his first letter:

"Do you not know that the wicked will not inherit the earth? Do not be deceived: Neither the sexually immoral nor idolaters nor male prostitutes nor homosexual offenders nor swindlers nor the greedy nor drunkards will inherit the kingdom of God. And that is what some of you were. But you are washed, you were sanctified, you were justified in the name of the Lord Jesus Christ and by the Spirit of God."[378]

Little of that earlier Greek period remained even when Paul's team arrived there, although the Doric Temple dedicated to Apollo still stood. Its Doric columns still stand today. The present ruins of Corinth seen by visitors to Corinth are mostly Roman. It was the Roman city–before it became today's ruins–which Paul's quartet knew. The earliest temple of Apollo might have been one of the less significant buildings of the Roman city.

As Corinth grew in importance, it attracted people from many ethic and racial backgrounds. Among the newcomers were Jews, who established a synagogue. And to their synagogue, in his usual fashion, Paul and company went first with their message of Good News.

Like the Jews of Athens, the Jews of Corinth found themselves in the midst of temples and statues to divinities that appalled them. Hermes was worshipped there; so were Poseidon, Tyche, Apollo, Octavia (the Emperor's sister), the Emperor himself, Hera, Asclepius and Aphrodite.

In addition, gleaming white and seen as far away as Cenchrea, the Acrocorinth held the incomparable sanctuary of Aphrodite. It was so large that its cult employed a thousand prostitute priestesses as part of their "communion" in "worship." Nothing remains of this temple today, although archaeologists have placed an imitation cement pillar marker atop the high hill to show where it probably was situated.

Nearby this Acrocorinth temple of Aphrodite were several other shrines used by the mystery cults–Demeter, Artemis, Kore, the Moires, the Great Mother (Magna Mater), Helios, Serapis and Isis. Like Athenians, Paul found that the Corinthians were very religious.

The practices of worship at these temples suggest why Paul had to instruct the Corinthians on a proper celebration of the Lord's Supper. Some of these pagan "worship" activities involved coitus with the priestesses, symbolizing fertility, success. The cult of Artemis bedecked its idol with strings of bull's testicles, also to symbolize fertility. Followers of the cult of the Great Mother were washed in the blood of a slain bull. These

[378] 1 Corinthians 6:6–9

practices must have deeply irritated the Jews and God-fearers whose own circumscribed lifestyle sharply contrasted with those of the idolaters.

First to the Jews

Again Paul recognized the importance of first going to the Jews. They understood God as Spirit. They knew that God does not inhabit temples made with human hands and dedicated to empty deities.[379] God is neither limited to depictions made by fleshly forms, nor does he accede to desolate prayers offered from many frantic pilgrims who misunderstood the true meaning of communion.

Jews in Corinth also shared a dream of welcoming their long-awaited Messiah. Paul arrived to tell them that Messiah had been born, lived, died and was resurrected. His name was Jesus. That was Paul's Good News. That was what brought him to Corinth, as it had earlier to Neapolis, Philippi, Thessalonica, Berea, Athens and Cenchrea.

Paul's fortuity improved in Corinth. He met two Jews named Aquila and his wife Priscilla. They were Jews recently exiled from Rome by the Emperor. They may already have been mature believers. They also plied the same trade as Paul. They were *kosher*-obeying leatherworkers, awning or tentmakers. The trio had a ready market in Corinth. The traditional Isthmian games requiring such workers were held at the time Paul came to the city.[380]

This married couple, Diaspora Jews who had become Christians, fled Emperor Claudius' possible persecution in Rome about 49 AD. They established immediate roots in Corinth where they set about to instruct Jews and pagans alike about the Gospel, Jesus' death, resurrection and return. They were in Corinth not long before Paul arrived there. Priscilla, Aquila and Paul were both "leatherworkers" or "tentmakers," so the three had much in common.

Paul wrote that he was the "father" of the Corinthian church. Did he mean the founder? Paul was not the founder. His wording suggests that Paul saw himself as a father-figure to the Corinthians.

> *"I am writing this not to shame you but to warn you as my dear children. Even if you had 10,000 guardians in Christ, you do not have many fathers, for in Christ Jesus I became your father through the gospel. Therefore I urge you to imitate me. For this reason I have sent to you Timothy, my son whom I love, who is faithful in the Lord. He will remind you of my way of life in Christ Jesus, which agrees with what I teach everywhere in every church."[381]*

Surely Priscilla and Aquila must be considered in the patrimony of the Corinthian Church. They were present there prior to Paul. Who knows that sailors, soldiers or traders–especially traders–all contributed to founding the Church in Corinth? When the Apostle arrived in Corinth, Paul went to see the couple. The married pair had no ego problems. They did not look for credit or special authority. They demonstrated humility.

---

[379] 2 Chronicles 6:18
[380] James L. Kelso. op. cit., p 73
[381] 1 Corinthians 4:15

These two aides of Paul were acknowledged in four different New Testament books, Acts, Romans, 1 Corinthians, and 1 Timothy. The references were always complimentary, *"my fellow workers in Christ Jesus,"* *"All the churches of the Gentiles are grateful to them."*[382] Evidently, they hosted a meeting place for believers to study and worship, *"Aquila and Priscilla greet you warmly in the Lord and so does the church that meets in their home."*[383]

Scriptures are ambiguous about their faith backgrounds. What is definitely known is that Emperor Claudius deported Aquila and Priscilla from the Empire's capital. He had issued an edict that centred in a Jewish concern over the preaching of a "Chrestus." In Corinth,

> *"He met a Jew named Aquila, a native of Pontus, who had recently come from Italy with his wife Priscilla, because Claudius had ordered them to leave Rome. Paul went to see them, and because he was a tentmaker as they were, he stayed and worked with them."*[384]

There is also some suggestion for what Luke does not say. Luke makes no claim that Paul was the instrument God used to convert either Aquila or Priscilla. They moved from Rome to Corinth and were already mature believers. Priscilla appears to have been an equal partner with Aquila in both tentmaking and in discipling the early Christians in the Corinthian church.

Her active witness seems surprisingly overlooked in Paul's later instruction to the Corinthians that women should be silent in the church. *"Women should remain silent in the churches. They are not allowed to speak, but must be in submission . . ."*[385]

Paul writes in this first letter to Corinth, that Stephanas was an early convert. *"You know that the household of Stephanas were the first converts in Achaia, and they have devoted themselves to the service of the saints."*[386]

This implies that by the time Paul and the other three apostles entered Corinth, the seed of the Gospel had germinated and already was sprouting. Was this seed sown prepared by fertile ground tilled by soldiers, traders or sailors reaching Cenchrea? Paul himself said to the Corinthian Christians, *"I planted the seed, Apollos watered it, but God made it grow."*[387]

Paul's newly-found friends Aquila and Priscilla offered their home to Paul (maybe also to the other three). They may have introduced him to the synagogue. Once there, he used the Scripture to tell his understanding of the truth that Jesus was the Christ (Messiah). Luke notes that Paul was in the synagogue each Saturday. *"Every Sabbath he reasoned in the synagogue, trying to persuade Jews and Greeks."*[388] He ministered to both Jews and Greek God-fearers.

---

[382] Romans 16:4
[383] 1 Corinthians 16:19
[384] Acts 18:2–4
[385] 1 Corinthians 14:34 *ff*
[386] 1 Corinthians 16:15
[387] 1 Corinthians 3:6
[388] Acts 18:4

After the other two missionaries, Silas and Timothy, who had remained in Macedonia joined Paul and Luke, Paul apparently became exclusively a preacher and teacher. The other three supplemented his work. Does this also mean that he put aside his leather crafting trade? Yet his trade was also an opportunity to witness his beliefs.

Then to the Gentiles

Eventually Paul alienated some Jewish community members. This scenario reverberated everywhere he travelled. Perhaps he had a prickly personality or perhaps the Jewish network caught up with him once more. Paul then announced to them that he would no longer accept responsibility for these Jewish people's salvation. *"But when Jews opposed Paul and became abusive, he shook out his clothes in protest and said to them, 'Your blood be on your own heads. I am clear of my responsibility. From now on, I will go to the Gentiles.'"*[389] That threat was Paul's favourite rebuttal to unaccepting Jews.

"Your blood be upon your heads" is a favourite Jewish formula for bringing God's wrath upon them. It was a phrase Paul would utter again in Ephesus and Rome. It stemmed from an Old Testament prophecy in which God holds the prophet accountable for proclaiming the urgency of repentance to sinners.

> *"When I say to a wicked man, 'You will surely die,' and you do not warn him or speak out to dissuade him from his evil ways in order to save his life, that wicked man will die for his sin and I will hold you accountable for his blood."*[390]

At this point Paul announced that he would offer this Good News message no longer to Jews. If Jews did not want to hear about their anticipated Messiah, Paul would spend his energies with those who were interested–the Greeks. He gave a similar threat to Jews he met for the first time in Rome. He had said much the same after being rejected in Asia Minor a year or two earlier: *"Since you reject* [the word of God] *and do not consider yourselves worthy of eternal life, we now turn to the Gentiles."*[391]

Luke writes that Paul's decision received affirmation in two ways. One was a revelation from the Lord. In that vision God told Paul not to fear. The Lord said, "Keep on witnessing." The Lord assured Paul that many believers now dwelt in Corinth. *"The Lord spoke to Paul in a vision. 'Do not be afraid; keep on speaking; do not be silent. For I am with you and no one is going to harm you, because I have many people in the city' So Paul stayed for a year-and-a-half."*[392]

A second divine confirmation came through the converts he made. Titius Justus, a Gentile God-fearer who lived adjacent to the synagogue, offered Paul accommodation for his preaching ministry. Luke writes that the synagogue's president, Crispus, also became a believer in Jesus as Messiah and Saviour. Crispus' household members, like the households of the Philippian jailer and of Lydia, also believed and were baptized. So

---

[389] Acts 18:6
[390] Ezekiel 3:18
[391] Acts 13:26
[392] Acts 18:8–10

were "many others." Paul remained 18 months in Corinth. Corinth had become a fertile field for the Gospel.

The opposition to Paul's teaching in the local synagogue is recounted by Luke: *"Then Paul left the synagogue and went next door to the house of Titius Justus, a worshipper of God. Crispus, the synagogue ruler, and his entire household believed in the Lord; and many of the Corinthians who heard him believed and were baptized."*[393]

Luke pinpoints the time of Paul's ministry in Corinth. It happened while Gallio was proconsul of Achaia.[394] From an inscription found at Delphi, we know that Gallio was appointed to that office in 51 AD–in July, to be precise. Gallio was famous for his family, especially his brothers Mela and Seneca. Mela was the father of the popular poet Lucan; Seneca was renowned as the tutor of Nero and as a Stoic philosopher. Gallio himself had a reputation of being kindly and accommodating.

In Paul's case, Gallio was more than accommodating. He made a landmark legal decision that benefitted the Apostle and greatly affected the preaching of the Gospel in Achaia. Jews made a legal charge against Paul and petitioned Gallio that Paul had overreached his grasp. They argued that Paul was persuading people to worship God, against Roman law. Roman law required citizens and non-citizens alike to worship the divine Caesar. *"The Jews made a united attack on Paul and brought him into court. 'This man,' they charged, 'is persuading people to worship God in ways contrary to the law.'"*[395]

Gallio judged that the charge was mischievous, and of a religious nature, to be settled within Jewish tradition. He dismissed the case. *"Gallio said: 'If you Jews were making a complaint about some misdemeanor or serious crime, it would be reasonable for me to listen to you . . . Settle the matter yourselves. I will not be a judge of such things.'"*[396] Gallio would not even allow Paul to articulate a defence.[397]

The judgment was unwelcome to the plaintiffs. It led to a small riot. A group took Gallio's advice to "settle it yourselves" and assaulted the new president of the synagogue. *"So he had them ejected from the court. Then they all turned on Sosthenes the synagogue ruler and beat him in front of the court."*[398] (The synagogue ruler was the elected one who presided or moderated events at the synagogue).

Luke is ambiguous about who did what to whom. Did the Jews attack Sosthenes as a new Christian, because they could not get at Paul? Or was Sosthenes beaten because they had failed to make an adequate case against Paul? Since a Sosthenes is named later in the Scriptures as a believer perhaps the first suggestion is more likely. *"Paul, called to be an apostle of Christ by the will of God, and our brother Sosthenes . . ."*[399]

---

[393] Acts 18:7, 8
[394] Acts 18:12
[395] Acts 18:12
[396] Acts 18:13–15
[397] see John Pollock's <u>The Apostle: A Life of Paul</u>, p. 176
[398] Acts 18:16, 17
[399] 1 Corinthians 1:1

In rendering that decision, Gallio legalized Christian faith and practice–at least in Achaia. He acknowledged it as having a legitimate place in the community.[400]

The location of that trial and tribunal can be pinpointed today. In fact, visitors to the site can stand roughly where Paul would have stood, facing Gallio. The trial took place at the bema,[401] the platform immediately in front of the tribunal's location, at the South end of the Lechaion Road. As one walks Northward "down" from the bema, one can see strategic buildings of the Roman period of Corinth: the fountain house of Pirene, the propylaea, the baths, the public toilets, and the Julian Basilica (a former law court).

The Fullness of Time

Paul declared that God had clarified to him that from this point forward, his ministry would be focused on the Gentiles. What he had begun in small measure in Asia Minor as an outburst of his frustration, grew in Macedonia, then in Athens, and now became more clearly intentional for him in Corinth.

In a later letter to the Christians in Galatia, Paul used a phrase which sums up what had happened to this point–"*in the fullness of time . . .*"[402] This instructive phrase describes how in God's eternal plan the prophecy of Isaiah came true: "*It is too small a thing for you to be my servant to restore the tribes of Jacob and bring back those of Israel I have kept. I will also make you a light for the Gentiles that you may bring my salvation to the ends of the earth.*"[403]

Somehow, this prophetic statement was focused here in Corinth. The world's common language at the time was Greek. As noted earlier in this document, the Greek language was the means by which Paul could preach anywhere. The road and sea transportation systems enabled Roman citizens to travel relatively safely and rapidly.

As a Roman citizen, Paul enjoyed the privileges of Empire. As a Jew, he understood the *Torah* law in its fullest detail. The Pax Romana meant that unhindered travel was available to these missionaries. Even the Roman law now protected the preaching of the Good News in Corinth.[404] It was, as Paul wrote, "*the fullness of time*"[405] as was noted earlier in a reference to Vergina. Philip II and his son Alexander contributed unwittingly to the furtherance of the Gospel by creating a Greek-speaking world.

All these factors, language, relative peace, travel, dissemination of print, inter-conducted, coming uniquely together to suit God's purposes of salvation for the world. "*In the fullness of time*," or as the NIV puts it, "*When the time had fully come, God sent his Son, born of a woman.*" Paul plays with the words "fully come" to emphasize the developing pregnancy of and delivery by Mary, who birthed Jesus.

---

[400] Nicos Papahatzis. <u>Ancient Corinth</u>. p. 57

[401] Nicos Papahatzis. <u>op</u>. <u>cit</u>., see map. p. 49

[402] Galatians 4:4

[403] Isaiah 49:6

[404] Acts 18:16

[405] Galatians 4:4; see also Ephesians 1:9–11

The word for "time" (*chronos*)[406] in this Galatian passage refers to linear, measured or chronological time. It can also be translated as "era," or "epoch," or what is denoted as a major historical event in cosmic history. Cronos (sic), a Titan, was the Greek deity in charge of time; in Rome he was titled Saturn. This deity devoured all his children except Jupiter, Neptune and Pluto.

"Thus Saturn," records Thomas Bullfinch, "who devours all his children is the same power whom the Greeks called Cronos (Time) which may be said to destroy whatever it has brought into existence."[407] Ergo "now" becomes "past" as soon as "now" is born. "Past" destroys "future" as soon as it appears. The line between past and future is nano-thin; at "present's" inception it is dead. Paul does not assign the meanings of Cronos and Saturn to this passage. But time is not a factor in Jesus' permanence. As stated in Hebrews, "*Jesus Christ is the same yesterday, today and forever.*"[408]

By referencing Jesus birth to chronological "human" time, Paul echoed what John's Gospel stated in its prologue–"*The Word was made flesh and dwelt among us.*"[409] Jesus lived among humankind! Paul underlines the truth that the kingdom of God has come, is now and is coming. Jesus is past, present and future. Or, as some officiators say when celebrating the Eucharist (communion), "This is the mystery of our faith: Christ has died. Christ is risen. Christ will come again." Note Paul's word to Colossae: *Kaì aùtós éstin pro pántōn kaì tà pánta èn aùtō synestéken*–"*He is before all things and in him (Christ) all things hold together.*"[410] Christ is the centre of everything!

"Time," as Paul uses the word, is God's unique exactly-timed intervention in human history that came with Jesus' birth–and with Saul's conversion.

We also are grateful to Paul, writing to Corinth with a universal truth for all time (not just the moment!):

> "*And now I will show you a more excellent way. If I speak in the tongues of men or of angels, but do not have love, I am only a resounding gong or a clanging cymbal. If I have the gift of prophecy and can fathom all mysteries and all knowledge, and if I have a faith that can move mountains, but do not have love, I am nothing. If I give all I possess to the poor and give over my body to hardship that I may boast, but do not have love, I gain nothing.*
> "*Love is patient, love is kind. It does not envy, it does not boast, it is not proud. It does not dishonour others, it is not self-seeking, it is not easily angered, it keeps no record of wrongs. Love does not delight in evil but rejoices with the truth. It always protects, always trusts, always hopes, always perseveres.*
> "*Love never fails. But where there are prophecies, they will cease; where there are tongues, they will be stilled; where there is knowledge, it will pass away. For we know in part and we prophesy in part, but when completeness comes, what is*

---

[406] See Mark 1:15 [*kairos*, not *chronos* –another Greek word for time, as used by Mark 1:15, i.e., God's special announcement of his purposes being fulfilled in the imminent "Kingdom of God," proclaimed by Jesus]
[407] Thomas Bullfinch. Mythology, p. 301
[408] Hebrews 13:8
[409] John 1:14
[410] Colossians 1:17

in part disappears. When I was a child, I talked like a child, I thought like a child, I reasoned like a child. When I became a man, I put the ways of childhood behind me. For now we see only a reflection as in a mirror; then we shall see face to face. Now I know in part; then I shall know fully, even as I am fully known.

"And now these three remain: faith, hope and love. But the greatest of these is love."[411]

The continuing maturing Paul placed love above all virtues. "We may be certain that he always advised love," wrote E. P. Sanders of Paul. "especially love of fellow Christians (1 Thess. 4:10; Gal. 13, 6:10) and that he urged his hearers to live by the Spirit and to abstain from evil and immortality."[412]

No one should be surprised to read the Twentieth Century psychoanalyst (logotherapist) Viktor Frankl agree with Paul:

"Love is the only way to grasp another human being in the innermost core of his personality. No one can become fully aware of the very essence of another human being unless he loves him. By his love he is enabled to see the essential traits and features in the beloved person; and even more, he sees that which is potential in him, which is not yet actualized but yet ought to be actualized. Furthermore, by his love, the loving person enables the beloved person to actualize these potentialities. By making him aware of what he can be and of what he should become, he makes these potentialities come true."[413]

C. S. Lewis, another Twentieth Century observer of unconditional love, pointed out that love calls for vulnerability. Paul allowed himself to be weak. *"That is why, for Christ's sake, I delight in weaknesses,"* the Apostle wrote, *"in insults, in hardships, in persecutions, in difficulties. For when I am weak, then I am strong."*[414] Note an observation by C. S. Lewis:

"To love at all is to be vulnerable. Love anything and your heart will be wrung and possibly broken. If you want to make sure of keeping it intact you must give it to no one, not even an animal. Wrap it carefully round with hobbies and little luxuries; avoid all entanglements. Lock it up safe in the casket or coffin of your selfishness. But in that casket, safe, dark, motionless, airless, it will change. It will not be broken; it will become unbreakable, impenetrable, irredeemable. To love is to be vulnerable."[415]

---

[411] 1 Corinthians 12:30–13:13
[412] E. P. Sanders. <u>Paul,</u> p. 103
[413] Viktor E. Frankl. <u>Man's Search for Meaning</u>. p 104
[414] 2 Corinthians 12:10
[415] C. S. Lewis. <u>The Four Loves</u>. p. 169

CHAPTER TWENTY
AGAMEMNON AND MYCENAE

Most tourists today will surely visit the ruins of Mycenae. Did Paul or Luke, Timothy or Silas take time during their 18 months in Corinth to walk a day's journey Southward, to one of the great cities of Greek history, especially of the poet Homer's literary history?

Mycenae is unimportant in biblical history. Yet it certainly was an important community for the Greeks in Paul's time. Because of Homer's Iliad, the story of Mycenae's role in the Trojan War was known to all Greek schoolchildren.

Surely Paul, someone exceedingly familiar with Greek philosophers, would have read Homer's striking saga. The epic describes, in part, the exploits of King Agamemnon, who led the fight against Troy. Moreover, Troas, the port from which Paul's troupe sailed to Macedonia, lies somewhat near (Southwest of) the ancient city of Troy. The community Troas derives its name from ancient Troy. Paul would not have been ignorant about Homer or Mycenae, especially if Luke's early residence was in Tarsus.

Mycenae dominated Greek history for over a millennium earlier. Though the name Mycenae may be unfamiliar to some, surely everyone had heard of the "Trojan Horse" built by the Mycenaeans as a clever ruse to enter Troy and seize it. The Trojan Horse was one episode in the ongoing wars between Mycenae and Troy. King Agamemnon of Mycenae appears to be a contemporary of Moses–although the dates of both leaders are inexact. Nevertheless, the mythical–if it is mythical–Trojan Horse may have been constructed about the time when Moses was attempting to free the Hebrew people from the power of Pharaoh in Egypt.

Mycenae reached its zenith during this time and left its impression on most of Greece, before fading into such obscurity that for centuries Homer's Iliad was considered to be a mixture of legend and fiction. Now Mycenae is laid bare by excavations for all to see its majestic keystone Lion Gate and royal tombs. Was Mycenae's beehive tomb the actual burial place of Agamemnon? Were the gold burial masks on display in Athens' National Museum really the death masks of Agamemnon and his offspring?[416]

The self-taught archaeologist Heinrich Schliemann explored these ruins in 1876 and offered his answers–likely they were. Later archaeologists disputed some of his conclusions and correctly severely criticized his scientific methods.

---

[416] S. E. Iakovidis. Mycenae–Epidaurus p. 61

CHAPTER TWENTYONE

EPIDAUROS, CAESAREA AND ANTIOCH

Had Paul or his friends hiked a further two days South from Mycenae, they would have reached Epidauros. Luke would have found it interesting because of its medical reputation. Such a visit was unlikely, of course. Had they travelled there, they would have visited a shrine centred around and dedicated to the healing deity Asclepius. This ancient sanctuary may have been "the largest healing centre of antiquity."[417]

This mythological deity was believed to be the son of Apollo. In turn, Asclepius, goes the legend, was schooled by the centaur Cheiron, who was wise and skilled. He taught Asclepius the arts of surgery and medicine. It was said of Asclepius that his powers were so great that he could resurrect the dead. This conjecture was in opposition to the general Greek tenet that discounted bodily resurrection. His powers, however, attracted the jealousy of Zeus who killed Asclepius with a thunderbolt. The dead deity, relates the legend, was buried at Epidauros.

Modern medicine copies something connected to this mythical god. A staff and a snake symbolized him and are emblems that still continue to herald healing today. In some centres of Asclepius worship, such as Epidauros and Pergamum, the sick and the devotees would lie on the sanctuary's surface and allow serpents to slither over them. This was therapy! For some it worked, especially when used with priestly positive pronouncements like, "You are getting better."

In Epidauros, the sick made offerings to the priests of the god, then slept on the skins of the animals that had been sacrificed to the deity. They believed that Asclepius would appear to them in dreams and heal them. Many healings were attributed to this cult centred in Epidauros. Apparently, even 2,500 years ago, medical priests understood much about psychosomatic illness, functional disorders, and the power of suggestion.

Like many other Greek cities, Epidauros held athletic games. Given the cult centred there, these were known as the Asclepiad Games.[418] The sports events were held every four years. Ruins of a racing track may be observed at the archaeological excavations.

The most astonishing element of Epidauros is none of these; it is the theatre.[419] Built 400 years before Paul's missionary beachhead into Europe, it holds 14,000 spectators in 55 rows, and boasts almost perfect acoustics. Even in the highest row, spectators can hear paper crumpled, a match lit, a coin dropped–and perfect enunciation of actors' lines–when these things are done centre stage.

Dramas performed in the theatre were related to the healing cult's activities. Medical priests and magistrates occupied the front rows. Devotion was offered to Asclepius and to Dionysos.

---

[417] S. E. Iakovidis, op. cit., p. 127
[418] S. E. Iakovidis. op. cit., p. 145
[419] S. E. Iakovidis. Mycenae–Epidaurus. op. cit., p. 130

Even if he didn't visit Epidauros, Paul would have been interested because of the resurrection myth about Asclepius and of the healings attributed to him. Certainly Luke, the physician, would have been curious too. Together, Paul and Luke could have used the connection to declare Jesus' resurrection and the redeeming, saving health he gave to humankind by the forgiveness of sin.

While no one really knows if Paul or Luke went to Epidauros (likely not!) modern tourists will miss a unique site if it is left off their itinerary. In Epidauros, an important centre in Greek history, we gain an insight into the Greeks' struggle for knowledge and understanding. The architecture gives witness of the advanced skills and abilities of Paul's time and what he had to deal with–and adjust his style to meet a need.

But Paul, with Luke, and perhaps others, probably skipped Mycenae and Epidauros. From Cenchraea, Paul and Luke headed to Caesarea and then to Antioch, reported to the Antiochenes, and soon returned to Ephesus on another mission. We have a significant insight into Paul's personality. Whatever the vow he made, he was adamant in attaining it. His was an earnest oath, not to be distracted once he zeroed in on his objective. Paul was locked in to conclude his vow. The oath preoccupied Paul. Once the commitment was completed, he had time for other pressing matters. But his vow was an immutable agreement with God. In that matter, Paul could not be moved. With the vow completed, Paul was spiritually healthy once more and able to move on.

Paul, accompanied by Luke, tramped inland, revisiting their charges in Galatia, "*strengthening the disciples.*"[420] Luke and Paul must have visited myriad small house church communities between Antioch and Ephesus–and it was an arduous trek of several weeks. Yet, he had the opportunity to visit and meet people along the way some of whom may already have known Christ as Saviour and Lord, and some who were ripe for conversion.

In Ephesus, Paul explained to the native Alexandrian Apollos, that he needed to know the Spirit's baptism (see the next chapter). That accomplished, Paul and Apollos traded places; while Apollos moved to Corinth, Paul advanced to Ephesus, a main community whose emerging church gave leadership to other growing churches inland.

---

[420] Acts 18:23

CHAPTER TWENTY–TWO
EVANGELIZING EPHESUS

Leaving Old Mission Stations

Paul returned from his European mission experiences to visit Ephesus briefly. He left Corinth with his two special instructors, Priscilla and Aquila.

Silas is not mentioned. They had been of enormous assistance to him while he sojourned for 18 months or more in Corinth. They brought their valued experiences in teaching and discipling to the burgeoning Corinthian Church. They added a maturity and stability which Paul and Silas desperately needed in maturing the adolescent Corinthian congregation.

That was especially essential possibly because of the influx of previously immoral temple devotees of Aphrodite, now converts (to whom Paul had advised to, *"keep silent in the churches"*).[421]

Or, perhaps Paul was addressing the phenomenon of glossolalia, where women were speaking in strange tongues without an interpreter as he insisted.[422]

Or, maybe the newly converted women, unaccustomed to a Jewish style synagogue "service" where men set and manipulated the agenda, spent their time disrespectfully yakking while disrupting any semblance of assembly propriety as worship progressed from praise through testimony to biblical exegesis and exhortation.

Or, maybe the Corinthian women added their "two cents' worth" to a *Torah* discussion about which they were mostly relatively ignorant, not having studied as the males would have done. Paul fretted that the new Corinthian believers did not understand that appropriate decorum was a sign of a stable church and church doctrine must conform everywhere.

Theological opinion must always give way to exacting exegesis. Wrote Paul, *"Everything should be done in a fitting and orderly way."*[423] We do know this: Priscilla, a woman who helped Paul both in Corinth and in Ephesus, was not "silent" in her ministry to the Corinthian and Ephesian churches. Her voice was essential to the Gospel work. Paul didn't forbid Priscilla either to speak or to teach (including men!).

Paul and Silas needed all the help they could get to help grow this adolescent congregation. Probably that explains why Paul spent so much time in Corinth, given his usual short-term evangelistic thrusts. Certainly Phoebe, the leader of the church in Cenchraea (some 16 kilometres Southeast) was not silent in that community's church and it appears unlikely she depended on a husband to explain things to her as Paul taught.[424]

---

[421] 1 Corinthians 14:34
[422] 1 Corinthians 14:27
[423] 1 Corinthians 14:40
[424] 1 Corinthians 14:35

Paul's Vow

The Southeastern cobbled road's trek to Corinth's Southern port of Cenchraea was a steady half-day's journey, circling around the soaring 575-meter Acrocorinth (Corinth's mound rising about 1,600 feet) to the wharves on Cenchraea's bay, also dubbed the "Bath of Helen."

Phoebe was the spiritual leader of the now-formed, spin-off (?) from the Corinth church at Cenchraea. As we noted, Paul called Phoebe a *diakonos* (deacon, minister, servant, sometimes translated "officer") who was very helpful to Paul.[425] Having reached that port, Paul completed an unknown and unreported vow, by shaving his head.[426] This act conveyed to everyone that now he had fulfilled the obligations of his private, undisclosed oath except one. The Apostle needed to finalize his sworn accountability within the House of the Lord in Jerusalem.

What was the vow? Who knows for certain? It may have been a Nazarite vow. The vow may have had to do with a form of ritual purity, such as touching a dead body. It is completed with an appropriate visit to the Temple in Jerusalem (and before that, the Tabernacle). Paul's detractors often claimed he was abandoning his insistence that Jews and Gentiles are the same, but here he was obeying a *Torah* requirement! Paul is not inconsistent here. He simply is deferring to a *Torah* instruction that is unrelated to the issue of salvation, and would not have insisted that Gentiles needed to observe it.

Then he, together with his precious partners Aquila and Priscilla, set sail on a convenient cargo carrier headed to Ephesus. Paul's immediate business was not in Ephesus. He left his friends to walk from the delta's dockside along the Caystor River in Ephesus while he caught a ship or connecting merchantman setting sail for Caesarea Maritima and ultimately, Jerusalem.

In Jerusalem's great Temple, Paul would have sealed his Nazarite vow.[427] With his obligation to the covenant completed, Paul felt he could return to his mission activity. Obviously, he understood that his first need was to his own spiritual pledge; that explains his quick visit to Jerusalem's Temple. Later,[428] Paul made an offering payment for others who also had made a vow similar to his.

As noted in the previous chapter, Paul soon returned to his Syrian Antioch Church base and subsequently to visit his Galatian churches. How he loved them! Luke records[429] that Paul spent some quality and quantity time in Antioch. He likely needed updating with his Christian friends. They may also have enriched him by prayer and study together.

You can't be "on the road" all the time without spiritual and physical replenishment. Apostles also needed ingrowth as well as giving output. Paul needed such refreshment. He was "on furlough," as mission boards like to describe missionaries when

---

[425] Romans 16:1
[426] Acts 18:18
[427] Numbers 6:1–21
[428] Acts 21:6
[429] Acts 18:21

they return to share their stories with those who commissioned them. It was again time for Paul's further spiritual renewal.

After Paul's spiritual sustenance, he sensed the divine urge and pastoral responsibility to revisit congregations in Perga, Pisidian Antioch, Iconium, Derbe and Lystra—"*from place to place, throughout the region of Galatia and Phrygia, strengthening all the disciples.*"[430]

Luke does not tell his readers what happened to Timothy. Timothy had joined Paul and Silas from his hometown of Lystra, to travel as the Lord led them. He had proven himself as a valuable team member in Thessalonika and Corinth but Luke gives no evidence that he accompanied Paul to Ephesus, Caesarea and Jerusalem. Luke, however, must have accompanied Paul.

That single journey was Paul's private undertaking, Luke excepted. Did Timothy return to Lystra to undergird the church there? We don't know. What we do know is that if Timothy was not immediately at Paul's right hand, he was always "on call."[431] Neither Paul nor his associates gave less than a full account of themselves. As Paul told the church at Corinth, "*I run with purpose in every step.*"[432] (NIV: "*I do not run like a man running aimlessly; I do not fight like a man beating the air*").

In due time, his need for pastoral work in these inland communities completed, the Apostle took an "interior route"[433] arriving in Ephesus to meet other challenges. His close friends Aquila and Priscilla were already there, perhaps with God-consigned mission-minds to share the Gospel in that great city.

These two had already proven their worth in Ephesus. They found an eloquent man teaching about Jesus who did not fully understand the Gospel. Apollos was an Alexandrian Jew who oddly did not know about or receive the Holy Spirit, even though he knew about Jesus. Apollos zeroed in on the Jewish contingent in Ephesus, doing much more than an unemotional, routine, ritual cleansing in a *mikveh* or the "living water" of a flowing stream, but urging an immersion in water as a genuine, heart-felt act of true repentance.

Apollos was rooted in John the Baptist's preaching of repentance. He was also entrenched in the Jewish interpretative style of allegory taught and practised by Philo. But repentance was only part of the Gospel. Paul's friends Aquila and Priscilla knew they must correct what Apollos was inaccurately teaching and preaching. Luke writes about his misunderstanding of the Gospel. Priscilla and Aquila "*invited him into their home and explained to him the way of God more adequately.*"[434] Apollos rejoiced in the correction. Luke does not record his "Christian" baptism.

With his skewed theology now corrected, Apollos indicated a strong desire to journey to Achaia to serve the church at Corinth. The Christians at Ephesus gladly

---

[430] Acts 18:23
[431] Acts 19:21
[432] 1 Corinthians 9:26a NLT
[433] Acts 19:21
[434] Acts 18:26

endorsed such a ministry and forwarded an introductory letter to the Corinthian Church with their imprimatur.[435] Apparently he was well-received in Corinth, so much so, that he took on a "star" importance.

Paul tried to correct the Corinthian cult of stardom in a letter to the Corinthian Church.

> *"My brothers and sisters, some from Chloe's household have informed me that there are quarrels among you. What I mean is this: one of you says, 'I follow Paul'; another, 'I follow Apollos'; another, 'I follow Cephas'; still another, 'I follow Christ.' Is Christ divided? Was Paul crucified for you? Were you baptized in the name of Paul?"*[436]

Paul returned to Ephesus after his "follow-up" pastoral call to his church infants in Asia and Europe. He maintained his usual method of beginning in a synagogue. It is likely that Ephesus had only one *shul* (synagogue), because Jews normally were reticent to perambulate in the city centre so replete with myriad statues of mythical pagan gods.

Nonetheless, a synagogue existed in this major city and Paul knew intrinsically where to find it, perhaps on the outskirts, and likely close to a water source where Jews could ritually immerse themselves before their worship activities. A meeting place for observant Jews necessitated some kind of water pool or flowing stream. Jewish rules insisted that preparatory washing and immersion precede worship, prayer and study activities. He would know its location anyway, because Paul's friends Priscilla and Aquila were already ministering in Ephesus.

Paul first had some theological "care-taking" with a dozen followers of Apollos who had not fully known the atonement that Jesus achieved on the cross.

About dozen of them needed correction even though Priscilla and Aquila taught Apollos the Gospel truth. The 12 people only knew John's baptism of repentance. Paul wasted no time in explaining that baptism in the name of Jesus, succeeds and trumps the repentance baptism of John "the Baptist." When they thus acknowledged Jesus' death, baptism and resurrection, the dozen converts received proper baptism and the gift of the Holy Spirit.

Paul and the Ephesian Synagogue

Then Paul attended to matters related to the synagogue. A big difference exists between the function of the synagogue in Paul's time and today. Five years after Paul's death, the Jerusalem Temple was fully destroyed, so some functions of the former Temple life have been reinterpreted for today's synagogues, i.e., sacrifices, which are now replaced by prayers. The work of the priests changed as well, since priests (*kohanim*) no longer shed sacrificial blood as an act of atonement for sins. Yet Jews continue to remember the Day of Atonement (*Yom Kippur*) with exceptional reverence even if many do not believe in the need of atonement.

---

[435] Acts 18:27
[436] 1 Corinthians 1:11–13

A form of synagogue began during the Jewish exile, when Jews were without a Temple and rued their loss.

> *"How can we sing the songs of the LORD while in a foreign land? If I forget you, O Jerusalem, may my right hand forget its skill. May my tongue cling to the roof of my mouth if I do not remember you, if I do not consider Jerusalem my highest joy. Remember, O LORD, what the Edomites did on the day Jerusalem fell. 'Tear it down,' they cried, 'tear it down to its foundations!'"*[437]

When Jews returned from their Babylonian captivity and when many Jews became part of a Diaspora, synagogues developed more fully. They became the main teaching places for God's people to learn their biblical instructions. As synagogues grew in numbers and vitality, rabbis grew in authority too. Soon the oral law led to different schools shepherded by differing interpreters.

The Greek word *synagoge* when translated into Hebrew is *beyt knesset*, the house of assembly. It is the same word for the current Israeli Legislature. Like the once central Jerusalem Temple, it is a "house of prayer" (*beyt t'fila*). Jesus called the Jerusalem Temple a house of prayer for *all* nations.[438] But it is more than that. Unlike the Temple, a synagogue requires a *minyan*, i.e., 10 Jews to congregate. It celebrates the *Torah*, i.e., the five books which contain Moses' law.

In most synagogues, when the Ark containing the *Torah* is opened among the *minyan*, the people rise as an act of respect. Those offering prayers usually face toward Jerusalem. Scriptures are read from a form of lectionary that congregants will study, especially on *Shabbat*. Worshippers recite the *Shema*.[439] *Torah* divides into 54 sections (and correlated readings from the Prophets), so that a section read every *Shabbat* allows a systematic reading for the entire year. In many synagogues prayers are an on-going ritual, offered three times daily–but some require a *minyan* to be recited legitimately.

Paul arrived in the engaging Ephesian synagogue with this extensive heritage and rich background. The *shul* was a quasi-democratic institution, moderated by an elected president allowing participants to offer explanations of the text for each day. In the book of Ecclesiastes, this president is called "preacher" or "teacher" (Hebrew: *Koheleth*).

That sanction for clarifying *Torah* and Prophets gave Paul three months' of exegesis and interpretation of the biblical truths as highlighted by Jesus' life and work. Synagogues were open to prayers and teaching on days other than *Shabbat*, and Paul also exploited that opportunity. That was something of a record for Paul; in Thessalonika he expounded for only three weeks. As Luke records, the *"obstinate"* unbelievers in the local synagogue *"publicly maligned The Way."*[440]

Paul, however, saw his critics as having tunnel vision. They opposed him but were not enemies. They lacked an insight into their purpose in life. Later, Paul wrote to the Ephesians to clarify their purpose and the role that God had given them. *"It is God himself who has made us what we are and given us new lives from Christ Jesus; and long*

---

[437] Psalm 137:4–7
[438] Mark 11:17
[439] Deuteronomy 6:3–5
[440] Acts 19:9

ages ago he planned that we should spend these lives in helping others."[441] This is a measure of Paul's healthy response to God's dealing with humanity.

One of Paul's teaching tenets was that the Gospel of Jesus included Gentiles. "*Is God the God of Jews only? Is he not the God of Gentiles too? Yes, of Gentiles too, since there is only one God, who will justify the circumcised by faith and the uncircumcised through that same faith.*"[442]

Paul used no double standard in his teaching. He also taught that, "*There will be trouble and distress for every human being who does evil: first for the Jew, then for the Gentile; but glory, honour and peace for everyone who does good: first for the Jew, then for the Gentile. For God does not show favouritism.*"[443] These instructions would not sit well with some Hellenistic Jews.

Paul did not neglect sacred days. He kept Sabbath but was open to others worshipping on Sundays (the first day of the week). Why not worship God every day? In Jerusalem, the first believers visited the Temple daily[444] but they had a special assemblage each Sunday to celebrate Jesus' resurrection.

Paul shows this keeping of the Lord's memorial when he also remembered what Jesus commanded his disciples to do,[445] i.e., remember Jesus' work on the cross, his resurrection and his promised return.

To Corinth, Paul instructed the church to gather their offerings on the first day of the week (Sunday)[446] The early Christians, not obliged as were Jews to celebrate their worship in a synagogue on Saturdays, had moved to a celebration of Jesus' resurrection each Sunday. Sometimes they met in homes.[447]

The "worship day" issue must have mattered in Rome. To the Roman church Paul wrote, "*One person considers one day more sacred than another; another considers every day alike. Each of them should be fully convinced in their own mind. Whoever regards one day as special does so to the Lord.*"[448]

Paul is ambivalent on this matter. That is a sign of Paul's developed "wellness." A rigid Pharisee would never have been that tolerant of such Gentile ambivalence.

The Lecture Hall

Paul would not have been shocked to be evicted from his synagogue endeavours. Expulsion was old hat to him. The Apostle always knew that God would provide a Plan B for him. The better alternative included a new and superior location, probably more

---

[441] Ephesians 2:10 TLB
[442] Romans 3:29, 30
[443] Romans 2:9–11
[444] Acts 2:46
[445] Acts 20:7; 1 Corinthians 16:2
[446] 1 Corinthians 16:2
[447] Philemon v. 2; Romans 16:5
[448] Romans 14:6; 1 Corinthians 8:3 ("*The man who loves God is known by God*")

central and ethnically neutral building for Paul's lectures and evangelism. He negotiated a daily, two-year lease.

Tyrannus, a Greek Philosopher,[449] was a citizen of Ephesus who owned a school and adequate facilities for Paul when he was evicted from the Ephesian synagogue. Tyrannus Hall was more than suitable for Paul to teach and instruct interested parties. It was neutral territory for Jews and Gentiles alike. Whether Tyrannus was a believer is uncertain but he had no compunction in allowing Paul to instruct Christians using some of his facilities.

Most modern tourists who to travel to Greece or Turkey will appreciate that most Mediterranean entrepreneurs open their shops about 7:00 am, and build into a daily agenda some pause time (siesta?) ranging from approximately 11:00 am to 4:00 pm. Businesses shutter for these five hours and re-open until a 9:00 pm dinner time at home. Mideastern heat is a factor in the mid-day extended power nap and refreshment period.

Tyrannus' Lecture Hall likely would have been available to Paul, maybe cheaply. The non-business hours during midday were perfect for Paul's purposes. Kelso cited a Codex D stating that Paul spoke from the fifth hour to the tenth."[450] The Apostle may have needed to ply his tent-making trade during the other hours. Paul seized the God-given ideal opportunity and turned it into a "school of evangelism and training" for two full years.[451]

Ephesian Ministries

The three years Paul spent in Ephesus generated solid productivity. That Priscilla and Aquila worked alongside him was good symbiosis–synergy. Miracles became obvious among the believers and sceptics alike, sometimes through peculiar methods with atypical results.

What is clear is that many people did not understand that only God had the power to heal and he did it through the Apostle Paul. Earlier in Acts,[452] Luke recounts that some Jerusalemites brought their sick to the disciples *"so that at least Peter's shadow might fall on them as he passed by."* This likewise was a misunderstanding of the cause of healing, yet it was still an act of their faith.

> *"God did extraordinary miracles through Paul, so that even handkerchiefs and aprons that had touched him were taken to the sick, and their illnesses were cured and the evil spirits left them.*
> *Some Jews who went around driving out evil spirits tried to invoke the name of the Lord Jesus over those who were demon-possessed. They would say, "In the name of the Jesus whom Paul preaches, I command you to come out." Seven sons of Sceva, a Jewish chief priest, were doing this. One day the evil spirit answered them, 'Jesus I know, and Paul I know about, but who are you?' Then the man*

---

[449] James L. Kelso. op. cit., p. 77
[450] James L. Kelso. ibid.
[451] Acts 19:8–10
[452] Acts 5:15

who had the evil spirit jumped on them and overpowered them all. He gave them such a beating that they ran out of the house naked and bleeding.
When this became known to the Jews and Greeks living in Ephesus, they were all seized with fear, and the name of the Lord Jesus was held in high honour. Many of those who believed now came and openly confessed what they had done. A number who had practised sorcery brought their scrolls together and burned them publicly. When they calculated the value of the scrolls, the total came to fifty thousand drachmas. In this way the word of the Lord spread widely and grew in power."[453]

The Silversmiths

Actions are always met with reactions. It is a fact of life. It is also Isaac Newton's Third Law. So, when many of Ephesus' citizenry ceased to believe in idols, the idol makers lost both business and income. The main idol in Ephesus was the mythical deity Artemis. She was revered as mother deity of the city, because they believed she founded the city, giving birth to it.

These moon worshippers of Ephesus saw her also as overseeing childbirth and the hunt, protector of virgins and alleviator of women's diseases. Her statue in the once world-famous temple, showed a woman with many breasts (some argue, eggs, some argue, testicles!), in other words, fertility symbols. One can imagine that anyone responsible for fecundity (read success) is not to be derided or despised but adopted and adored.

The Temple of Artemis was an admiration of the ancient world. The locals thought their deity's idol likeness had fallen from the sky, perhaps from their sighting a meteor.[454] Ephesians erected a glorious temple and sanctified it to her. The *temenos* (sanctuary) existing in Paul's time was the decaying third iteration of the temple. A flood destroyed the first temple, then it was rebuilt. The second temple was burned by an arsonist. The new version was a world wonder, some considering it to be among the official "seven wonders of the ancient world."

At its most beautiful, it displayed 127 large columns each at a height of almost 60 feet (17.5 meters) tall. The high roof protected the idol. Goths had destroyed much of the temple by the time Paul arrived, so the locals were very prickly about anyone dissing their favourite deity. Today, only one pillar of the temple remains and it teeters precariously in a swamp.

Copies of the idol were a financial resource to the city's silversmiths who made replicas of the idol for local homes. They were amulets for myriad blessings, such as good hunting, successful marriages, booming births, financial proliferation and copious crops. Silversmiths not only protested their losses of income due to Paul's preaching but they objected to the perceived disparaging of their matronly goddess.

---

[453] Acts 19:11–20
[454] Acts 19:35

The Riot

The silversmiths, led by a trade spokesman, Demetrius, connected the loss of sales directly to the teachings of The Way, especially to Paul. Trades formed unions or guilds, and likely the silversmith craftsman's guild's deity was Artemis to whom they paid faithful obeisance at their monthly meetings (monthly, because this was a moon-worshipping society). Thus, as their household miniature idol sales slackened, they concluded that Paul was denigrating their patron. Hence they created a riot.

The silversmiths excelled at fomenting the civil disorder. The populace streamed into Ephesus' 25,000-seat theatre and intoned chants to Artemis. *"Great is Artemis of the Ephesians,"* they chanted in synchronized voice[455] for two hours. They claimed not only that Paul had diminished the stature of Artemis but that this would ultimately discount the celebrated reputation of the city around the Mediterranean world.

The city clerk intervened to calm the protesters after two hours of focussed intoning. He told them that Paul had said nothing against the city's god. Paul was completely innocent of the accusation. No one in the crowd dared to bring formal charges against Paul or the two captured colleagues. The city clerk dismissed the masses. Paul edged down Harbour Street, slipping from the waterfront on a vessel, aware that the Gospel foundation could be damaged if he tried to re-enter Ephesus.[456]

Paul was now nowhere to be found. But officials grabbed two of his close travelling and teaching associates, Gaius and Aristarchus, and brought them into the Great Theatre of Ephesus. The mob also pushed Alexander to the stage area of the theatre.

Paul had heard the roar and wanted to join his colleagues but wiser friends, some Roman officials whom Paul knew, but not from a faith standpoint, stepped in. They would not allow it. They begged him to not intervene.

They told him the time had come for Paul to leave Ephesus. Paul's associates found transport for him to reach Macedonia.[457] Paul had already sent Timothy and Erastus to Greece, so it was a good destination for him too. Paul may have sent the two to Greece to collect an offering from Gentiles which Paul could deliver to the needy Jewish Jerusalem Church. It is possible.

Paul's Farewell Tour

Timothy and Erastus helped Paul avoid trouble in Macedonia too. An ambush awaited him in Greece, but he heard about it. Some of the disciples agreed to meet him in Troas about the Passover time.

After sailing five days from Philippi or its port Neapolis, Paul arrived at Troas. Here his friends gathered and encouraged each other. Paul stayed a week in Troas.

---

[455] Acts 19:29
[456] Acts 19:31, 32
[457] Acts 20:1

Luke specifically mentions that on the first day of the week the church family of Troas met to celebrate communion. The practice of keeping the Lord's Supper or Eucharist on a Sunday had by now been firmly established among early Christians.

Paul had much to say. He was still sermonizing at midnight when a young man fell from a niche at the third floor of the building in which they met.[458] Eutychus was deemed to be dead but Paul wrapped himself around the youth, and told the audience that he was still alive.

Eutychus was aptly named, meaning "fortunate." Indeed he was fortunate; he fell while listening to Paul's overextended sermon from a wall niche by the third floor of the large building. He was not the last person to sleep during a sermon, but "fortunately" not all suffered the same results as Eutychus.

The result of his "deep sleep," as Luke writes, was that, *"He fell to the ground from the third story and was picked up dead. Paul went down, threw himself on the young man, and put his arms around him. 'Don't be alarmed,' he said. 'He's alive!' . . . People took the young man home alive and were greatly comforted."*[459] Trust it to a physician to relate this episode. Paul and Luke cared.

Paul set his agenda to arrive in Jerusalem in time for *Shavuot*. Perhaps his urgency to be at the Temple on *Shavuot* was to celebrate the anniversary of the church's birthday. He also had a collection to offer and alms to pay. Paul "had collected a substantial sum," and his dozen or so companions represented hundreds of people who were funding his sacrificial pilgrimage.

He wanted to get to Jerusalem for Pentecost (Acts 16:20, *Shavuot*) when Christians there celebrated God's Spirit pouring through the risen Christ on all humanity. It was the perfect moment for Paul's sacrifice."[460] On Paul's personal, yet God-guided schedule, that gave him about a month to make the rest of the trip.

Pesach was behind them. He already spent some of the 50 days sailing from Greece and staying in Troas with the believers. On this journey, Passover was important but Pentecost was essential for the Apostle Paul. None can quite underestimate Paul's urgency.

Paul and some of his companions footed it (*pedzeuein*) to Assos almost a marathon's distance South from the coastal city of Troas. Moreover, the hike was over rocky and hilly terrain, not near the coastal paths, although the sea was always visible to the West. The seashore route was longer because of its inlets and coves. The over-hill passage was more direct and faster.

Still, there were travellers to meet along the way and faith to share with them, right? Paul travelled solo on this trek. Luke and other accompanying disciples sailed to Assos where they met one another again.

With his limited time encroaching like an imperious dictator, Paul boarded a ship or ships once more, and taking a circuitous route, he stopped at, or sailed by many ports.

---

[458] Acts 20:9
[459] Acts 20:8–12
[460] Bruce Chilton. op cit., p233

If the ships happened to land as crews transferred goods, Paul would spend the time intercepting anyone who would listen about Jesus who died on a cross, was buried, resurrected and promised to return. He loved to talk atonement and resurrection.

Miletus

The Apostle arranged with messengers to invite–require–the Ephesian leaders to sail North to meet him in Miletus.[461] Ephesus, with all its rioting outbursts, was no private place to discuss uninterrupted, significant shared words to elders and leaders in this extraordinary church. The city of Miletus, which already enjoyed a noteworthy corpus of Christians, offered both the safety and seclusion necessary for in-depth discussions of God's plans–past, present and future objectives for his church and for the agenda the Lord was providing for Paul.

The Miletus colloquy was something of a retreat in order to advance Christ's cause. No doubt it featured long periods of prayer, study of scripture, singing psalms, exhortation, table fellowship and mutual encouragement. The assembly understood it would be their final visit with Paul. Likely, the gathering mirrored the preparation for oncoming spiritual battles written about the Jerusalem Church after the birthday of the Church at *Shavuot* about 30 years previously.

"They devoted themselves to the apostles' teaching and to fellowship, to the breaking of bread and to prayer. Everyone was filled with awe at the many wonders and signs performed by the apostles. All the believers were together and had everything in common. They sold property and possessions to give to anyone who had need. Every day they continued to meet together in the Temple courts. They broke bread in their homes and ate together with glad and sincere hearts, praising God and enjoying the favour of all the people. And the Lord added to their number daily those who were being saved."[462]

Isn't it fascinating that Paul's last words to the church family assembled here was a saying of Jesus? *"We must help the weak, remembering the words the Lord Jesus said, 'It is more blessed to give than to receive.'"*[463]

The separation and departure was especially emotional. Paul knelt and prayed with the church family. Then, they all cried a lot. They embraced and kissed him. Luke's comment: *"What grieved them most was his statement that they would never see his face again."*[464]

The Last Lap

Luke and Paul *"tore themselves away"* from the crowd[465] and completed their voyage to Jerusalem. In the process, they criss-crossed the Aegean Sea, suggesting they

---

[461] Acts 20:17
[462] Acts 2:43–47
[463] Acts 20:35
[464] Acts 20:38.
[465] Acts 21:1

caught more than one freighter to reach the shore of Palestina. Their circuitous route took them to Cos, Rhodes and Tyre, passing Samos, and Patmos.

Paul spent seven days in Tyre with the disciples living there. They tried to convince him not to visit Jerusalem. He delayed by one week going to Jerusalem. Finally he and Luke left, amid another weepy farewell. *"All the disciples and their wives and children accompanied us out of the city, and there on the beach we knelt to pray. After saying goodbye to each other we went aboard the ship, and they returned home."*[466]

Paul and Luke's new carrier took them to Tyre, Ptolemais (today's Akko) and finally, Caesarea Maritima on the Palestinian mainland. The two visited Philip and his family of four spinster daughters and remained there a week. There was much to share, not only by Paul and Luke but by the deacon cum evangelist Philip.

In mid-week, the visitors had a visitor themselves. It was a disciple name Agabus.[467] Agabus foreknew the fate of Paul in Jerusalem. He took the sash from around Paul's waist and tied it with his own hands into a belt, suggesting to Paul what would befall him in Jerusalem. Agabus warned Paul of his arrest by Roman guards and his impending imprisonment.

The pleading of the Christians at Caesarea did not deter Paul. He knew God had prepared him for whatever would occur. *"'Why are you weeping and breaking my heart,'* questioned the Apostle. *'I am ready not only to be bound but also to die in Jerusalem for the name of the Lord Jesus.' When he would not be dissuaded we gave up and said, 'The Lord's will be done.'"*[468]

Obviously, the friends of Paul loved him very much, and he them. The miracle begun on the Damascus Road was still bearing fruit as Paul was concluding his apostolate.

But Paul did not die in Jerusalem. Luke and Paul walked from Caesarea's port to Jerusalem. Paul had come to the Temple to bring an offering. *Shavuot* was the festival of first-fruits and Paul came to honour that feast with an appropriate offering. *"I came to bring alms to my nation and to offer sacrifices . . . While I was doing this, they* (the rabble-rousers) *found me in the Temple, completing the rite of purification without any crowd or disturbance."*[469] Once at the Temple, Roman soldiers arrested Paul on a false charge, jailed him and escorted him back to Caesarea Maritima for "protective custody."

He spent the remainder of his life as a prisoner. Paul was relatively content with that, except for comments in his letters that he was "in chains." He happily had been a prisoner of the Lord much of his adult life.[470] He had more witnessing to do before Roman officialdom. He died in Rome, and fulfilled a hope he harboured to be in the Empire's capital before his life was over.

---

[466] Acts 21:5, 6
[467] see Acts 11:28 where Agabus predicted a famine.
[468] Acts 21:13, 14
[469] 2 Timothy 1:18; Philemon v. 9; Ephesians 3:1, 4.1
[470] Acts 24:18

PART FIVE: FROM MYTH TO FAITH

CHAPTER TWENTY–THREE
DÉNOUEMENTS

Samos

"The day after that we crossed over to Samos and on the following day arrived at Miletus."[471] Paul left Corinth and Cenchrea, then spent three years in Ephesus in Asia and moved on to revisit Philippi and Macedonia. He and Luke travelled widely over three months to encourage the churches from which he had departed almost five years previously.

Paul learned of a plot against him, sailed again to Greece, and sent word to his friends of his change of plans. Paul had many acquaintances and believers to accompany him at this reunion. Shortly after Passover, Paul and Luke left Neapolis, the port of Philippi, and set out for Troas.

Thus Paul avoided a confrontation by Jews in Syria (perhaps Antioch?). He felt God's leading to return to Jerusalem. En route, he paused for a week at Troas, his once departure point some few years earlier to begin his team's European Gospel invasion.

He transferred to a ship at Assos, and because Ephesus was its usual inhospitable self to him, he asked the elders of the Ephesian church to meet him at Miletus. It was a tearful reunion and departure. These verses in Acts, chapter 20, unveil the dramatic growth of the Gospel. It now possessed competent leaders to pastor people and proclaim the Good News.

With Luke, he sailed from Miletus and came to the Island of Samos as he journeyed to Judea. Paul may have used this convenient transfer point to rest for the night and to share his vibrant faith while awaiting a ship for the next leg of his Island-hopping journey in and out of Greek and Asia Minor ports. *"The day after that we crossed over to Samos, and on the following day arrived at Miletus."*[472]

The pair of travellers (Paul and Luke) likely went ashore in Samos for the night while sailors unloaded their vessel. Perhaps he needed a different ship for the next leg of his voyage to Jerusalem. He certainly did not place himself in the way of longshoremen doing their duty.

Samos is a delightful, hilly island with an attractive sheltered harbour as its main port. Like most Aegean Islands today, it sports whitewashed houses with pastel-coloured trim. That counteracts the summer heat. The coast of Turkey is clearly visible most of the time. It is only a few kilometres away.

Samos was acknowledged in Greek myth as the birthplace of the mythical Hera. Six centuries before Paul, the Island was the centre of a powerful political system with a

---

[471] Acts 20:15
[472] Acts 20:15

large influence in the area. It succumbed to the Persians, then to the Greeks and eventually to the Romans by the time the apostles Luke and Paul overnighted there.

Rome ruled Samos during Paul's travels. The Island grew famous for four of its sons who had distinguished themselves in the fields of mathematics, philosophy, astronomy and art.

The philosopher Epicurus was best known. His disciples were dubbed "Epicureans." They were among those who reasoned with Paul in Athens. Pythagoras, the mathematician, gave the world his theorem about right-angled triangles, a truth still taught in schools. ["In a right angled triangle, the square of the hypotenuse is equal to the sum of the squares of the other two sides"]. An artist who lived a century after the mathematician also bearing the same name of Pythagoras, likewise lived in Samos. He earned distinction for his sculptures. Aristarchus, an astronomer, developed theories similar to those of Copernicus–who lived 18 centuries later.

Some ruins, especially its aqueduct, are visible in Samos today. A museum holds some treasures of antiquity.

Cos (Kos)

"*After we had torn ourselves away from them* (the elders who met Paul at Miletus: see the previous chapter) *we put out to sea and sailed straight to Cos.*"[473] The verb "torn" is pregnant with emotions. On the same voyage from Philippi to Assos, Troas, to Samos, and to Miletus, the tiny group sailed into Cos for an overnight break. The Bible reveals little about Cos (Kos).

Paul had his thoughts fixed on his agenda for Jerusalem and likely that was topmost in his mindset. Cos provided a pause of convenience. Paul was felt pressed to return to Jerusalem. He needed transport to help him reach Jerusalem as rapidly as possible. One can imagine him configuring what ships were headed for what ports and which ones best served his personal schedule. He wished to keep his vow to sacrifice at the Great Temple for the festival of first fruits, *Shavuot*, Pentecost.

Long before the Christian era, Cos became the focus for the cult of Asclepius after the cult declined in Epidauros. The temple to Asclepius claimed "healing waters from the surrounding springs–especially dermatological disorders."[474] One of its medical priests became known as "the Father of Modern Medicine." Hippocrates was born on the Island about 500 years before Paul. Like Paul, Hippocrates concerned himself about morality. His 10-point oath (or series of moral codes; see p. 68) became the ethical framework for medicine and remains its foundation today.

Remnants of a significant temple complex show how deeply Greeks felt about the Father of Modern Medicine. It spreads over a wide area near the present port and obviously was a remarkable sight to see in its heyday. This was a medical school topping all medical schools.

---

[473] Acts 21:1
[474] A. Alexandri. Kos, Hippocrates Island, pp. 66, 69

Today, Cos looks more medieval than classical Greek. The Knights of St. John built a fortress here about the same time Columbus was born. Cos is a walled city. Some stones were removed from the ancient Asclepieion temple to fortify their castle.

Some other ancient relics remain, columns of a Corinthian period and places of a temple once dedicated to Aphrodite. The most important ancient site is the Asclepieion, built partly to honour Hippocrates, its most famous doctor-priest. Perhaps Luke walked over to see it?

Patmos

Paul centred his mission mostly in urban areas, and we should not be surprised that his visit to an Island such as Cos was mainly as a port stopover. However, the rural-oriented Jewish feasts were a part of his life. Jewish roots were deep in agriculture events as is noted by their special feasts of First Fruits and Tabernacles.

With Paul's influence, Christian centres moved from rural to urban points of reference. Paul was not easily sidetracked! Paul had his face set for Jerusalem and an agricultural-based sacred rendezvous. Necessary stops delayed him from his agenda. A stop at Patmos was "iffy."

Patmos was not an Island visited by Paul so far as we know–yet he must have known about it, sea traveller that he was. It is situated in the Dodecanese Islands of Greece. According to mythological tradition, this Island was originally a sanctuary for the worship of Artemis (Diana). Its original name was Letois. Later, the name became Patnos that morphed into its present name, Patmos, supposedly because Neptune-Poseidon set his foot (*pato*) there.

In the Bible, the Island is best known for the disciple John who penned what we now call "The Book of Revelation of Jesus Christ." When John wrote this book-letter under the direction of the Lord himself, to the seven churches of Asia Minor, the Emperor was Titus Flavius Domitianus, commonly known as Domitian.

The Apocalypse was scripted a generation after Paul had sailed by. However, if John sought a refuge and home there, a Christian community must have already existed. A collection of large stones (fenced in) near the harbour are labeled by the Orthodox priests on the Island as a basilica begun by John, dated late in the First Century AD. Dare we speculate that Paul had a remote hand in founding such a community? Or is that a leap too far?

Other traditions suggest that John the Evangelist began a mission on Patmos and led converts in building a faith community and a church building.

For persons interested in its religious history, Patmos has two important locations to visit. One is a cave, part way up the volcanic hill from the harbour. A series of monastery chapels are built around this Cave of the Apocalypse or Grotto of the Revelation, consecrated as a "church" by the Greek Orthodox priests to venerate both St. John and the biblical book of Revelation. Except for the many icons, the cave is simple, visitors are welcome and the priests are friendly.

One tradition offers that this Island with its significant grotto probably was once a penal colony in which John the Divine was imprisoned. His book was written in a kind of symbolic code that scholars refer to as apocalyptic language.

From the port Skala on Patmos Island, the coded letter was carried to the mainland, perhaps even entrusted to Caesar's royal mail ship, and dispatched to Ephesus. From there, the book was forwarded to six other churches–Smyrna, Pergamum, Thyatira, Philadelphia, Sardis and Laodicea in an elongated and ragged circle on the map. No doubt Hierapolis and Colossae congregations, perhaps other churches too, also read it.

The second site on Patmos worth visiting is the fortress-like monastery of John the Theologian on top of the Island's main hill. The founding monk, Holy Christodoulos, began the monastery mission. His name means "Christ's slave." He initiated it in 1088, 22 years after the Norman Conquest of England–on property ceded to the monk by the Emperor.

The monastery itself was constructed later than that and was remodelled more than once. Its treasury exhibits icons, clothing and vestments worn by its clergy as well as parchment manuscripts, copies of Scripture, ornaments and vessels used during the Eucharist. Some captivating and mind-blowing mosaics, murals, and friezes in the chapels and courtyards of the monastery depict biblical events.

Best of all is the view that the monastery affords. The harbour of Patmos, the town of Skala and the distant Turkish coastline are exceptionally photogenic in the Aegean sunlight.

Rhodes

"The next day we went to Rhodes and from there to Patara."[475] Paul caught another ship from Cos to Rhodes. This was a full day's sail. If Paul bypassed Patmos, he did not miss Rhodes. Moreover, it was a straighter and faster route than sailing by way of the Dodecanese Islands. Paul was in a rush.

Luke relates nothing of Paul's activities there. This was a quick stop, while either they obtained a new ship heading East from Rhodes to Patara or they waited while cargo was laded or transshipped. Local tradition claims that the point of landing in Rhodes was not at the main port of Rodos in the Northeast corner of the Island once the site of the renowned Colossus of Rhodes, but at a small bay near the town of Lindos on the Southeast coast.[476]

Above the bay stood the acropolis of Lindos and the venerable temple dedicated to the main deity, Athena. Entrance to the semi-enclosed bay is difficult to see from land but it was a safe and secluded harbour. Someone has named it, "The Bay of Saint Paul."

Local tradition also claims that Paul preached in Lindos during his brief stopover in Rhodes and that a church was birthed here. A white chapel dedicated to St. Paul, together with an annual festival on 28 June honours that occasion. The date of Paul's visit

---

[475] Acts 21:1
[476] Dorling Kinderoey Travel Guides. The Greek Islands. p.193

here, by local tradition is 43 AD. That surely is erroneous; Paul's visit is at least 15 years later than the local tourist guide book suggests.

Lindos is a beautiful community of whitewashed houses and shops. As tourists climb from the roadway to its acropolis, they pass by stalls displaying linen handcrafts woven by the women of the city. On their way to the acropolis they also pass by a sculpted ship, chiseled along the solid rock face at the entrance to the fortress and temples above.

This art was crafted by the Rhodian artisan, Pythekritos, who is better known for giving the world the famed "Victory of Samothrace," now in the Louvre Museum in Paris. The prow of the ship in the rock face at Lindos was dedicated to Agesandros, one of Poseidon's priests.

Atop the acropolis of Lindos are ruins of Genoese buildings, a Knights Hospitaler fortress, as well as a very old (10th Century BC) Doric temple to Athena. At this particular temple, the cult of Athena worshipped "with fire."

Historians are uncertain of the meaning of "with fire." This could mean that these devotees belonged to a rare Grecian group that offered burnt sacrifices on an altar. There are shades here of the *Torah*: ". . . *Burn the entire ram on the altar. It is a burnt offering to the LORD, an offering made to the LORD by fire.*"[477]

Nanno Marinator, Director of Archaeology at Lindos, spells out what he thinks, "with fire" means.

1. The priests who are going to perform the ceremony, undergo a special preparation. They purify themselves by bathing and adorn themselves. The animal also may be especially adorned, for example its horns may be gilded. This preparation stage marks the beginning of the ceremony and the 'sacrilization' stage.
2. The animal is led to the altar. A basket is brought into which the sacrificial knife is hidden beneath corn, fruit and/or cakes. Music is played.
3. The participants stand around the altar, which is situated in front of the temple. They take the corn from the basket and throw it at the animal. The priest says a prayer.
4. The knife, the actual instrument of death, is revealed from the basket. Some hair from the animal is cut and thrown into the fire of the altar.
5. The actual killing follows. Smaller animals are held above the altar, while their throat is slit. Large animals are stunned first, and then their throat is slit. The women utter a cry at the moment of death. This marks the climax of the action.
6. The animal is skinned. Its bones, fat and entrails are burned on the altar, whereas the meat is distributed to the participants The feasting often took place in the sanctuary. In Lindos it took place in the Propylaea.[478]

Ruins of a Christian basilica are obvious near the remains of the larger, newer Athena temple. This Church of Saint John represents the so-called "dark ages" period when the Knights had possession of the area. It also mirrors a transition. After Paul had left Lindos a metamorphosis took place. The worship at Lindos moved from myth to faith. Worship of Athena died; worship of the resurrected Christ lives on.

---

[477] Exodus 29:18
[478] Nanno Marinatos. Lindos. p.46

The Colossus of Rhodes

Chares, another sculptor from Lindos, designed the celebrated Colossus of Rodos, at the capital city of Rhodes. Vying with Alexandria's Pharos lighthouse, the great statue stood at the Island's Northern tip. At one time, this humungous statue was considered one of the "seven wonders of the ancient world." The Colossus of Rhodes reflected the prosperity of Rodos.

Both factual and fictional stories surround the storied Colossus. They were legion. The money to build it came from spoils gained from a battle against Demetrios Poliorketes the Besieger in 305 BC.[479]

Soon after this, Chares began his work. The statue, a bronze figure of the sun god Helios, stood astride the harbour of Rodos (some of the story may be exaggerated) so that ships had to sail under the splayed legs of the statue. A torch with a burning flame served as a lighthouse and was held by a left arm.

A series of earthquakes destroyed the statue in 225 BC. The ruins of the statue were still visible when Paul sailed past Rodos to moor on the other side of the Island at Lindos. Jewish salvagers picked up the pieces and sold them. Nevertheless, the Colossus, although erected for only 95 years, developed a worldwide and long-lasting reputation. Though it has not stood for more than 20 centuries, the phrase "like the Colossus of Rhodes" still lingers in our language.

If Paul stopped at Rodos, instead of Lindos, only God knows. It is unlikely. Certainly Rodos was the largest of all the ports on the Island since the Fifth Century BC. Rodos has left us a legacy. Rodos had some kind of assembly, or *ekklesia*–the Greek word Paul and Jesus used to describe the church. The earliest manuscripts of the gospels attribute the same word to Jesus, when he refers to a community of faith.

"Jesus replied, 'Blessed are you, Simon son of Jonah, for this was not revealed to you by man, but by my Father in Heaven . . . and I tell you that on this rock I will build my church (ekklesia), and the gates of Hades will not overcome it.'"[480]

Today Rodos is a city of roses, bougainvillea, and other flowers of unequalled beauty. The city is protected by thick mediaeval walls, an inheritance from its former Venetian governorship. It contains Arabic mosques, a legacy of Turkish rule–all mixed under a searing sun, with sizzling sand and sparkling sea. The indulgent pleasure boats now moored in Rodos' idyllic harbour emulate the tourist magnetism of modern Rhodes.

At Sea and Reaching Port

Silas and Timothy were now absent. Much of Luke's reporting about Paul's travels relates to the sea. That was natural. Greece was and is a seafaring nation. While travelling the sea was only a means to an end, Paul did use his sea voyages as opportunities of ministry. *"Three times I was shipwrecked. I spent a night and a day in the open sea."*[481]

---

[479] Nanno Marinatos. op. cit., p. 14
[480] Matthew 16:18

We do not know everything about Paul's maritime experiences. In his second letter to Corinth we learn that the Apostle had been shipwrecked three times and that he had spent some time afloat on debris and wreckage. We do not know whether that includes the reference by Luke recounting how Paul was brought by sea and shipwreck near Malta on his way to Rome.

Still, Luke says enough in Acts about Paul shuttling back and forth across the Aegean Sea that he must have been quite familiar with sailing. In addition, as a "tentmaker" or "leather worker," he probably often found employment in the merchant marine in some ways, perhaps by mending or manufacturing sails at wharves in various seaports, maybe even on ships underway at sea. Tarsus must have offered such an opportunity, perhaps Cenchrea and Lechaion also. As well, Paul may have worked at the Olympic or the Isthmian Games that were held while he was sojourning at Corinth.

At one point we see something of Paul's sailing savvy. As his ship approached Crete, Paul now a prisoner, warned his Roman guard that the journey would be disastrous. The centurion, presumably a landlubber, decided to ignore Paul's nautical expertise, and heeded instead the advice of the captain and ship owner. After all, what does a jailbird know?

Luke noted that the ship had "difficulty" as it passed along Crete's protective Southern shore. The sacred Mount Ida (snow capped in winter) in West-central Crete is high enough to control the weather to the South. Paul must have known the weather would only worsen. He dared to suggest to the ship's captain that they harbour at Kali Limenes (Fair Havens),[482] where the modest harbour might somewhat protect them for a short anchorage. One wonders how Paul knew about Fair Havens and its pocket-sized harbour!

Paul could not resist an "I-told-you-so" when his forecast proved much more accurate than the recommendations of the ship's commander. Although Paul had been humiliated by having his counsel rejected, he clearly was a person with whom to be reckoned. In the middle of a howling gale Paul seized the authority to call the crew together and offer them God's reassurance.

"Paul stood up before them and said: 'Men, you should have taken my advice not to sail from Crete; then you would have spared yourselves this damage and loss.'"[483]

One must conjure up one's imagination to see images of the variety of craft Paul and his companions used for transport. It was easy for him when the centurion was escorting Paul as his prisoner. It may not have been an oar-powered military naval vessel. More likely they found a ship or ships headed in the general direction of their desired destination. Once selected, the centurion commandeered passage on it. He could do that in the name and purposes of Caesar.

However, neither Paul nor the centurion could command sleeping quarters if they embarked on a freighter. Sleeping space was reserved only for consuls and senators.

---

[481] 2 Corinthians 11:25
[482] Acts 27:8
[483] Acts 27:21

Berths, as such, were not for mere army personnel, certainly not for prisoners or criminals. This group became deck passengers.

In his missionary work, Paul may have bartered passage on any ships he serviced with sail repairs. It was "contra," an exchange of passage for darning sails. He would have walked along the waterfronts looking for ships about to embark, and asking captains where they were headed or if they needed sail repairs.

A slight detour was no challenge for Paul. For him there were no detours. Every journey had a purpose. Each stop gave him opportunity to be a "babbler." He could buttonhole sailors, captains and travellers alike with the Good News that God had commissioned him to share.

CHAPTER TWENTY–FOUR
CRETE

It was no pleasure yacht that carried Paul and Luke on the Apostles' last sea journey to touch Greek territory. Indeed, the idea of boats for self-indulgence was alien to sailors of his day. Ships were for business, cargo or military transit. They were not for pleasure.

Nor was Paul's last voyage a pleasure trip in any way. He was a prisoner. Some years had passed since Paul paused at Lindos on Rhodes. His journeys had taken him to Caesarea Maritima in Palestina, then to Jerusalem. Paul was arrested in Jerusalem on a trumped-up charge of desecrating the Great Temple.

He was indicted and jailed. Paul then was transported covertly by Roman soldiers back to Caesarea where he first landed. Following that was a series of trials–no habeas corpus then. Finally, after an appeal to Caesar, Paul was sent on several lesser vessels and finally to an enormous freighter-ship presumably intended to dock and unload its cargo at Rome's port, Ostia.

From that harbour the ship's cargo, without Paul, Luke and Julius, would be transported by land to Rome, some 25 kilometres East of Ostia, Rome's port. It did not work out quite that way. His travel agent was Julius, an elite Roman Imperial Regiment centurion who was officially charged with accompanying him for the entire distance from Caesarea to Rome.

The journey was long and complicated, not to mention life-threatening. It involved slow ships, detours, transfers to other ships, and fitful weather. The route Julius charted meant finding ships to get them to Rome. So, from Caesarea, Julius, Paul and Luke embarked on a freighter stopping at Sidon. The kindly Julius permitted Paul to go ashore where he greeted believers–evidence that the church had greatly expanded by that time, and that a burgeoning believers' network existed among the followers of Jesus who knew Paul was coming and when. This obvious church expansion must have elated Paul when he was already in chains.

The next leg of the voyage to Rome was to Cyprus, probably on the same ship. The freighter hugged the lee of Cyprus, and then roughed it on open water until the ship landed at Myra in the district of Lycia within Asia Minor. Luke records that the seas were turbulent.

Julius found a humungous grain ship that had just arrived in Myra from Alexandria. Once loaded and boarded, it carried 276 passengers. Some of them, like Paul, probably were prisoners on their way to a Roman trial. This ship veered South and West sailing South of Crete, using the lee of the Island to insure better weather. Crete has a 2,453 m. (8,058 ft.) high mountain. Mount Ida (aka Lefka Ori, 2453 m.) creates its own weather system even when winter storms are absent.

A major late autumn storm developed–a "Nor'wester." Paul asked if the captain would put into Kali Limenes ("Fair Havens") for a safe harbour. Luke: *"We came to a place called Fair Havens near the town of Lasea."*[484] This Cretan harbour was not large, barely big enough for a ship the size of Paul's current transportation to winter. This could have been a brief respite from the post-Yom Kippur October storm.

A millennium-and-a-half earlier, Paul's shipmates would have landed in Minoan territory. The chief city of that region was Phaistos,[485] and it was a city-state, second only in power and renown to the city-state of Knossos on the Northeast side of Crete. Minoans and their civilization ceased to exist after the massive pyroclastic volcanic eruption at Santorini which buried Santorini deep within the earth."[486]

The Minoan Civilization

Two very large excavations in Crete reveal much about the Minoan civilization. Add to that the fantastic Bronze Age excavations at Akrotiri on the Island of Santorini, and you get a picture of a remarkable civilization wiped out by a magna-disaster volcanic pyroclastic eruption circa 1,500 BC.

Knossos is about five kilometres inland from Crete's Northern coastal city of Iraklion. Excavator and Oxonian Arthur Evans was scolded by some archaeologists for spoiling what he uncovered by attempting a restoration to demonstrate what Knossos once might have looked like. Despite the purists' denouncement of Evans, the dig of Knossos is worthy of considerable inspection, as is the Museum in Iraklion.

Phaistos, 30 kms. North of Fair Havens on Crete's South shore, shared the Minoan culture. It was not destroyed to the degree of a thick volcanic blanket over Santorini's Akrotiri. Its different buildings reveal what was important to the once-Phoenician trading nation. Phaistos had a throne room as well as an immersion tank ("lustral basin")[487] used by those preparing to enter into the divine king's presence in a regal sanctuary. [488] The region surrounding Phaistos produced food of differing sorts.

The Knossos version of Minoan culture centred its worship in the adoration of the bull. It had power. Myth or history? Readers might keep in mind the reputation of citizens of Crete who were challenged by Paul about their honesty. In Paul's letter to Titus, he wrote, *"Even some of their own prophets have said, 'Cretans are always liars, evil brutes, lazy gluttons.'"*[489]

Visitors to Knossos must sort truth from fiction. The name Minos appears to be legend. Minos, says the myth, was a son of Zeus who likewise was born on Crete. This astonishing civilization sprang from that myth and took the name Minoan.

The Minoan culture spread far and wide, mirroring former sea and trading routes pioneered by Phoenicians. Soon the Island became the centre of shipping lanes that extended in every direction across the Mediterranean Sea.

---

[484] Acts 27:8
[485] Nanno Marinatos. Crete. p.143
[486] Christos G. Doumas. Santorini. p. 3
[487] Despina Hadzi–Vallianou. Phaistos. Greek Ministry of Culture, p. 31, 32
[488] Nanno Marinatos. op. cit., p. 145
[489] Titus 1:12

Minoan civilization came to an abrupt end with a massive pyroclastic eruption near Thera on what is now called the Island of Santorini in the Aegean. The blast sent shock waves, volcanic ash and giant tidal waves throughout the Mediterranean. So great was the eruption that the ash and tsunami were known to reach Egypt. Was this tsunami connected to the Red Sea events where Israelites escaped to dry land and Egyptian chariots were mired in the mud?

According to legend at the time of this eruption, the city of Atlantis sank beneath the sea near Thera. A caldera–a volcanic crater some kilometres wide–at Thera plainly marks the area where the volcano gave its largest incredible performance. On an Island in the caldera, the volcano's remnant still smolder's and exudes sulphuric fumes.

The zenith of Minoan culture must have been reached in Knossos and Phaistos. Knossos' legends centre on the Minotaur (the bull) and the Labyrinth (the maze). The palace of Knossos itself has remarkable proportions and scores of rooms. Arthur Evans, an acknowledged archaeologist from the Ashmolean Museum in Oxford, England, excavated it in 1900. Evans also made a disputed attempt to restore the palace.

Essentially, what Evans uncovered was a civilization contemporary with the biblical Joseph. It was advanced, progressive and intelligent. Its religion centred on the sacred bull. Evidence of the bull as an object of worship is everywhere. Miniature models of bulls' heads and bodies are displayed at the Iraklion Museum. Also shown are its monoliths and horn altars that are displayed *in situ* at Knossos.

Forms of baptism as a cleansing ritual were adhered to, especially when one entered the presence of the deity-king.[490] Some archaeologists consider these to be "ordinary baths." The Minoans thought that their kings held divine properties. They respected and treated them as such. Some phrases in the psalter suggest that in subtle ways, Jews shared the concept of a king who was also afforded the reputation of Messiah.

Archaeologists continue to dig, probe and draw conclusions at Knossos and Akrotiri on the Island of Santorini. The final word is not yet in. The jury has not yet met. What is known is that the Minoans developed a remarkably advanced civilization. Their time links with biblical events will make for interesting studies when new information is gradually made available through the exhausting work of diggers working within the precincts of Minos' court. Paul missed all that but then, he was not on a tourist trek. *"I run with purpose in every step."*[491]

---

[490] Costis Davaras. The Palace of Knossos, p. 8; illustration #24 (p. 32); Nanno Marinatos. Crete, p. 75, 80
[491] 1 Corinthians 9:26a NLT

CHAPTER TWENTY–FIVE
MALTA

This book concerns Paul's life, travels, contacts, theology manners, attitudes and ability to cope, especially his spiritual health and recovery from his distracting Damascus disaster. The evidence is in the history told by Luke and in the letters he wrote to churches and individuals. Malta is not in Europe or Asia or Palestina, yet it was an unwanted destination as Paul took the long convoluted voyage to Rome. Thus this book includes Malta, once a dominion answering to Carthage, but since 264 BC, now in 60, 61 or 62 AD whenever Paul stopped there, was under the sovereignty of Imperial Rome. Paul's Malta experience is a marvellous way of evaluating how far the Apostle had come from his excretory Damascus turnabout.

Malta was an unsolicited, unnecessary yet not unwarranted stop on the ship's journey to Rome. It was almost a disastrous break from the voyage. "Break" is an appropriate word, for the ship came apart and survivors clung to flotsam as the ship disintegrated. The crew tried to prevent that.

They lowered ropes around the sides of the ship to tighten, seal and prevent the side planks from coming apart. Yet after 14 days at sea, constantly pounded by rogue waves, the Mediterranean took a terrible toll on the capacious grain ship that carried Paul, Luke, Julius, a number of prisoners, some army personnel and a ship's crew.

Paul anticipated that this would happen. He began to take charge of the situation. He addressed captain, prisoners, army people and crew with "I told you so!"

After they had gone a long time without food, Paul stood up before them and said:

> "Men, you should have taken my advice not to sail from Crete; then you would have spared yourselves this damage and loss. But now I urge you to keep up your courage, because not one of you will be lost; only the ship will be destroyed. Last night an angel of the God to whom I belong and whom I serve stood beside me and said, 'Do not be afraid, Paul. You must stand trial before Caesar; and God has graciously given you the lives of all who sail with you.' So keep up your courage, men, for I have faith in God that it will happen just as he told me. Nevertheless, we must run aground on some Island,"[492]

The ship broke up in what the Maltese believe to be at San Pawl Milqghi cape leading into a sheltered bay at Qawra Point.[493] In English, it is now called Saint Paul's Bay. The Maltese were charitable people. Being familiar with shipwrecks, they provided hospitality for all who came ashore–none was lost, as Paul prophesied.

They built a fire, provided blankets and nourishment to everyone. Paul added wood to the fire and an asp bit him, clinging to his hand. At first the Maltese thought a god was judging Paul for evil deeds. He shook the serpent off and suffered no damage. The Islanders now considered him to be a god.

---

[492] Acts 27:21–26
[493] Aldo E. Azzopardi. <u>Malta and Its Islands</u>. p. 9

In an estate nearby, the governor of the Island was delighted to welcome Paul and the others into his villa. He hosted them for three days. Paul prayed for and laid hands on Publius' ailing father who was restored to health. Luke tells what followed: *"When this had happened, the rest of the sick on the Island came and were cured. They honoured us in many ways; and when we were ready to sail, they furnished us with the supplies we needed."*[494]

Paul spent three months on Malta, preaching and teaching on the Island. The significance of this divine coincidence was that Malta became a thoroughly Christian community. Today some 90% of the population attend church service every Sunday.

---

[494] Acts 28:9–10

CHAPTER TWENTY–SIX
ROME

After the Apostle's enforced hiatus, Paul again was on his way to Rome. With winter storms now slacked and freighters resuming their traffic, the veterans of the shipwreck embarked on a wintered-berthed ship from Alexandria that had unloaded its cargo in Malta. The ship had wintered in the safety of a Maltese port. The time had come for Paul, Luke and the centurion Julius to resume their itinerary.

Luke describes it as a ship whose prow featured figureheads of Castor and Pollux.[495] Luke and Paul may have been mildly amused about this since the twin Roman deities were patron gods of travellers, especially of sailors. Paul and Luke's Deity had already been at work protecting them in their travels.

The first stop was at Syracuse in Sicily. They now were back in Europe. Syracuse boasted some exceptional notables. They included Archimedes, the mathematician and scientist, Aeschylus the playwright, and Pindar the poet.

None reached the world-contribution level of the missionary who stepped onto the Syracuse wharf and stayed for three days while sailors exchanged cargoes. What did he do with his three days in Syracuse? Likely he became an Athenian babbler again–a *spermologos*–talking to anyone who would listen about Jesus.

A straight sail run along the Southeast coast of Sicily brought the three, past the volcanic Mount Etna, to Rhegium (now S. Giovanni) on the Italian mainland, across from Messina in Sicily.

The ship was blessed with welcome warm winds that enhanced their voyage. Their vessel quickly passed Stromboli's volcano and they arrived at Puteoli on mainland Italy. Passengers debarked here; cargo remained on board until the ship reached Ostia The three, Paul, Luke and Julius, spent a week there. Today the city is called Pozzuoli. It is close to Anzio where in 1944 Allied forces held a deafening invasion much unlike that of the two missionaries with their quiet, unheralded revolution.

Paul's sea journeys ended at this port. The three, Paul, Luke and Julius, had a new experience. They were welcomed for the first time in a place where Luke and Paul never before had set foot. They met some new Christian friends who awaited them, likely also meeting for the first time. *"There we found some brothers who invited us to spend a week with them."*[496]

What did they do? Maybe they discussed the letter Paul had sent to the church in Rome to clarify his Summa Theologica, his theological view of the gospel. It is encapsulated in the Letter to the Romans. Summa Theologica is the name for a tome later used by Thomas Aquinas, 1,200 years after Paul, to set down his theology based on Aristotelian and Pauline teachings. Aquinas had no copyright on the phrase. The title belonged to Paul as much as to anyone, maybe more.

---

[495] Acts 28:11
[496] Acts 28:14

Since Paul had never been to Rome, he wanted to answer the Romans' questions about what he believed. They seemed to need to know if Paul was theologically correct or not. Thus, the week may have seen Paul "in teaching mode." No doubt he reported his experiences and the successes of growth in places he had preached. The substantial Christian network already may have circulated some of these matters.

"*And so we came to Rome*," wrote Luke.[497] "*The brothers there had heard we were coming, and they travelled as far as the Forum of Appias and the Three Taverns to meet us.*" The brothers encouraged Paul, elating him that the faith he hoped to find in Rome was vibrant, strong and solid. "*When we got to Rome*," wrote Luke," "*Paul was allowed to live by himself, with a soldier to guard him.*"[498] Julius' work was done; he had delivered Paul safely to Rome for a trial before Caesar.

The Apostle Paul would not have been surprised that a reception committee came to welcome him. He had a long contact list in Rome. Claudius may have expelled Christians along with Aquila and Priscilla in his 49 AD expulsion of some Jews. But with Claudius' death by 54 AD, Christians in great numbers arrived or re-surfaced in Rome.

The New Testament, especially Acts and the Epistles, provides an extensive list of people drawn to Jesus of Nazareth. Some of these individuals seem to play small roles. No one among the people of God plays a picayune position in the Gospel work. None are unimportant. Every member of Christ's church is God's trophy equally as valuable to him as any other.

Look at the names–some familiar in other parts of the New Testament. We recognize Priscilla and Aquila in the list, as we do Timothy. Most of the others are valuable to the Gospel growth and especially beloved by Paul. They have worked in bit parts in the powerfully rapid growth of the church and the salvation of "lost" people. All of them are the heritage of the saints and are as pertinent to every Christian's faith family tree as the Bible's "begats."[499] These are believers' spiritual and salvation ancestors. It is important that all believers know of them. Christians will meet them in glory.

Here are a few names Paul knew in Rome, some women and some men, weak and strong, yet all are equals in Christ's mission and God's grace: Epaenetus (the first Asian convert); Mary; Andronicus and Junias (believers before Paul was converted); Ampliatus; Urbanus; Stachys; Apelles; Herodion (Paul's relative); Aristobulus; Narcissus; Tryphena; Tryphosa; Persis; Rufus and his mother; Asyneritus; Phlegon; Hermes; Patrobas; Hermas; Philogus; Julia; Nereus and his sister; Olympas. We mention them because Paul loved them and knew they were part of the heritage deriving from the Gospel and producing their own Christian progeny–reproducers, all of them. These names represent the Christian faith family tree. Believers should know their spiritual family's ancestry.

There other lists of course, such as in the letters to Timothy. Moreover, the list is incomplete; many saints were likely unknown to Paul and were unlisted in the Epistles'

---

[497] Acts 28:14 *ff*
[498] Acts 29:16
[499] Matthew 1:1–17; Luke 3:23–38

documentation. The church has many unsung servants whose names are always known to God and recorded in the "book of life."[500]

Paul's mission was yet unfinished. He summoned local Jews to meet him. Despite his earlier insistence that he would turn only to the Gentiles, he could never forget the Jews. In Rome, he found them open and welcoming for they had no dispatches from any other Jews about his teaching. He explained what had happened to him by Jewish persecution, but they listened.

They said, *"Nobody wrote warning us about you. And no one has shown up saying anything bad about you. But we would like very much to hear more. The only thing we know about this Christian sect is that nobody seems to have anything good to say about it."*[501] Luke says that some Jews were convinced by what Paul told them. Yet others would not believe about his proclaiming that Messiah had already come.

Paul also faced disappointments to daunt and test his genuine "wellness." As the book of The Acts of the Apostles reaches its last chapters, readers learn of an expanding, vibrant, growing list of disciples connected in some way to the Apostle Paul. Augmenting the stories told by Luke in Acts, the references in the Epistles broaden the increasing scope of the Gospel partners in the flourishing church. The growth is impressive; the biblical platform cannot include them all in the many biblical references.

Yet not all those listed in the church growth were helpful to the body life of the early church. Two who would not want their names promoted in the church press were Ananias and Sapphira who made public promises about their generosity to the Jerusalem Church but defaulted on them in an act of fraud. The moral? Don't mess with your promises to God!

Others seemed to fail in different ways. Alexander of Ephesus was one flounderer who was apparent to the Apostle Paul. He proposed that Christians need not be moral, proposing that matter itself was evil, so humans are free from its punishment!

Another developing heretic was Hymenaeus, like Alexander, an antinomian, who Paul said he had "handed over to Satan." The early church had a collection of lone, self-important theological wolves who attempted to skew the apostles' teachings by their own versions of a perceived truth. Paul spoke of them as "shipwrecks." Paul became harsher. Since they did not believe in a bodily resurrection, Paul accused the trio of Philetus, Alexander and Hymenaeus' teaching as "gangrenous."[502] This criticism was coming from a man, who as a young Pharisee, tried to destroy the church himself!

The early church had many shipwrecks. This should not have surprised anyone because Jesus' parable warned of believers' bents to buckling.

"A farmer went out to sow his seed. As he was scattering the seed, some fell along the path; it was trampled on, and the birds ate it up. Some fell on rocky ground, and when it came up, the plants withered because they had no moisture. Other seed fell among thorns, which grew up with it and choked the plants. Still

---

[500] Philippians 4:3; Revelation 3:5, 13:8, 22:19
[501] Acts 28:21, 22
[502] 1 Timothy 1:20

other seed fell on good soil. It came up and yielded a crop, a hundred times more than was sown."
When he said this, he called out, "Whoever has ears to hear, let them hear." [503]
Jesus/The Spirit anticipated dropouts

And then there was Demas. He appears to have been a once-valued travelling companion of Paul and Luke. Paul mentions him in two letters. In Paul's note to Philemon, Paul describes Demas as a "fellow worker." In the letter to Timothy, Paul rues the allegation that Demas has sold himself out to commercialism, *"Demas has loved this world and has deserted me and gone to Thessalonika."* [504] What did Paul mean by that?

No one knows the allegation's meaning, of course. Has Paul lost his perspective? Is he so "down" while a prisoner that he thinks ill of his former friends and close co-workers. Perhaps.

Paul's writing to Philemon reveals even more about Paul than it does about the letter's recipient. Paul described himself as a slave (*doulos*) of Christ[505] with the inference that Philemon likewise was "owned" by Christ. Philemon was a personal and wealthy friend of Paul, a convert under his ministry. He now lived in Colossae. He allowed and encouraged a church to meet in his home. Paul refers to "fathering" him in the faith. Philemon owned a runaway slave, who by now was also a convert of Paul's, and ministering to him while in prison. Paul did not lecture Philemon on the slave trade but reminded him of the principle that, *"in Christ there is neither slave nor free."* [506] Paul must have urged Philemon to realize both he and Paul belonged to God who was their master. Paul's owner was *"the God to whom I belong and whom I serve."* [507]

Paul sent the escaped slave back to Philemon with a letter, trusting that the former owner would "obey" Paul and receive him as a "brother in Christ." Paul petitioned, *"Perhaps the reason he was separated from you for a little while was that you might have him back for good–no longer as a slave, but better than a slave, as a dear brother. He is very dear to me but even dearer to you, both as a man, and a brother in the Lord."* [508] Philemon's response is unknown.[509]

---

[503] Matthew 11:8 *et. al*; see also Revelation 2:7 etc.

[504] 2 Timothy 4:11

[505] Philippians 1:1

[506] Galatians 3:24

[507] Acts 27:23

[508] Philemon 15, 16

[509] A questionable and disputable entry in a Serbian Orthodox account (Prologue from Ochrid) quoted by Bishop Nikolai Velmirovic, claims Onesimus became a bishop. "Onesimus was later made bishop and received the see of Ephesus after the death of the Apostle Timothy. This is recorded in the epis-tles (sic) of Ignatius the God-Bearer. At the time of the persecution under Trajan, Onesimus, by then an old man, was arrested and taken to Rome. There he testified before the judge Tertylus, was imprisoned and finally slain. A wealthy woman took his body, placed it in a silver coffin and buried it, in the year 109. Source: syrianorthodox.net."

Paul led Onesimus to faith in Christ. He was Philemon's runaway slave, now ministering to the prisoner Paul. His name meant "profitable, useful." He wasn't very useful to his master Philemon while he was on the lam but Paul wanted to return him to usefulness.

A subtle hint in the letter [v. 18, 9] suggest that Onesimus may have stolen from Philemon, but Paul offers a payment if there was a loss. Thus Paul and Timothy sent a letter to his owner to ask for reconciliation and forgiveness for him.

Tychicus accompanied Onesimus to Colossae to carry the letter to Philemon.[510] Paul does not write a treatise on the rights and wrongs of slavery. Perhaps that was because he knew God owned him. To Corinth he had written, "*You are not your own; you were bought with a price.*"[511]

On another note, some have speculated that the "*thorn in the flesh*"[512] he mentioned was an illness like malaria or epilepsy or developing blindness. Any of these ailments would cloud the perspective of an imprisoned person like Paul. Whatever the challenge, Paul felt crippled by the ordeal. Yet he accepted the situation once the Lord told him that God's gift to him was grace.

He was troubled, however, by the thought that some believers had regressed in their faith. There were others like the now-despised Demas whom Paul sensed had marooned him. Paul felt deserted, not only by Demas, but by other close friends such as Crescens and even Titus. Again, Paul may have badly misunderstood and misinterpreted their absence. He certainly missed them.

Paul's venting to his protégé student Timothy about the actions and reactions of some friends is a lesson to all the church members everywhere. Christians, selfishly not thinking of other Christians, are capable of harming each other. Demas may never have known how much he hurt Paul and upset people in various churches. None of us may ever fully know how much our actions or even our words, may injure someone else. When one is hurt, all are hurt. As Paul said, "*The body is a unit . . . not made up of one part but of many . . . if one part suffers, every part suffers with it; if one part is honoured, every part rejoices with it.*"[513]

Heeding James' admonition is good advice for any church. "*The wisdom that comes from heaven is first of all pure; then peace loving, considerate, submissive, full of mercy and good fruit, impartial and sincere.*"[514] English translations call him James but his real Hebrew name is Jacob, the patriarch. This is not the fisherman brother of John, the child of Zebedee, but the brother of the Lord Jesus. He is often referred to as James, "the brother of the Lord," or "James the Just." Nor is James the Just, the son of Alpheus, a disciple of Jesus also dubbed "James the Less."[515]

---

[510] Colossians 4:9
[511] 1 Corinthians 6:19, 20
[512] 2 Corinthians 12:7
[513] 1 Corinthians 12: 2, 13
[514] James 3:17
[515] Luke 6:15; Matthew 10:3; Mark 3:18

This James authored the book of James in the New Testament. It is a "straight from the shoulder" epistle, citing the need of believers to square their words with their actions, to "Walk the walk, not just talk the talk."

Every cause has its casualties. But it also has its spectacular successes. The cause was not ultimately hampered by its losses, although looming theological controversies such as Hymenaeus' and Alexander's creeping Gnosticism would dog authentic Christian dogma for years, even for centuries to come.

But the Bible cheers for those who "hang in" and continue yet to become seed falling into fertile furrows.

"Blessed are you when people insult you, persecute you and falsely say all kinds of evil against you because of me. Rejoice and be glad, because great is your reward in heaven, for in the same way they persecuted the prophets who were before you."[516] To which James adds: *"Perseverance must finish its work so that you may be mature and complete, not lacking anything."*[517]

As for those who denied what Paul argued, he left them with this thought: *"I want you to know that God's salvation has been sent to the Gentiles, and they will listen."*[518] Luke tells us that Paul continued his work from a house he rented in Rome.

That ministry lasted two years.

Luke concludes: *"He lived there two whole years at his own expense, and welcomed all who came to him, proclaiming the kingdom of God and teaching about the Lord Jesus Christ with all boldness and without hindrance."*[519] It completed his dream about sharing the Good News in Rome. *"I am eager to preach the gospel also to you who are at Rome."*[520] Dream fulfilled!

Whatever Paul's circumstance, he had a healthy attitude to accommodating it. To Rome, in which he now had arrived to meet Nero's justice, he wrote: *"We know that in all things God works for the good of those who love him."*[521]

What happened to Paul? Luke does not tell, perhaps because Luke also probably lost his life for the Gospel. Two hundred years later, Eusebius, bishop of Caesarea (c. 263–339 AD) in a questionable comment describes what happened to Paul after his first imprisonment:

"After defending himself, [Paul] was again sent on the ministry of preaching, and coming a second time to the same city suffered martyrdom under Nero. During this imprisonment he wrote the second epistle to Timothy, indicating at the same time that his first defence had taken place and that his martyrdom was at hand."[522] Was Eusebius factual or opining something?

[516] Matthew 5:11, 12
[517] James 1:4
[518] Acts 28:28
[519] Acts 28:30, 31
[520] Romans 1:5
[521] Romans 8:28 NIV
[522] Ecclesiastical History 2:22.2

The End

A tradition (not always reliable) tells that both Peter and Paul were incarcerated in the same holding cell near the Foro Romano, a stone's throw from the Arch of Septimum Severus. The prison is under the present church of San Giuseppe Felegname. The lower part of the church, the dungeon, is marked on the exterior:

MAMERTIUM. PRIGIONE DEI APOSTOLIC PETRO E PAOLO.

This prison once held those who would never be released. The next stop was execution.

Perhaps this prison is where Paul languished before his death. He sent a farewell epistle: "*Recalling your tears, I long to see you, so that I may be filled with joy. I have been reminded of your sincere faith, which first lived in your grandmother Lois and in your mother Eunice and, I am persuaded, now lives in you also.*"[523]

Tradition suggests that Paul died in 67 or 68 AD. He was a victim of Nero's excuse for a conflagration started in Rome so he could beautify the city and place blame elsewhere. In the Annuls of Tacitus, it is recorded:

> "No human effort . . . could make that infamous rumour disappear that Nero had somehow ordered the fire. Therefore, to abolish that rumour, Nero falsely accused and executed with the most exquisite punishments those people called Christians, who were infamous for their abominations. The originator of the name, Christ, was executed as a criminal by the procurator Pontius Pilate during the reign of Tiberius; and though repressed, this destructive superstition erupted again, not only through Judea, which was the origin of this evil, but also through the city of Rome . . . first those were seized who admitted their faith, and then, using the information they provided, a vast multitude were convicted, not so much for the crime of burning the city, but for hatred of the human race. And perishing they were additionally made into sports: they were killed by dogs by having the hides of beasts attached to them, or they were nailed to crosses or set aflame, and, when the daylight passed away, they were used as nighttime lamps. Nero gave his own gardens for this spectacle and performed a Circus game . . . Even though they were clearly guilty and merited being made the most recent example of the consequences of crime, people began to pity these sufferers, because they were consumed not for the public good but on account of the fierceness of one man."[524]

Also according to unprovable tradition, Paul was taken three kilometres South of the city, near the third milestone of the Ostian Way, or Via Ostensis the way to the port of

---

[523] 2 Timothy 1:4, 5

[524] William M. Ramsay, op. cit., p. xxxiv–p. xxxvi. Ramsay cites, "High authority has been assigned to a statement ascribed (falsely) to Chrysostom, Vol. VIII, p. 621 . . . that Paul served God 35 years and died at the age of 68. This represents an early tradition current in Asia Minor; and it affords a good chronological argument in the year of Paul's death can be fixed . . . Some months after the great fire of Rome (August 64) Paul was arrested (in winter 64, 65) presumably at Nikopolis) and there ensued a formal trial in Rome . . . all was over before the end of 65. Therefore the conversion must be dated in 31, then the first visit to Jerusalem in 33, and the second in 44, *viz* the 3rd and 14th year of Paul's new life.

Ostia, and beheaded at a site with three springs known as Aquae Salviae, now the Trappist monastery of San Paolo alle Tre Fontane (Three Fountains). After three years of digging under the altar of St. Paul Outside The Walls basilica in Rome, archeologists found a sarcophagus in a vault with words likely carved in the Fourth Century, PAULO APOSTLEMART, meaning Paul, Apostle, Martyr. The excavators presume this may be Paul's earthly resting place–or maybe not. Presumption is not fact.

CHAPTER TWENTY–SEVEN
SUMMARY: WELLNESS AND ATTITUDINAL DEVELOPMENT

This book has attempted to describe an incredibly important and rapid transition point in human history.

Within 20 years of the life, death, burial, resurrection and ascension of Jesus the believers had moved in a dramatic way to change the world. In the words used of the reaction from Thessalonian critics, *"Those who have turned the world upside down have come here also."*[525] God had also moved his Apostle in a dramatic way from being a young terrorist to be part of the inversion group that "turned the world upside down."

More important to this study is the incredible turnaround in the Apostle Paul's life. These missionaries did much of their work in the pagan Greek culture. They had to learn foreign social graces as well as learn how to tell their story so that Europeans would accept it. Paul adjusted remarkably quickly to act out God's requirements of him.

Judaism was the root and the soul of the new faith. It taught that temples made by human hands can neither contain nor control the Eternal God.[526] From this concept of God who is Spirit came a further truth, that God is neither whimsical nor capricious, like Greek and Roman deities. God's dominant characteristic is love. *"His banner over me is love!"*[527]

Believers in the life, death and resurrection of Jesus articulated this understanding still further. They said that the example of God's love dwells supremely in the person of Jesus, who though crucified, was sinless and did not deserve death. His life and death provided the means by which humanity and deity can join together in unity.

By willing his own life (*"No one takes it from me, but I lay it down of my own accord. I have authority to lay it down and authority to take it up again"*)[528] as an atonement for human sin, his death, Jesus–the Christ, the Jew's Messiah, the Spirit of the living God–removed from everyone that persistent sin that had built a wall between God and humanity. On the cross, Jesus broke down that dividing wall of hostility between God and man, between man and man.[529] He atoned for the sin of all who trusted in the validity of Jesus' sacrificial atonement on the cross.

The Apostle also knew spiritual death and resurrection. As Saul, he was so alien to God's business, that only God's miracle brought him around to shape him up as a slave for Christ. As Paul, no longer Saul, he grew dramatically to reach the purpose for his life that God revealed to him. He grew from guilt to grace. He matured from an abominable adolescence into a corroborated maturity. He had foolishly tyrannized the Lord but he later came to defer to Jesus without reservation.

---

[525] Acts 17:6b KJV
[526] 2 Chronicles 8:18
[527] Song of Solomon 2:4
[528] John 19:30; John 10:18
[529] Ephesians 2:17

Jesus' followers believed that he was Lord. The first creed simply affirmed, "*Jesus is Lord.*"[530] That truth Paul proclaimed with an undeniable total trust in this Lord who had given him the gift of humility to replace his previous braggadocio. Paul was now the loyal and reliable instrument God used to transmit his grace to humanity.

In a few short years, some special messengers spread this faith. Saul/Paul of Tarsus, and an assortment of associates and companions slogged the roads and plied the seas so that the cities of Asia and Europe could have a vibrant, wholesome faith. Paul especially demonstrated the meaning of conversion, transformation, and growth from negative faith to a new "rejoicing faith."

Saul had died on a roadway near Damascus. Saul discovered what John later wrote to the church at Sardis: "*I know your works; you have the name of being alive, and you are dead. Awake, and strengthen what remains and is on the point of death.*"[531] God raised Paul from that death to a new, joyous life as a servant of the Gospel. He applied what he wrote to Ephesus to his own transformation:

> "*But because of his great love for us, God, who is rich in mercy, made us alive with Christ even when we were dead in transgressions—it is by grace you have been saved. And God raised us up with Christ and seated us with him in the heavenly realms in Christ Jesus, in order that in the coming ages he might show the incomparable riches of his grace, expressed in his kindness to us in Christ Jesus.*"[532]

The world's movement from myth to faith was breakneck. The Greek and Roman divinities soon were easily seen to be fabrications, illusions containing only fractional truths. Within 275 years of Paul's team landing at the piers of Neapolis, the entire Roman Empire became officially "Christian." Paul, the earlier vacuous incendiary en route to Damascus, had become the steadfast captain for God's mission to all peoples of the world.

Wellness and Attitudinal Changes

Several results from Paul's transformed life are reflected in the turnarounds during his life. The evidences are found in the 18 points that follow. They are not the only signs of attitudinal development but they are significant ones.

They are, in random order: (1) A total conversion; the turnaround at Damascus; (2) Needing help from God; (3) A learned power of humility; (4) A sense of being; (5) An exhibition of *agape*; (6) A salvaged optimism; (7) The new world order: Spirit trumps law; (8) Christ is everything; (9) An open book; (10) A community of faith; (11) A conciliatory attitude; (12) A sense of humour; (13) No sense of quit; (14) Grace makes amends; (15) Saved from guilt; memory becomes a "heads-up"; (16) Acceptance; (17) Networking and contacting; (18) Synthesizing Gospel theology.

---

[530] Philippians 2:12
[531] Revelation 3:1, 2
[532] Ephesians 2:4–7

1. A Total Conversion: The turnaround at Damascus

Psychologists link a Positive Mental Attitude (PMA) to shalom-wellness; a Negative Mental Attitude (MNA) to devastating illness. Psychotherapist Sidney Jourard, a professor of Psychology at the University of Florida, summarized the concept this way: "There is growing reason to suspect that hope, purpose, meaning and direction in life produce and maintain wellness, even in the face of stress, whereas demoralization by the events and conditions of daily existence helps people become ill."[533] "Life is a quest for meaning," wrote Viktor Frankl.[534]

Surely that applies to the traumatic episodes in Paul's life beginning on a widely used path the terrorist Saul travelled to root out all the traces of the fledgling Christian Movement. At the onset of his mean-spirited journey, Saul was spiritually sick, ill unto death. When God found him and he found God, the mood reversed and he began a tough trek toward a tonic. The finis of Paul's life was a reversal of how it began. He moved from hatred to love, from ungrace to grace, from vengeance to mercy.

It came about because Paul realized he was the problem, and not the Christians. The passage from illness to wellness was an inward journey. Paul embarked on it immediately he was converted and turned his travels into a dangerous joy.

2. Needing Help from God

Young Saul had a serious personality flaw when Luke first introduced him to the world in Chapter Nine of Acts. As Bruce Chilton described him, "Paul is the most complex, brilliant, troubled figure in the New Testament. He speaks for himself–inviting us to trace his turbulent dramatic life."[535]

Anyone in a seven or twelve step program (i.e., Alcoholics Anonymous) knows that one must admit to a need before help can be achieved in solving the challenge. One rung of the "step program" lays out a simple yet profound confession. "The spiritual focus of Step 7 [536] is humility, asking a higher power to do something that cannot be done by self-will or mere determination. (Step 7: Humbly asked Him to remove our shortcomings").

"Him," AA interprets, as a higher power. "This step is the culmination of a great deal or preparation of working the 'middle steps' of the 12-step programs. After carefully taking a moral inventory, admitting our faults and becoming willing to have them removed, the final step in the process is to humbly ask for help in removing those character defects that may have been in effect for many years."

The AA Big Book suggests, "When ready, we say something like this:
'My Creator, I am now willing that you should have all of me, good and bad. I pray that you now remove from me every single defect of character which stands

---

[533] Sidney M. Jourard, The Transparent Self. p.75
[534] Viktor Frankl. op. cit., p. 104
[535] Bruce Chilton. op. cit., p. xvi
[536] Alcoholic Anonymous. Big Book, p. 76

in the way of my usefulness to you and my fellows. Grant me strength, as I go out from here, to do your bidding. Amen.' We have then completed Step Seven."

In Saul's instance, he immediately recognized the higher power as God. *"Who are you Lord,"*[537] Saul replied to Jesus' confrontation with him, already recognizing the "higher power" as Jesus. Saul desperately needed God's help–a first step to his wellness.

3. A Learned Power of Humility

God has a way of converting pride into humility. He did this in several ways, first by Saul's knock-down, blinding event on the Damascus road and secondly by placing Saul in the hands of Ananias, the very person representing The Way that Paul set out to annihilate. The Lord quickly got Saul's undivided attention. Enforced blindness can do that! His attitudes and prejudices had come under the Lord's review.

Paul's continuous take was to keep his humility as a guiding star. He achieved this in several ways. One was to admit his failure publicly. Another was to describe himself as the "least of all the saints."

> *"I became a servant of this gospel by the gift of God's grace given me through the working of his power. Although I am less than the least of all the Lord's people, this grace was given me: to preach to the Gentiles the boundless riches of Christ . . . For this reason I kneel before the Father . . ."*[538]

Most important, was the assertion he claimed as his own banner, requiring it of all believers, to acknowledge "Jesus as Lord."

In that way Paul acknowledged that God owned him and that was God's servant-slave. He saw himself like a serf in the slave market, bought by a new owner and redeemed from the slavery of his past sins that once had possessed him.

In reminding the Corinthians of who they really were, he reminded himself of his purchase from a form of slavery by a bad owner to slavery by the most acceptable one: *"You are not your own; you were bought at a price."*[539]

Paul had learned the power of humility. He blazed onto the world stage as a "big shot," a Pharisee with a king's famous name. Then he learned he had it all wrong. Braggadocio and power were not suitable styles for the Spirit's servants. He gradually toned down his manner and by the time he was part way through his first mission in Cyprus, Saul had morphed into Paul (whose name meant "insignificant" or "little") and without guile reminded all who heard him that he was the "least of all the saints."

4. A Sense of Being

As he was growing in faith and maturing in personality, Paul clearly identified himself as being "in Christ." This is a recurring concept that Paul offers to his letter recipients.

---

[537] Acts 9:5
[538] Ephesians 3:7–14
[539] 1 Corinthians 6:20, 7:23

To Alec Vidler, interpreting "in Christ" to Malcolm Muggeridge, that phrase means that, "Christ was, as it were, the new atmosphere in which he was going to live and breathe and which he always was going to depend upon. And he wanted everyone else to live in this atmosphere and to breathe it."[540]

But it also means that Paul saw reality as Christ being in him. *"It is no longer I who live,"* he wrote to Galatia, *"but it is Christ who lives in me. And the life I now live in the flesh I live by faith in the Son of God."*[541] And to Colossae he wrote, *"To them God has chosen to make known among the Gentiles the glorious riches of this mystery, which is Christ in you, the hope of glory."*[542]

Paul used another metaphor to expand this understanding. He referenced the Jerusalem Temple where only the high priest could offer sacrifice. Then he likened believers to the building itself, in which God allows his name to dwell. *"Do you not know that you are God's temple and that God's Spirit dwells in you?"*[543]

Of course the implications of that are tremendous. This concept determines how we act and how we speak and how we honour God who indwells us.

In his unique, droll way, C. S. Lewis expresses his sensing of being as such:

"I was driven to Whipsnade one sunny morning. When we set out I did not believe that Jesus Christ is the Son of God, and when we reached the zoo I did. Yet I had not exactly spent the journey in thought. Nor in great emotion. "Emotional" is perhaps the last word we can apply to some of the most important events. It was more like when a man, after a long sleep, becomes aware that he is now awake."[544]

5. An Exhibition of *Agape* (Love)

Paul came to realize that love *did* make the world go round. So he tried it on himself. He learned to like himself. Then he tried it on others. He learned to like them. The people he hated, he now loved. He enjoyed their company, their community and their way of living. Love allowed Paul to deal with life!

"As servants of God we commend ourselves in every way: in great endurance; in troubles, hardships and distresses; in beatings, imprisonments and riots; in hard work, sleepless nights and hunger; in purity, understanding, patience and kindness; in the Holy Spirit and in sincere love; in truthful speech and in the power of God; with weapons of righteousness in the right hand and in the left; through glory and dishonour, bad report and good report; genuine, yet regarded as impostors; known, yet regarded as unknown; dying, and yet we live on; beaten, and yet not killed; sorrowful, yet always rejoicing; poor, yet making many rich; having nothing, and yet possessing everything."[545]

Paul found God because God sought him out. Following his conversion, and because of it, Saul realized the extent of God's unconditional love, not only for him, but

---

[540] Malcolm Muggeridge and Alec Vidler. Paul: Envoy Extraordinary. p. 47
[541] Galatians 2:20
[542] Colossians 1:27
[543] 1 Corinthians 3:16
[544] C. S. Lewis. Surprised by Joy. p. 189
[545] 2 Corinthians 6:4–10

for the world. He both appropriated it for himself and extended it to all his contacts. *"Oh, the depth of the riches of the wisdom and knowledge of God! How unsearchable his judgments, and his paths beyond tracing out!"*[546]

Psychiatrist Karl Menninger noted Paul's recovery to wellness, especially based on the positivity of love. Wrote Menninger:

"Paul (or another early Christian) once preached a sermon by mail which he advised renewing our minds and heart, discontinuing our lying and adhering to the truth. And if any of us is angry, he said, let him avoid aggressive revenge and make peace before the sun sets. Cease stealing, he said, (it was going on then, you see), discard envy and greed, and direct our energies into constructive and benevolent activities. Renounce all malice. Yes, and be kind to one another, kind and gentle and forgiving, so that we ourselves can be forgiven. "And walk in love."[547]

6. A Salvaged Optimism

In the Rogers and Hammerstein musicale South Pacific, nurse Nellie Forbush, sung by Mary Martin, has a great sense of "up" in the midst of a paralyzing war. Her song goes, "I have heard people rant and rave and bellow that we're done and we might as well be dead, but I'm only a cockeyed optimist and I can't get it into my head."

Paul was like a cockeyed optimist: *"God can do anything, you know–far more than you could ever imagine or guess or request in your wildest dreams!"*[548]

He knew what had happened in his own life and he believed anyone in sin or despair could be resurrected. He was also a person of realism–*"the wages of sin is death,"*[549] he wrote to Rome, but he completed that threat with a hope, *"but the free gift of God is eternal life in Christ our Lord." "A man reaps what he sows."*[550]

Paul told the Galatians believers, *"Do not be deceived, God is not mocked; for whatever a man sows, that he will also reap. For he who sows to his flesh will of the flesh reap corruption,"* but Paul countered that truth with a positive response, *"but he who sows to the Spirit will of the Spirit reap everlasting life."*[551]

7. The New World Order: Spirit Trumps Law

Paul saw the *Torah*, not as the final authority, but as a teacher introducing the Jews to Christ. *"The Law was put in charge to lead us to Christ that we might be justified by faith."*[552]

"Christ redeemed us from the curse of the law by becoming a curse for us, for it is written: 'Cursed is everyone who is hung on a pole.' He redeemed us in order

---

[546] Romans 11:33
[547] Karl Menninger, op. cit., p. 97
[548] Ephesians 3:20 MSG (The Message)
[549] Romans 6:23
[550] Galatians 6:7,8 NKJV
[551] *ibid*
[552] Galatians 3:24

that the blessing given to Abraham might come to the Gentiles through Christ Jesus, so that by faith we might receive the promise of the Spirit.[553]

"Those who are led by the Spirit of God are Sons of God,"[554] wrote Paul to his Roman audience. Paul was telling the Roman Christians that with the age introduced at *Shavuot*, God had given the church a new template, the Spirit, who was now the guiding principle of all believers. He reminded the Galatian audience that they will know how the Holy Spirit will indwell them by what the Spirit produces in their lives. The Holy Spirit is our wisdom and our guide. As Jesus promised and Paul understood, *"I will ask the Father, and he will give you another Counsellor to be with you forever–the Spirit of truth."*[555] The evidence of the Spirit's role in our lives is found in the legacy we issue.

> *"But the fruit of the Spirit is love, joy, peace, forbearance, kindness, goodness, faithfulness, gentleness and self-control. Against such things there is no law. Those who belong to Christ Jesus have crucified the flesh with its passions and desires. Since we live by the Spirit, let us keep in step with the Spirit. Let us not become conceited, provoking and envying each other."*[556]

Paul was saying what Jesus told his disciples, *"You did not choose me but I chose you and appointed you to go and bear fruit–fruit that will last."*[557]

8. Christ is Everything

Being "in Christ" gave the Apostle Paul a genuine reason for accepting any predicament, loss, suffering or setback. And he did suffer. His chronicles include beatings, shipwrecks, imprisonment, taunting, stoning–name the abuse.[558] Viktor Frankl, in his woebegone sojourn in the Nazi prison camp Auschwitz, expressed his own sense of meaning in what he had been through. Wrote Frankl, "When we are no longer able to face a situation–just think of an incurable disease such as inoperable cancer–we are challenged to change ourselves . . . that is why man is even ready to suffer, on the condition, to be sure, that his suffering has meaning."[559]

Paul came to know that Christ meant everything and knowing that he found meaning in every part of his life. He believed that nothing in his life was in vain. *"Your labour in the Lord is not in vain."*[560] The apostle punctuated that belief in his letter to Roman Christians. *"For from him and through him, and to him are all things. To him be the glory forever."*

Again, Paul echoed that tenet to Philippi: *"For me to live is Christ."*[561] To Colossians believers he had never met in person, he penned a letter underling that Christ

---

[553] Ephesians 3:8–10
[554] Romans 8:14; 15:13
[555] John 14:15–16
[556] Galatians 5:22–26
[557] John 15:16a
[558] 2 Corinthians 11:25 Colossians 2:20
[559] Viktor Frankl. op. cit., pp. 105, 106
[560] 1 Corinthians 15:58
[561] Philippians 1:21

was the centre of life, even the cosmos: *"In Christ you have been brought to fullness. He is the head over every power and authority."*[562]

9. An Open Book

Paul developed a profound sense of both needing and wanting to share his journey. Paul's life was open for any and all to see, his strengths and weaknesses, as Oliver Cromwell, stated, "warts and all."[563] Paul's life was an open book. He hid nothing from following friends or doubting distracters. He also encouraged new Christians to be equally open about their victories and struggles.

Openness is a critical underlying part of Paul's apostolic message. Christians have nothing to secrete from each other. Let them hide nothing. Let them be fully honest, fully transparent about their past, their present and their future. Let others see them as God sees them. Paul learned to be absolutely candid with his various audiences. He believed nothing should be hidden about his life.

To Corinth he wrote: *"We have spoken frankly to you Corinthians; our heart is wide-open to you. There is no restriction in our affections, but only in yours . . . open wide your hearts also."*[564] He was fully open about his wrong attitudes and his persecution of those in "The Way." He was not proud of that behaviour. Yet he did not allow it to give him a never-ending guilt trip. He knew the reality of his sins being "nailed to the cross."[565]

Writing to the Colossians, he also appropriated his notes to himself:

"When you were dead in your sins and in the uncircumcision of your flesh, God made you alive with Christ. He forgave us all our sins, having canceled the charge of our legal indebtedness, which stood against us and condemned us; he has taken it away, nailing it to the cross. And having disarmed the powers and authorities, he made a public spectacle of them, triumphing over them by the cross . . . Therefore do not let anyone judge you."[566]

Paul did not wallow in guilt. He simply told his story to remind himself of where he had been and what the Saviour had done for him personally. Perhaps that would help others in confessing their sins, accepting Jesus as Saviour and freeing themselves from both sin and guilt, allowing the Lord to nail all sins to his cross.

---

[562] Romans 11:36

[563] The phrase "warts and all" is attributed to Oliver Cromwell, via Horace Walpole. In his 1764 book Anecdotes of Painting in England, Walpole reported an alleged conversation between the Duke of Buckingham and the architect of Buckingham Palace, William Winde. Winde related to the Duke that while Cromwell sat for a portrait by Sir Peter Lely, he said, "Mr. Lely, I desire that you use all your skill to paint my picture truly like me, and not to flatter me at all; but remark all these roughnesses, pimples, warts and everything you see in me, otherwise I will never pay a farthing for it."

[564] 2 Corinthians 6:11–13

[565] Colossians 2:14

[566] Colossians 2:14c–16a

10. A Community of Faith

As Paul matured he developed a rich sense of community (together=*kononia*). He saw the church as an organism, not an organization. He saw that the individuals within the church contributed to the spirituality of all other members.

> *"Just as a body, though one, has many parts, but all its many parts form one body, so it is with Christ. For we were all baptized by one Spirit so as to form one body—whether Jews or Gentiles, slave or free—and we were all given the one Spirit to drink.*
>
> *Now you are the body of Christ, and each one of you is a part of it. And God has placed in the church first of all apostles, second prophets, third teachers, then miracles, then gifts of healing, of helping, of guidance, and of different kinds of tongues. Are all apostles? Are all prophets? Are all teachers? Do all work miracles? Do all have gifts of healing? Do all speak in tongues? Do all interpret?"*[567]

Moreover, Paul knew that his Lord approved of and invested himself in the church in the same way a husband approved of, invested in–and loved his wife. *"Christ loved the church and gave himself up for her."*[568]

Paul did not live or work in private seclusion. He nourished his friends with his own spirituality; they very much contributed to his. Paul was no isolationist. "With" is one of Paul's major prepositions.

"Together" is one of Paul's favourite words. *"In him* [Christ] *the whole building is joined together and rises to become a holy temple in the Lord,"* wrote Paul to the Ephesians believers. *"And in him you are being built together to become a dwelling in which lives by his Spirit."* Then he added, *"Through the Gospel the Gentiles are heirs together with Israel, members together in one body, and sharers together in the promises of Christ Jesus."*

The Apostle depended upon many co-workers, including Barnabas, Silas, Luke and Timothy, without whom the several missions could have taken many different turns including failure. This writing however, mainly concerns Paul's psychological and spiritual development, which the book refers to as "wellness and developing attitudes."

His friends, allies and supporters may indeed have contributed in a large part to his spiritual, psychological and physical health. That cannot be discounted. But Paul had come a long way from being unable to bear believers as reported in Acts 9, to becoming totally affirmatively absorbed in their lives.

11. A Conciliatory Attitude

Over the years of his apostolate, Paul learned that a conciliatory approach would aid and ameliorate obnoxious individuals in their ready protests with others. The apostle's now acquired sweet-tempered attitude advanced several light years away from the proud cadet Pharisee. Had not Saul strutted imposingly en route to Damascus with his Temple quasi-military reinforcements to capture Christians and annihilate them?

---

[567] 1 Corinthians 12:27–30
[568] Ephesians 5:25

"Though I am free and belong to no one, I have made myself a slave to everyone, to win as many as possible. To the Jews I became like a Jew, to win the Jews. To those under the law I became like one under the law (though I myself am not under the law), so as to win those under the law. To those not having the law I became like one not having the law (though I am not free from God's law but am under Christ's law), so as to win those not having the law. To the weak I became weak, to win the weak. I have become all things to all people so that by all possible means I might save some. I do all this for the sake of the gospel, that I may share in its blessings.[569]

12. A Sense of Humour

Normally, a man as neurotically obsessed as was Saul when he left Jerusalem to hunt believers in Damascus does not have a sense of humour. But the Apostle Paul, developed a wry humour during the years of his spiritual maturity. Here are some instances of his learned wit:

First, note the comment in 1 Corinthians 3:5. *"What then is Apollos? What is Paul? . . . I planted, Apollos watered, but God gave the growth."*

What sense of humour is in that?[570] It is in the word "water." (*èpòèstin*=water, irrigate) Paul reminded his Corinthian audience that before he was corrected by Aquila, Priscilla and Paul, Apollos was obsessed with repeated baptisms as after the manner of John the Baptist. The Corinthians, including Apollos, would have chuckled at Paul's oblique reference. Paul probably wanted to introduce a small measure of levity to compensate for the heavier matters he had to say later in the epistle.

Second, Paul, using his humour, cushioned the heavier items in his letter to the Galatians by commenting on the Jewish insistence of circumcision for new Gentile believers. He joked (Galatians 5:12), *"I wish those who unsettle you would castrate themselves!"* That wry humour allowed Paul to vent some of his frustrations in dealing with the pesky Galatians.

Third, as previously noted earlier in his letter to the Philippians, Paul humorously references the link connecting Epaphroditus and the pagan deity Aphrodite and Syntyche to Tyche, Aphrodite's daughter, the goddess of "chance." Paul noted that Epaphroditus, the letter carrier, had "gambled" his life for the Gospel. Aphrodite was the deity respected by gamblers. That would make the Philippians smile!

And then there's Onesimus. He was the runaway escaped slave who was evangelized by Paul and became a believer in Christ as Saviour and Lord. His name means "useful one." Paul applied his sense of humour in playing on the meaning of his name. In sending him back to Colossae with a letter, Paul tells Philemon, *"formerly he was useless to you but now he has become useful to me."*[571] With this small pun, Paul surely softened Philemon to receive back and welcome his once-slave.

---

[569] 1 Corinthians 9:23–30
[570] Bruce Chilton. op. cit., p. 200
[571] Philemon v. 11

Without doubt, Paul had a become a cheerful person. He told the Corinthians that, "God loves a cheerful giver."[572] Paul's Greek word for cheerful is *hilaron (ilaròn)*, giving the English word "hilarious." Who could give this kind of advice to a church except from a transformed Paul? He also had developed a cheerful attitude:

"Rejoice in the Lord always. I will say it again: Rejoice! Let your gentleness be evident to all. The Lord is near. Do not be anxious about anything, but in every situation, by prayer and petition, with thanksgiving, present your requests to God. And the peace of God, which transcends all understanding, will guard your hearts and your minds in Christ Jesus.

Finally, brothers and sisters, whatever is true, whatever is noble, whatever is right, whatever is pure, whatever is lovely, whatever is admirable—if anything is excellent or praiseworthy—think about such things. Whatever you have learned or received or heard from me, or seen in me—put it into practice. And the God of peace will be with you."[573]

13. No Sense of Quit

There developed no sense of "quit" in Paul's life; he had established sheer tenancy. He showed signs of this steadiness when he set out to attack the Damascus believers. God let him keep this character by "baptizing" his "no surrender" aspect of his life. Paul learned to be rock steady in the face of any and all situations. In turn, he conveyed this virtue in his several letters to the fledgling churches he counselled. "Be strong in the Lord and in his mighty power."[574]

To Ephesus he wrote:

"Therefore put on the full armour of God, so that when the day of evil comes, you may be able to stand your ground, and after you have done everything, to stand. Stand firm then, with the belt of truth buckled around your waist, with the breastplate of righteousness in place, and with your feet fitted with the readiness that comes from the gospel of peace. In addition to all this, take up the shield of faith, with which you can extinguish all the flaming arrows of the evil one. Take the helmet of salvation and the sword of the Spirit, which is the word of God."[575]

Note how many times the instruction indicates "no quit"–"stand your ground," "after you have done everything, stand," "stand firm then." Add to this evidence of Paul's "no quit" policy, something similar he told the Corinthians: *"Therefore, my dear brothers and sisters, stand firm. Let nothing move you. Always give yourselves fully to the work of the Lord, because you know that your labour in the Lord is not in vain."[576]*

14. Grace Makes Amends

Paul had many issues in his life, both personal and in relation to "his" churches. he tried very hard to coax, prod, encourage and support these congregations he helped

---

[572] 2 Corinthians 9:7
[573] Philippians 4:4–9
[574] Ephesians 6:10
[575] Ephesians 6:13–17
[576] 1 Corinthians 15:58

bring into being. Sometimes his frustrations got the better of him, especially when his people did not get the proper message. One issue that continually irked him was the role of the Judaizers who insisted that Gentiles become proselyte Jews. At one point we read of Paul's full frustration in which he is pointedly direct so much so that he seems cross:

> *"You foolish Galatians! Who has bewitched you? Before your very eyes Jesus Christ was clearly portrayed as crucified. I would like to learn just one thing from you: Did you receive the Spirit by the works of the law, or by believing what you heard? Are you so foolish? After beginning by means of the Spirit, are you now trying to finish by means of the flesh? Have you experienced so much in vain—if it really was in vain? So again I ask, does God give you his Spirit and work miracles among you by the works of the law, or by your believing what you heard?"*[577]

The same issue was unresolved when he wrote to the Philippians from his Roman prison. He not only is thwarted by the teaching of the Judaizers, he also realized he was running out of time here on earth and therefore unable to visit and correct the erring Christians in person. Once again, readers see his choler rising as he pens his letter: *"Beware of the dogs, beware of the evil workers, beware of those who mutilate the flesh,"* he penned.[578] To call people dogs, in that part of the world is insulting to the Nth degree because dogs inhabited the trash piles in the outskirts of the community. Paul was angry when he wrote those words, very angry.

Yet Paul advocated grace as God's unmerited love to those who knew Christ as Saviour. Surely Paul can be forgiven for venting about the Judaizers. When he penned a letter to those in the region of Ephesus, Paul reminded everyone that that God's grace allowed each believer to receive God's gift of service and each on a separate service. Paul placed an emphasis on grace: *"a grace has been given to each one of us."*[579] God gave his redeemed people such grace, *"because of his great love for us."*[580]

Best of all, Paul appropriated such grace to himself when he needed victory over some unknown ailment God did not heal the situation the way Paul wanted but he accepted God's alternative to Paul's plea. *"But he* (the Lord) *said to me, 'My grace is sufficient for you, for my power is made perfect in weakness.' Therefore I will boast all the more gladly about my weaknesses, so that Christ's power may rest on me."*[581]

Ultimately Paul states what has become his way of life–his *halakah*. *"So we are always confident; even though we know that while we are at home in the body we are away from the Lord–for we walk by faith, not by sight. Yes, we do have confidence."*[582] Surely the former terrorist once travelling the Damascus highway has come a long way in healing his attitudes–or more accurately, has allowed God to refashion them in him.

---

[577] Galatians 3:1–5
[578] Philippians 3:2
[579] Ephesians 4:7
[580] Ephesians 2:4
[581] 2 Corinthians 12:9
[582] 2 Corinthians 5:7

15. Saved from Guilt; Memory Becomes a "Heads-Up"

Paul had a need to remember his failings–not to feel guilt or remorse, but to remind him of what God had done for him. The scars he earned through life served to remind him that he was forgiven, and therefore guilt-free.

It was propaedeutic for Paul to review his life, remembering the hard lesson learned from his sinful treatment of Christians. But he need not grovel by looking at his scars. *"Having cancelled the charge of our legal indebtedness, which stood against us and condemned us; he has taken it away, nailing it to the cross."*[583] The past was past and entirely in God's forgiving love. He accepted what he could not change.

The same was true for others who previously had succumbed to sin but through Christ had been justified by their faith. They were not required to wallow in their guilt but in Christ's liberty, to rejoice in their new freedom from sin and guilt.

> *"Do you not know that wrongdoers will not inherit the kingdom of God? Do not be deceived: Neither the sexually immoral nor idolaters nor adulterers nor men who have sex with men nor thieves nor the greedy nor drunkards nor slanderers nor swindlers will inherit the kingdom of God. And that is what some of you were. But you were washed, you were sanctified, you were justified in the name of the Lord Jesus Christ and by the Spirit of our God."*[584]

The key phrase in that Corinthian passage is, *"Some of you were."* They were no longer what they were! Paul saw no need for the redeemed of God to slosh in a pig-pen style of remorse once God had forgiven them and forgotten their past iniquities. With Christ, they could hold their heads high because they were completely forgiven and sanctified in God's sight. He felt that way about himself too.

16. Acceptance

The young Pharisee Saul who stormed North from Jerusalem to create havoc among members of The Way, recognized his wrong and began learning to accept situations that called for sober thought instead of rashness.

Yet Paul did defend himself when necessary, such as insisting that Philippi's magistrates apologize to him and escort him properly to the city limits. He defended himself often, in Jerusalem, for example, when a mob attempted to do him harm, and he told the riffraff that he had a right to access the Temple and that those accompanying him met all the requirements to worship in the Temple.

Paul defended himself against Agrippa, Festus and Felix in Caesarea Maritima and finally asked permission to defend himself against accusations aimed at him before the emperor himself! Did Paul have nerve or chutzpah?

His imprisonments in Caesarea Maritima and Rome were a new phase in the Apostle's itinerant missionary life. He felt that God allowed him to be in prison for a godly reason. Imprisonment becomes an opportunity–he was now addressing people no

---

[583] Colossians 2:14
[584] 1 Corinthians 6:11

ordinary citizen could readily do. Moreover, he had friends inside the army Pretorian guard and could witness to other soldiers not yet believers.[585]

He complained as any normal person would of the shackles he must wear. But he showed no bitterness. He accepted imprisonment without bitterness. Talking to the region's king (Herod Agrippa) and to his political friend Festus, about the stretched-out time of his trials, Paul reflected: *"Short time or long–I pray to God that not only you but all who are listening to me today may become what I am, except for these chains."*[586] When Paul retired each night, he could say with Samuel Pepys, "I went to bed late with great quiett."[587]

17. Networking and Contacting

Paul developed a strong urge to network and maintain relationships. Paul had developed a masterful pastoral connection with the entire flock he had begun to shepherd. As one reads Paul's itinerary in Acts, and his connections in his letters, one is amazed at the contacts he has made and the mutual confidences he has enjoyed.

Combined with these connections, one sees the remarkable growth of the church, a part of which came from Paul's vigour, faith and enthusiasm. The personalities are clearly cited in the letters, i.e, Syntyche in Euodia in Philippi, several greeters who welcomed him to Italy at Puteoli[588] as he debarked from the ship carrying him to his Roman trial. The list of connections cited in the last chapter of Romans is a case in point.

Many of the connections were through his pastoral work, whether in person, carried by his growing list of associates (Tychicus, Onesimus, Epaphroditus) or by Caesar's mail. Among fellow believers, Paul was hailed as a convincing leader, a model of love, and a dutiful partner. Paul had developed loving friends without number.

So, Luke recognizes their affection for the Apostle as he stopped briefly at Miletus or along the coastal area of Palestina. Their farewells were weepy events.[589]

These were signals of a beloved friend, one deeply loved and fondly cherished. Among fellow believers, Paul was hailed as a convincing leader, a model of love, and a dutiful partner. Paul had developed loving friends without number. No wonder he needed an amanuensis to pen the multiple epistles he sent to friends and churches! Did this affection come insincerely from people who had been touched by him as an impulsive insurgent? Hardly!

18. Synthesizing Gospel Theology

The Gospels[590] tell of a disturbed cave-dwelling man near the village of Kursi along the Eastern hillsides of Lake Galilee (today's Golan Heights). He was so confused

---

[585] Acts 21:8. 10. 16; Philippians 4:22
[586] Acts 26:29
[587] Samuel Pepys. Samuel Pepys Diary, February 5, 1664
[588] Acts 28:14
[589] Acts 20:36–38

that he didn't know who he was. His neighbouring Gentiles who were swine herders called him Legion because he showed so many personalities. Jesus healed him. When his neighbours saw him later, the Gospels reported that, they found the man *"sitting at the feet of Jesus, clothed and in his right mind."*

This account is much like that of the Apostle who neither knew who he was nor behaved sanely. In Paul's transformed life, aided by wisdom gleaned from God's desert tutor, the Holy Spirit, Paul was able to assimilate the Gospel's implications. In a sense he was a fireman called on to douse explosions in various congregations. In reality his teaching became the synthesis of Gospel truths.

Paul had no intention of expecting his work would become a large part of what later came to be known as the New Testament. But that's what happened. Paul's letters became "Canon" fodder! This once mixed-up incendiary became the one person who would offer a full theological concept of the Gospel, the work of Jesus. Paul, in his many epistles synthesized the Gospel so that believers would have a delineated road map for Christian attitudes and behaviour.

When Emperor Constantine was converted, he represented the truth that Europe was under new spiritual management. From a Christian perspective, the continent had moved from darkness to light. Long before, Isaiah said it would happen, didn't he? Paul's part in this transformation was critical. *"The people walking in darkness have seen a great light; on those living in the land of deep darkness a light has dawned."*[591]

---

[590] Matthew 8:28–34; Mark 5:1–20; Luke 8:26–39
[591] Isaiah 9:2

Bibliography

Books

Alcoholic Anonymous. The Big Book, (on-line or hard print from AA) 2001

Alexandri, A. Kos. Sotiri Toumbi Publishers. Athens, Date unlisted (198?). pp. 96

Alexis, Nikos. Rhodes. Athens. Efstathiadis Group Publishing. 1985

Andronicos, Manolis. Thessaloniki Museum. Athens, Ekdotike Athenon S. A. Publisher, 1986.

Andronicos, Manolis. The Acropolis. Athens. Ekdotike Athenon S. A., publishers. 1982

Ariel, David S. Spiritual Judaism, Hyperion Press, New York NY, 1998. 319 pp.

Armstrong, Karen. St. Paul: The Apostle We Love to Hate. New Harvest Houghton
Mifflin Harcourt. New York 2015 143 pages

Azzopardi, Aldo E. Malta and Its islands. Florence. Campo Stampa Editoriale, 2003

Barth, Karl. The Epistle to the Romans. Oxford, Oxford University Press, 1933.

Beers, Clifford Willingham. A Mind That Found Itself. 1908, Published most recently by Amazon.com. (Ebook). Also Pittsburgh, and London, Pittsburgh University Press, 1994

Bettenson, Henry. The Early Christian Fathers. Oxford, Oxford University Press,. 1969 .

Bright, John. A History of Israel (Revised Edition), London UK, SCM Press, 1972/1979.

Belgum, David. Alone, Alone, All Alone. Concordia Publishing House.1972. St. Louis MO. pp. 77

Blaikie, William Garden. Dictionary of National Biography, Fuller, Andrew 1885-1900, Volume 20. 1885, updated 2004. Oxford University Press, Oxford UK.

Broadman Bible Commentary, Vol. 11 Broadman Press Nashville, Philippians 1972.

Buber, Martin. I and Thou. (re-translated as I and You by Walter Kaufmann 1970) New York, Touchstone Press (Simon & Schuster Inc.)

Bullfinch, Thomas. Bullfinch's Mythology. New York, 1855? Thomas Y. Crowell Company.

Burkert, Walter (translated by Raggan, John) Greek Religion. Cambridge MS, Harvard University press.

Caillet, Emile. Journey Into Light. Grand Rapids MI. Zondervan Publishing House. 1968

Calvin, John. Institutes of the Christian Religion. Edited by John T. McNeill. Translated by Ford Lewis Battles. 2 vols. Louisville KY: Westminster John Knox Press, 1960.

Chilton, Bruce. Rabbi Paul. New York, Doubleday (Random House), 2004

Colson, Charles. The Body: Being Light in Darkness. Dallas, Word Publishing, 1992

Crossan, John Dominic and Reed, Jonathan L. In Search of Paul. HarperSanFrancisco. New York, 2004 447 pp.

Danby, Herbert. The Code of Maimonides. Book Ten: The Book of Cleanness. New Haven: Yale University Press, London, Oxford University Press

Davaris, Costis. The Palace of Knossos. Athens, undated (1986?), Hannibal Publishing House. 1960

Dixon-Kennedy. Mike. Encyclopedia of Greco-Roman Mythology. Santa Barbara CA .

Doumas, Christos . Santorini. Editions Hannibal Publishing. No date given (possibly 1983?)

Eliyahu, Mordechai. The Paths of Purity. New York and Jerusalem. Friends of Sucath David. 1986

Gager, John G. Reinventing Paul. Oxford. Oxford University Press, 2000.

Frankl, Viktor. Man's Search for Meaning. Boston, Beacon Press, 1959 reprinted several times (previously titled, Say Yes to Life).

Freud, Anna. The Ego and Mechanisms of Defence. London, Karnak Books revised. 1936, reprinted 1993.

Grant, Michael and Hazel, John. Classical Mythology. London, Rutledge Publishers, 2002

Hadzi-Vallianou. Phaistos. Athens. (Greek) Ministry of Culture. 1989

Harris, Thomas A. I'm OK–You're OK. Harper and Row, Publishers New York, 1967, 1969

Hofmann, Hans (ed.) The Ministry and Mental Health. 1960. New York NY: Association Press.

Hopkins, Keith. A World Full of Gods: Pagans, Jews and Christians in the Roman Empire. London, Weidenfield & Nicolson, 1999

Iakovidis, S. E. Mycenae–Epidaurus. Athens. Ekdotike Athenon S.A. Publishers. 1978

Irwin, Jane and De Visser, John. Old Canadian Cemeteries, Toronto Firefly Books, 2007.

Jocz, Jakob. The Spiritual History of Israel. London, Eyre & Spottsiswoode, 1961.

Jones, William H. Jewish Ritual Washing and Christian Baptism: Evolution or Revolution? Toronto. ChiRho Communications, 2010. pp. 191

Jourard, Sidney M. The Transparent Self. (revised ed.) New York, D. Van Nostrand Co., 1971

Kaplan, Aryeh. E. Waters of Eden: The Mystery of the Mikvah (sic). New York. NCSY / Orthodox Union, 1982, 1988, 1992, 1994, 1997

Kelso, James L. An Archaeologist Follows the Apostle Paul. Word Books, Publishers, Waco TX 1970

LaHaye, Tim. Why You Act The Way You Do. Living Books, Tyndale House, Wheaton Ill. 1984

de Lange, Nicolas. Judaism. Oxford, Oxford University Press 1986

Lefkowitz, Mary, Women in Greek Myth. Baltimore MD, John Hopkins University, 1986, 2007

Lewis, C.S. Surprised by Joy. London, Collins Fount Paperbacks, 1955, 1959

Lewis, C.S. The Four Loves. London, Glasgow, Harper & Collins Publishers Ltd., 1960 (reprint 2002)

Longenecker, Richard N. Word Bible Commentary, Vol. 41: Galatians. Grand Rapids MI, 1990.

Longenecker, Richard N. Biblical Exegesis in the Apostolic Period. Grand Rapids MI, William B. Eerdmans Publishing. 1875

The Interpreter's Bible Commentary, Vol. 11 Philippians. Abingdon Press Nashville 1951, 500 pp.

Lüdemann, Gerd. Paul: The Founder of Christianity. Amherst NY, Prometheus Books, 2002

March, Jenny. Cassel. Dictionary of Classical Mythology. London. Cassel Wellington House, 1998

Marinatos, Nanno. Lindos, Athens Greece, D. & I., Mathioulakis, Publishers, 1983

Marinatos, Nanno. Crete. Athens Greece, D. & L. Mathioulakis Publishers, 1986

Mavromataki, Maria. Paul: The Apostle to the Gentiles. Athens, Greece, Editions Haitalis, 2003

Menninger, Karl. Whatever Became of Sin? New York, Hawthorn Books Inc. Publishers, 1973, 1975

Mikalson, Jon D. Ancient Greek Religion. Oxford, Blackwell Publishing, 2005

Mikolaski, Samuel J.. Theological Sentences. Green Bay WI, BookWhirl.com Publishing. 2012.

Mikolaski, Samuel J.. St. Paul and Free Speech: Then and Now. North Charleston SC, CreateSpace Independent Publishing Platform, 2015.

Miller, John Homer. Why We Act That Way. 1946. Nashville TN, Abingdon Press. pp. 222.

Morton, H. V., In the Steps of St. Paul. London, Methuen & Co. Ltd. 1936, 1955.

Morford, Mark P.O and Lenardon Robert J., Classical Mythology. New York, Longan Publishers, 1999

Murphy-O'Connor, Jerome. Paul: His Story. Oxford. Oxford University Press 2004

Neysner, Jacob (ed.). Rabbinic Literature. Toronto, Doubleday,. 1994. pp. 720

Oesterley, W. O. E. A History of Israel, Vol. II. Oxford, Oxford University Press, 1932.

Ogden, Daniel (ed.).) A Companion to Greek Religion. Oxford, Blackwell Publishing, 2007

Orr, James. The Resurrection of Jesus. Grand Rapids MI. Zondervan Publishing House, 1965

Papahatziz, Nicos. Ancient Corinth. Athens. Ekdote Arhenon S.A., Publishers. 1977

Petrakos. Delphi. Athens. Clio Editions Publishers. 1977

Pinnock, Clark (ed.) with Richard Rice, John Sanders, William Hasker, David Basinger. The Openness of God. Downer's Grove IL, InterVarsity Press 1994

Pollock, John. The Apostle: A Life of Paul. Colorado Springs CO, Chariot Victor (Word Books. 1985 US edition).

Pepys, Samuel. The Diary of Samuel Pepys. New York, London. Random House Modern Library, version 2001

Price, Simon and Kearns, Emily (ed.). The Oxford Dictionary of Classical Myth and Religion. Oxford. Ford University Press. 2004

Ramsay, William M.. St. Paul the Traveller and Roman Citizen. Grand Rapids MI, Baker House, 1925, 1866, 1982.

Reeves, Nicholas, Taylor, John H. Howard Carter Before Tutankhamen. London, British Museum Press; 1992 UK

Reinhold Meyer, Past and Present: The Continuity of Classical Myths. Toronto, Hakkert Publishers, 1972.

Roetzel, Calvin J. Paul: The Man and the Myth. University of South Carolina Press, Columbia SC 1998

Rosenberg, Stuart. To Understand Jews. Toronto ON: PaperJacks, 1972.

Sanders, E. P. Paul. New York, Oxford University Press. 1991, re-issued 1996
Simon, Marcel. Jewish Sects at the Time of Jesus. Philadelphia, Fortress Press, 1966.

Simons, Jane (project editor). The Greek Islands. London, Dorling Kindersley Travel Guides, 2000.

Shacter, Helen. Understanding Ourselves. Bloomington IL. 1952.

Sissa, Giulia and Detienne, Marcel. The Daily Life of the Greek Gods. Stanford CA, Stanford University Press, 2000.

Tetrakos, Basil. Delphi. Athens, Clio Editions Publisher, 1977.

Tournier, Paul. The Meaning of Persons. London, SCM Press. 1963 (third impression).

Tournier, Paul. <u>A Listening Ear.</u> Minneapolis MN. Augsburg Publishing House 1984, 1987

Toynbee, Arnold J. <u>Greek Historical Thought</u>. New York NY, A Mentor Book., 1952

Vidler, Alec and Muggeridge, Malcolm. <u>Paul: Envoy Extraordinary</u>. London, Collins, 1972.

Warren, Rick. <u>The Purpose Driven Life: What On Earth Am I Here For?</u> Grand Rapids MI Zondervan Publishers (Harper Collins), 2002

Whiston, William (translator). <u>The Life and Works of Flavius Josephus</u>. New York, Holt Rinehart and Winston, (date not given)

Wouk, Herman. <u>This Is My God</u>. New York. Fontana Books 1976

Vanier, Jean. <u>Becoming Human</u>. The Massey Lectures Series. Toronto: Anansi Press, 1998.

Zaphiropoulou, Photine. <u>Delos: Monuments and Museum</u>. Athens.<<Krene Editions>> Publishers. 1983

Zammit, Themistocles. The Temples of Malta and Gozo. Malta S. Masterson Publisher. 1995

Zeitlin, Irving M. <u>Ancient Judaism</u>. Polity Press and Oxford University Press, Oxford UK. 1984.

Periodicals

Borchert, Gerald. <u>Review and Expositor</u>, Vo. 85, No. 3 Summer 1988 "The Gospel of John"

Andronicos, Manolis. <u>Regal Treasures from a Macedonian Tomb, National Geographic Magazine</u>, July, 1978

Charles C. Mann. <u>Birth of Religion – National Geographic Magazine</u>, Vol. 219. No. 6, June, 2011.

Places Personally Visited and Cited in this Document

Cyprus

Famagusta/Salamis

Egypt

Alexandria

Greece

Apollonia; Amphipolis; Athens; Epidauros; Kavala (Neapolis); Vergina; Pella; Veria (Berea); Cenchrea; Corinth; Corinth Canal and Diolkos; Cos; Delphi;; Crete: Fair Havens (Kali Limenes); Phaistos (Festos) Iraklion (Knossos); Lechaion; Mycenae; Epidauros; Rhodes (Rodos and Lindos); Philippi; Samos; Sounion; Thessalonika

Israel

Caesarea Maritima; Jerusalem; Joppa (Yafa); Acco (Akko, Acre, Ptolemais); Azotus (Ashdod); Gaza

Italy

Forum of Appius; Puteoli; Ostia; Rhegium; Rome; Syracuse; Messina; Three Taverns

Lebanon

Sidon; Tyre; Baalbek

Malta and Gozo

Qawra Point and Saint Paul's Bay

Palestinian Authority

Bethlehem; Samaria (Sebaste)

Syria

Damascus

Turkey

Assos; Ephesus; Miletus; Troas; Troy

Made in the USA
Charleston, SC
25 March 2016